The Day We Almost
Bombed Moscow

The Day We Almost Bombed Moscow

The Allied War in Russia 1918–1920

-3. MAY 1986

Christopher Dobson and John Miller

HODDER AND STOUGHTON
LONDON SYDNEY AUCKLAND TORONTO

British Library Cataloguing in Publication Data

Dobson, Christopher
  The day we almost bombed Moscow: the allied
  war in Russia, 1918–1920.
  1. Soviet Union—History—Allied
  intervention, 1918–1920
  I. Title   II. Miller, John, *1932–*
  947.084′1   DK2654

ISBN 0-340-33723-0

Contents

Illustrations

General Denikin's cavalry in retreat across the Russian Steppes
(photo: by courtesy of Vic Clow)

The victorious Red Army marches into Irkutsk, March 1920
(photo: by courtesy of John Massey Stewart)

Maps

Foreword

One Sunday morning four years ago at Highwoods Golf Club in Sussex, Vic Clow, a big, handsome chap whose bearing belies his years, started talking in Russian to Christopher Dobson. Dobson, who had been a foreign correspondent in the Soviet Union, asked him where he had learnt the language and Clow then told the story of how he had almost bombed Moscow in 1919. This book stems from that conversation. Luckily, John Miller, who had spent some eight years in Moscow as the *Daily Telegraph*'s correspondent, was returning to Russia for one more year. He undertook to research the Russian end of the book while Dobson worked on the Western archives.

Very early on in the work it became apparent that what at first seemed a simple project was in fact immensely complicated and that almost every received idea about the Allies' intervention in Russia was wrong. The first myth to go was that cornerstone of Soviet propaganda which teaches that the intervention was a carefully concerted effort by "Capitalism and Imperialism" to strangle Communism at its birth. What emerged was a story of an unco-ordinated reaction to a series of events which actually started with the British Army fighting alongside Bolshevik troops and helping to protect the new Communist state against German-led incursions from Finland.

Admittedly, this phase did not last long and the Allies and the Bolsheviks were soon at each others' throats. Even so the Allies were more concerned with ensuring the defeat of Germany and counteracting what they regarded as the treachery of the Bolsheviks in making a humiliating peace with the Germans than in over-throwing the new rulers of Russia. America, in particular, was most reluctant to interfere in Russia's affairs; the French, bled white by the war of attrition on the Western Front, were desperate for the Russians to draw off the Germans by reopening the Eastern Front; even the Japanese, cynically taking advantage of their allies' prob-lems to pursue their own plans for occupying the maritime pro-vinces of Russia and China, had no ambitions in Russia beyond those provinces; and the British, main supporters of the White Russian armies, soon realised the political and military dangers of their involvement. It was only when Winston Churchill became

Minister of War in January 1919 – nine months after the first British troops landed at Murmansk – that the intervention took on the atmosphere of an anti-Bolshevik crusade. But even his oratory and drive could not persuade his Cabinet colleagues to pursue that crusade.

Wherever we dug, especially in unpublished papers and diaries and letters we found new and startling stories, many of which had been deliberately left out of the official accounts and the "sanitised" memoirs of the Allied and Russian generals involved. The stories of what lay behind the mutinies of the Yorkshire Regiment and the Royal Marines, for example, have never been told before; and, in the case of the Marines' mutiny it is still difficult nearly seventy years later to get anybody to admit that it ever took place.

In these circumstances we came to rely very much on private individuals sending us family papers and it gives great pleasure to thank them for their help: Mrs Betty McKeown for the diary and photographs of her father, Captain Peter Crawford, MC, "The King of Restikent"; Mr David Clegg for Colonel Johnson's letters and other material and his unfailing interest in the project; Mr Roy Rundell for his expert advice and contemporary material; Mrs Edward Sutro for her husband's story – and her hospitality.

We also had the good fortune to find another survivor of the intervention, Mr Arthur Waide, who remembers vividly what it was like to soldier in the Siberian winter. He lives only a mile from Vic Clow but they had never met.

We would not, of course, have been able to contemplate writing the book without the help of the Public Record Office at Kew, and the staff of the Imperial War Museum were, as always, unfailingly kind and helpful. The material they produced for us was invaluable. We must also thank Mary Jo Pugh of the Bentley Historical Library of the University of Michigan who sent us the diaries of the American soldiers on the Archangel front which throw so much light on that confused campaign. Our thanks are also due to the Royal Air Force Museum at Hendon, the Tank Museum at Boving-ton and the Royal Marines Museum at Eastney. Chatham House and the London Library provided their usual excellent service, as did the British Museum Reading Room.

The problems of researching "from the other side of the hill" were another matter. The policy governing archives in the Soviet Union is well known; all foreigners are suspect, and most foreign historians are considered to be bourgeois falsifiers. All doors are not closed, however, if they are pushed in the right way and some research facilities were made available to the authors by the Central

Museum of the Armed Forces, and the RSFSR State Historical Library which John Miller was allowed to join.

These facilities have provided some new material about the Soviet side of the fighting, but it must be frankly said that the Soviet Union has a long way to go before it can present an objective analysis of the historical background to the Intervention, of the Red Army leaders involved, and of the events themselves.

Much of this results from Lenin's ideological impositions on Soviet historiography. Much more is due to Stalin's cult of personality, his rewriting of his own role (and his writing out of Trotsky's), and the almost total elimination of the Red Army leadership during the Great Purge of the 1930s. We discovered in Moscow, for example, that a commander who had fought against the British Army on the Northern Front had published a popular book about his experiences. But after he was arrested, and shot in the Lubyanka, he became a "nonperson" and his books were destroyed. Only one copy still exists, and that remains under lock and key in the Lenin Library.

Even worse, the Soviets published falsified material and documents which, for example, had Stalin organising the fight against the British south of Archangel, including the successful Shenkursk offensive, when he was, in fact, being defeated by Baron Wrangel at Tsaritsyn in South Russia.

It is no longer fashionable as it was after Khruschev's denunciation of Stalin to declare in Soviet newspapers and books that specific individuals were killed under Stalin, but a recent publication gives the game away. *The Soviet Encyclopaedia of the Civil War and Military Intervention in the USSR*, published in Moscow at the end of 1983, presents dozens of short biographies of army personalities. With rare exceptions they are shown to have died between 1936 and 1940; and it is more than likely that they finished up in the cells of the Lubyanka or the Gulag.

Thus, but for Stalin's Purge, it is possible that some survivors of the Intervention still alive in the Soviet Union would have been able to tell their stories. Alas, most of the published accounts have been so heavily coated with ideology that the truth only occasionally shines through. There are no Vic Clows in the Soviet Union.

Among those in the Soviet Union who assisted in some way in the writing of this book – without having any responsibility for its opinions – the authors would particularly like to thank Mr Boris Ozhgibesov, the Director of the Order of the Red Star Central Museum of the Armed Forces, Mr Theodor Gladkov, a specialist on the history of the Cheka, and Mrs Vinogradova for her excellent and extensive translations from official documents.

If there is anyone we have forgotten, then please forgive us. It is a slip of the mind and not of the heart.

Explanatory Note

Four main socialist parties were in existence in Russia at the time of the 1917 Revolution. These were the Bolsheviks, the Mensheviks, the Socialist Revolutionaries and the Left Socialist Revolutionaries. The Bolsheviks, led by Lenin, were those of the radical faction of the Russian Social Democratic Workers' Party when it split in 1903. The Mensheviks were the non-Leninist faction and were established as a political party only in August 1917 at a congress of several Social Democratic groups. The Socialist Revolutionaries were founded in 1902 by the supporters of revolutionary Populism. A section of the party, the Left Socialist Revolutionaries, supported the Bolsheviks in 1917 and played a part in the government until the Treaty of Brest-Litovsk. By August 1918 there were about thirty different governments functioning on Russian soil.

CHAPTER I

"Permission to Bomb?"
South Russia, December 1919

One bitterly cold day in December 1919 Squadron Leader Joe Archer, commanding "Z" Flight, an undercover unit of the Royal Air Force fighting on the very edge of legality for General Denikin's White Russian Army against the Bolsheviks, halted the flight's special train in the heart of the Russian steppe north-east of Kharkov.

Parked alongside the railway line were two well-used RE8 reconnaissance bombers while four more, their wings strapped to their fuselages, rode on flat cars towed by the train. Mechanics, bundled up in a weird assortment of uniforms against the cold, clambered down to refuel the bombers – called "Harry Tates" in Cockney rhyming slang after a music-hall comedian.* Armourers checked their Lewis and Vickers guns. Signallers unloaded their equipment and strung their aerials.

Archer debriefed the pilots and observers of the waiting aircraft then encoded a message for transmission to Taganrog on the Sea of Azov where the British Military Mission to the White Russians had its headquarters.

The message was simple. It read: "In position to bomb Moscow. Await instructions."

He may have been somewhat ambitious in his estimate of the distance to Moscow and the venerable RE8's ability to fly to the capital of the hard-pressed Bolsheviks. To have accomplished the bombing he would probably have needed to set up a refuelling base a long way behind the Red Army's positions. But the country was so open and the opposing forces so scattered it was possible that by using half his planes to fly fuel to an isolated staging post, the rest could have made the attack.

Navigation was no problem; the pilots would simply follow the railway. The danger lay in being surprised by Red cavalry patrols while refuelling, or of an engine "conking out". The pilots of "Z"

---

* Harry Tate was a popular music-hall comedian. It was natural for the ARREEE (Harry) EIGHT (Tate) to become known as the "Harry Tate".

Flight had heard too much of Bolshevik cruelty to relish falling into their hands. They therefore awaited the answer to Archer's request with the mixture of excitement and trepidation common to young men at war engaged in special operations.

Moscow had not been attacked since Napoleon had captured it with all the might and splendour of his Grande Armée. Now, just over a hundred years later, a handful of scruffily dressed young Englishmen were planning to shower the city with a couple of dozen 20 lb bombs from decrepit biplanes held together by glue, piano wire and much faith.

Lieutenant Vic Clow was one of those young men and like all those who took part in the Allied intervention in Russia he recalls everything about it with absolute clarity. His experience was typical of the mixture of restless young men and the professional "aces" from the Western Front who now found themselves fighting over Russia during that momentous year.

Clow had joined the Army at the outbreak of World War I at the age of seventeen, and served as a clerk on General Smuts' staff in the East African campaign before transferring to the Royal Flying Corps. Trained at Heliopolis in Egypt, he ended the war at Alexandria flying obsolete BE 2c aircraft on escort duty for ships using the Suez Canal. He was then posted to ferry duties in England. Asked if he wanted to go to Russia for "a bit of a stunt", Clow jumped at the chance – "I was young and foolish then and thought it would be an adventure."

He was sent to the Caucasus, then thinly occupied by British forces whose ostensible task was to enforce the terms of the 1918 Armistice under which the Turks and the Germans gave up the territory they had occupied there during the war. But the British presence was also designed to prevent the Bolsheviks interfering with the new states of Georgia, Armenia and Azerbaijan which had proclaimed their independence from Russian rule.

After an adventurous journey by train and boat across Europe and the Black Sea Clow eventually joined 221 Squadron in June 1919 at Petrovsk, now known as Makhachkala, a busy port on the Caspian, north of Baku. The Squadron's duties included supporting a White Russian naval flotilla on the Caspian and keeping watch for Bolshevik ships ferrying agitators south into Baku and Persia.

A brisk little war was going on between the Bolsheviks and the British around the Caspian. 221 Squadron flew patrols in DH9a aircraft, then the most modern reconnaissance bombers of the newly established Royal Air Force. They also bombed the Bolsheviks in their Astrakhan stronghold. Clow took part in two of these raids in which five single-engine aircraft travelled 250 miles over enemy territory, to drop two 240 lb bombs on the city, ten in all, "quite an achievement in those days."

Part of the pilots' duties was to take it in turns to spend two weeks at a two-plane outpost on Chechin Island, little more than a sandbank, uncomfortably close to the Bolshevik positions and within range of their cavalry patrols.

However, Clow's Caspian adventure only lasted two months. There was growing opposition in Parliament and throughout the country to a foreign entanglement which promised only harm and which Britain was finding increasingly difficult to sustain. Thus, on the grounds that Turkey was abiding by the terms of the armistice and that British troops were needed elsewhere, all British forces were withdrawn from the Caucasus by August 1919, except for the strategically important port and railhead of Batum on the Black Sea.

221 Squadron returned to England where they were re-formed and sent out to Somaliland to deal with the Mad Mullah. "They did it in six weeks and covered themselves in glory," says Clow. But that was another story. The Squadron's circuitous route home took it by train from Baku to Rostov and then to Novorossiysk. All this was in territory under the control of General Denikin and his White Russian Army. On the way Clow fell in with Lieutenant-Colonel A. C. "Cissy" Maund, commanding officer of an RAF training mission based at Taganrog whose job was to teach White Russians to fly a fleet of 130 RE8s given to them by the British.

Maund, in need of experienced pilots, asked Clow to join the mission. Still "young and foolish" and tempted by the equivalent of a lieutenant-colonel's pay, he agreed and became a flying instructor. Training was brief in those days. "They gave you about four hours' dual flying, then the instructor said, 'go on – go out and bloodywell try to kill yourself' . . ." The Russians took somewhat longer to train. It transpired that they knew all about the faults of the RE8, and were disappointed that the British had not sent them something better. It was well known that in 1914 when the Russian Air Force had sought aircraft to take on the Germans, the British and French had donated only those planes unsuited for use on the Western Front, including the notorious Spad A2 which had a sort of pulpit for a gunner mounted in front of its propeller. Not many gunners survived a crash in a Spad. Neither were the Russian would-be pilots encouraged by the notice stencilled on the rear cockpit of the RE8s: "Do not fly with less than 150 lb in the gunner's compartment when getting off the ground."

To prove that the RE8s were airworthy the British instructors flew in close formation over Rostov with their 150-horsepower engines churning four-bladed propellers at full revs, the curious chimney-like exhaust belching fumes back above the cockpit. The demonstration, however, was not a total success: the citizens of Rostov made an official complaint that the RE8s were flying too close for safety.

The RAF training programme was part of a strong military mission comprising 356 officers and 1,102 other ranks, sent to help Denikin by Britain's Minister of War, Winston Churchill. Commanded by a forceful Major-General, Herbert Holman, it included a contingent from the Tank Corps engaged in training Denikin's men to use six Mark V heavy tanks and six Medium "Whippets" which, like the RE8s, were British army surplus left over from the war.

The mission's role was supposedly a purely advisory one, but this was a fiction designed to placate British public opinion which was becoming increasingly restive at what the *Daily Express* described as "Mr Churchill's own little war."

British officers were also allowed to serve with Denikin's forces on a "voluntary basis" and it was under this particular fiction that No. 47 Squadron was despatched from Salonika, where it had ended the Great War flying against the Bulgarians, to Novorossiysk, the Black Sea port through which Britain poured supplies to Denikin. Some of the long-serving Squadron members were none too happy with this arrangement as the real war had ended and all they wanted was to go home.

The Air Ministry picked a formidable character to lead the squadron – Raymond Collishaw – who, with no less than sixty victories over the Western Front, was the third highest scoring British fighter ace. A Canadian, he was eventually to be made a Companion of the Bath, an Officer of the Order of the British Empire, and to be awarded the Distinguished Service Order, the Distinguished Service Cross and the Distinguished Flying Cross. In World War II he became an Air Vice-Marshal. In his younger days he had been a hell-raiser who, it was said, "would walk over the bodies of his pilots" on Mess nights.

In London Collishaw gathered together a "Flying Circus" of ace pilots to join his new squadron. Among them was the much decorated South African, Flight-Lieutenant S. M. "Kinky" Kinkead who had shot down thirty enemy aircraft over the Dardanelles and the Western Front during the war. He was also to win the DSO in South Russia for destroying a Red Army cavalry formation, thus bringing his collection of medals to the DSO, the DSC and bar and

18

the DFC and bar. He achieved yet more fame in peacetime as a member of the RAF's High Speed Flight which won the Schneider Trophy in 1927. But his luck ran out on March 12th, 1928, when he was trying to break the world air speed record in a Supermarine-Napier S5, one of the fast seaplanes from which the Spitfire was developed. For some reason which still remains unexplained, he suddenly nose-dived into the Solent off the Isle of Wight and was killed instantly.

Collishaw's "Flying Circus" disembarked at Novorossiysk on June 8th, 1919. After travelling cross-country by train, it set up its base at Gniloakaiskaya about sixty miles south-west of Tsaritsyn, a city on the Volga which had been renamed the "Red Verdun" by its Bolshevik garrison. They thereby signified their intention to defend it against the White Army as the French had defended Verdun against the Germans. However, it was not until twenty-three years later that Tsaritsyn was to become famous for the steadfastness of its defenders when it became the rock on which Hitler's invasion of Russia foundered – only then it was called Stalingrad.

How ironic that it was bombed first not by the Luftwaffe but by the Royal Air Force, although the objective was the same – to drive out and defeat the Bolsheviks.

Although Collishaw did not get up to the front immediately, Kinkead and his colleagues were in action straight away. They flew DH9s for reconnaissance and bombing missions and Sopwith Camels to protect the bombers and strafe the Bolshevik positions. On one raid against Tsaritsyn a DH9 scored a direct hit with a 112 lb bomb on a building in which the local Soviet was meeting. Only two of the forty-one Red officers present survived.

The "Red Verdun" did not live up to its name, partly because Stalin, then a member of the Politburo who had been sent to help defend Tsaritsyn, undermined the authority of the former Tsarist officers who were actually conducting the defence. He considered them all to be potential if not actual traitors to the Bolshevik cause. Morale in the city collapsed and by the evening of June 19th the White Russian Cossacks of Baron Wrangel's army, supported by tanks and armoured cars, had fought their way into the streets. However the Red Cavalry hovered just a few miles to the north and the Bolsheviks organised a fleet of gunboats on the Volga in an attempt to retake the city.

Tsaritsyn's importance lay in its position between the White Armies of Denikin in the south-west and of Kolchak in the north-east. Only if the Whites held the city would it be possible for their two Armies to join forces. It was inevitable, therefore, that the

Bolsheviks would make every effort to recapture it. It was in fact almost as important in the Russian civil war as it was in World War II.

This meant that there was plenty of work for the pilots of 47 Squadron. They had taken possession of four special trains, one for each flight with the fourth being used as a mobile headquarters. They were thus able to get their aircraft right up to the battlefield and were soon in the thick of the fighting.

On July 30th they were involved in an extraordinary exploit. Three DH9s took off to bomb and strafe river barges and cavalry concentrations and to take photographs for General Wrangel's intelligence officers. Captain Walter Anderson and his observer Lieutenant John Mitchell were taking photographs when they were shot up and began to leak petrol. Mitchell climbed out on the wing and plugged the holes with his fingers. But then the machine flown by Captain William Elliot and Lieutenant H. S. Laidlaw was hit in the engine and Elliot had to force-land. Red Cavalry galloped up, swinging their sabres, but Laidlaw fought them off with his Lewis gun from the rear cockpit. Anderson landed alongside with Mitchell still plugging the holes in the petrol tank. Once down, Mitchell manned his Lewis gun while Elliot set fire to his machine. Then, when Elliot and Laidlaw scrambled into Mitchell's cockpit, he resumed his place on the wing and stuck his fingers back in the holes. Anderson opened up his engine and all four flew off to safety though for Mitchell the flight was a painful as well as a dangerous one: he was wearing shorts and was burned by the hot exhaust gases as he rode on the wing. He and Anderson were awarded the DSO and, later, the DFC. Collishaw, writing about this incident in his book, *A Fighter Pilot's Story*, commented that they should have got the Victoria Cross. Collishaw himself got into action by bombing a Red gunboat on the Volga with a pair of 230 lb bombs and literally blowing it out of the water. Later he added to his score when he shot down an adversary he had faced before on the Western Front, an Albatros DV.

Kinkead won his DSO after leading four Camels of B Flight in a devastating victory over cavalry of the freebooting Red Commander Dumenko when they caught some 5,000 horsemen in the open about forty miles west of Tsaritsyn. It was a massacre. Using bombs and machine-guns the Camels destroyed Dumenko's force. Dead and dying men and horses were strewn across the killing ground and as the survivors fled they were cut down by the White Cossacks. Later the Whites claimed to have counted 1,600 casualties. The pilots worked out of a system of close co-operation with the White Cossack General Ulayai. The Camels would attack first; flying just above the ground they were like horsemen themselves. Then the cavalry would charge with their sabres flashing, with the Moslems among them carrying green banners bearing quotations from the Koran.

Collishaw's pilots scored another important victory in September when they gathered all their machines at Beketova only a few minutes' flying time from Dubovka, a town on a loop of the Volga where the Reds had assembled a fleet of some forty boats to bombard Tsaritsyn with guns as large as 9.2 howitzers. The British planes bombed and machine-gunned this fleet for two days without respite. By the third day eleven of them had been sunk and the rest forced to withdraw up the river. Lieutenant Howard Mercer, an observer with C Flight, was awarded the DFC for his "work on this occasion". He had already won the military Cross and been decorated with the Cross of St George by General Wrangel.

Naturally, these exploits could not be kept quiet and while the bravery and expertise of the pilots received a full measure of praise at home there was great pressure from opponents of the intervention for the squadron to be withdrawn. Thus, on October 1st, No. 47 Squadron of the Royal Air Force changed its name to "A" Squadron and officially became part of the training mission. All its members, both officers and men, were required to sign a form explicitly volunteering for service in South Russia with Denikin. A flimsy façade, it nevertheless meant that those who had "been volunteered" before were now able to go home if they so wished.

While all this action had been taking place around Tsaritsyn, Denikin, striking north through Kharkov and Kursk across the battlefield where Russian and German tanks were later to fight the greatest tank battle the world has yet seen, had swept the Red Army aside and, advancing north of Orel, was just over two hundred miles from Moscow. He promised his men that they would be in the capital for Christmas and Lieutenant Charles Roberts, an artillery instructor with the British Mission who was attached to Denikin's staff, later ruefully reminisced that when they took Orel on October 13th "we were deciding which horse we should ride during the triumphal entry into Moscow."

It really did seem that the Bolsheviks were on the point of defeat, but Denikin had overstretched himself. The Anarchist guerrilla leader, Nestor Makhno, attacked his lines of communication, the reorganised Red Army inflicted a series of reverses on his forces and by the end of 1919 he found himself tumbling back in defeat.

Harried by the 1st Cavalry Army, commanded by General

Semyon Budenny, a former sergeant in the Imperial cavalry, Denikin was in desperate need of aerial support. But with certain shining exceptions the newly trained Russian pilots showed a marked reluctance to fly; it was as if merely acquiring their wings was the end of the affair. "They were covered with medals," says Clow, "but they refused to go up the line." It was in these circumstances that Maund gathered his instructors together and said: "We want some of you to go up the line and work with the Russians." Scenting adventure, nobody raised any objections and, hiding from Parliamentary displeasure behind the name of "Z" Flight, they set out to give battle to the Red Army.

The men were allocated one of the special trains. It was made up of flatcars for carrying the aircraft, living accommodation and workshops. It carried everything they needed; a sickbay, a bakery, ammunition wagons for bombs and bullets, carriages filled with drums of fuel. The men had bunks in the third class while the officers slept four to a first class compartment and set up their Mess in a stripped-out third class carriage. The train also had a horse-box complete with two horses, to give the officers exercise.

So "Z" Flight left the comforts of Taganrog with its Yacht Club and theatre where Denikin's own string orchestra played two or three times a week, and steamed north towards the fighting, establishing themselves for some days at Valuyki, north-east of Kharkov. They would take off from flatland alongside the train, carry out their mission and then, if the train was moving on, would scout out another landing ground by a siding where the train could pull in for a few days. These sidings provided centres of activity on the never-ending open plains. They were essential for trains to be able to pass one another on the single track line. Usually situated close to villages, they were also equipped with telegraphs, and provided water and fuel for the trains.

The Flight's first task on arriving at a siding would be to organise its communications, setting up the wireless with its collapsible mast. Equipment would be unloaded, cooking fires built, foraging parties sent into the village to trade for eggs and milk and butter. (One tablet of Pears soap would buy one pound of butter.) And work would start on the "Harry Tates", tuning their engines, restringing wires and occasionally patching a bullet hole.

The day's work over, the men would chat over a pipe after dinner – usually bully beef or a tin of Maconnachie's meat and two veg. Bronzed by the long hot days of summer in Southern Russia, they were glad of the campfire's warmth as it grew colder on the steppes. One of the pilots had a "Decca" and the tunes from London

shows such as *Chu Chin Chow* and *Maid of the Mountains*, would float through the Russian night, until the records became hopelessly scratched. Some of the pilots had taken their shotguns and trout rods to war with them and would supplement their rations with grouse, duck and hare and the occasional fish although the trout were caught more readily by being stunned by hand grenades.

Except for railway troops and passing patrols of cavalry, the pilots had little contact with the army they were fighting for although they sometimes carried Russian officers on reconnaissance flights. They led a strangely isolated life, self-contained, a little piece of England chuntering through the heart of Russia.

One of "Z" Flight's operations was against Semyon Petlyura the Ukrainian nationalist opposed to both the Whites and the Reds who, like Makhno, was attacking Denikin's communications. They caught Petlyura and his men drawn up on a village green with his baggage train of horses and "drozhki" wagons and shot them up. But Clow, flying with a Russian colonel as observer, was unpleasantly surprised to find their fire was being returned. Petlyura had acquired some German machine-guns on anti-aircraft mountings and was using them enthusiastically. Clow's aircraft was peppered but, despite a burst tyre, returned safely. Petlyura, notorious for his anti-semitic pogroms, survived that encounter and many others, but was eventually murdered in Paris by a Jew seeking revenge for the Ukrainian's past cruelty to his people.

This was just one of the cross currents of whose complexities the young pilots were innocent: as far as they were concerned Petlyura was a "bandit". And so the battle of the steppes swirled about them with Red fighting White for the possession of Mother Russia, with Cossacks changing side as the mood took them and with nationalists, anarchists and bandit gangs fighting their own wars for land and loot and ideologies. The young Britons were physically part of it, risking their lives, flying and bombing and strafing, but at the same time this was not their war. They had by now seen enough of atrocities committed by both Whites and Reds to wish a plague on both their houses. They were totally opposed to Bolshevism but the behaviour of Denikin's men, especially the cruelties inflicted on the Jews, appalled them.

This then was the situation when Squadron Leader Joe Archer set up his wireless by the railway line somewhere north of Valuyki and asked for permission to bomb Moscow. Archer and his pilots did not know, however, that their request had been anticipated a month before. On September 19th, Churchill, then Minister of War,

taking eager note of Denikin's advance on Moscow, had telegraphed a warning to Major-General Holman: "I think it inadvisable that British airmen should be used in present circumstances to
bomb Moscow." There was, he added "no military value in this
operation."

That may well have been so, but the real reason was political
rather than military. Churchill was under attack from almost every
quarter in Britain over what was seen as his reckless determination
to drag Britain into another major war before the widows had
stopped crying over the last one. If Joe Archer and his men had
flogged their decrepit "Harry Tates" up the railway line to drop
their tiny bombs on Moscow it would have been seen as proof that
Churchill was indeed running "his own little war". The *Daily
Express*, leading the campaign against the Allied intervention in
Russia, had insisted that the situation was intolerable. "We are
starting a new war the end of which cannot be seen." It was an
argument which had great popular appeal and one with which the
Prime Minister, David Lloyd George, had come to agree.

Major-General Holman was fond of his pilots. He called them
"my boys" and indulged their somewhat overplayful idiosyncra-
sies, making sure they had enough whisky and jars of strong rum
and demanding the dirtiest of ditties at their well-lubricated sing-
songs when he visited them in their railway carriage Mess on the
"Z" Flight Special.

But even the most indulgent of generals could not turn a blind eye
to such specific indications of his political master's wishes as those
which Churchill had telegraphed. And Holman was no political
novice. So that when the morse key chattered its response to
Archer's request it was short and stark: "Permission refused.
Withdraw immediately."

Clow recalled the pilots' reactions: "We were very disappointed.
We had come all this way to do a job and now we were being
ordered to go back . . . But I must admit there was also an
underlying feeling of relief because the old Harry Tates would have
been flying at the very limit of their range, we would only just have
been able to make it with a small bomb load and we were very
frightened of being forced down and captured by the Bolos [the
British nickname for the Bolsheviks]."

So they got on their train and steamed south, not realising that
they were leaving a battlefield on which the future of Russia was
being settled, nor that when the battle was over the Bolsheviks
would be the masters and Communism would have acquired the
base to attempt to realise its dream of world revolution.

CHAPTER 2

"Treacherous Desertion" Russia, 1914–1918

It had started five years before on August 1st, 1914 when, at seven o'clock in the evening, Count Friedrich von Pourtalès, German Ambassador to Russia, drove up to the Ministry of Foreign Affairs in St Petersburg's Palace Square.

Formally dressed, the picture of diplomatic nicety, but with his pale blue eyes brimming with tears, he presented Germany's declaration of war to his friend, Sergei Sazonov, Foreign Minister of His Imperial Majesty, Tsar Nicholas II of Russia.

Sazonov accepted the declaration and then, as he later told the French Ambassador, Maurice Paléologue, said to Pourtalès: "The curses of the nations will be upon you."

"We are defending our honour," replied Pourtalès.

"Your honour was not involved. But there is a divine justice," said Sazonov.

Pourtalès began to weep. "That's true," he quavered, "a divine justice."

The two men then embraced, with Sazonov comforting the distraught Pourtalès as he ushered him out into the warm summer evening.

It was in this manner that the Great War started, a war which was to tear apart empires and destroy kingdoms which had endured nearly a thousand years. Ten million men were to be killed, destroyed by the products of the technological age which had promised to free them from toil and misery. And revolution would lurk in every European capital, waiting to seize power in countries bled white of men and resources and, it was supposed, the will to resist. When it started the Russian generals told their War Office that there was no need to order new typewriters because it would be over before the existing ones would need replacing. But when it ended the generals themselves had been replaced by men who would not have dared talk to them in August 1914.

The Russia which mobilised its brave but ignorant army and sent it into battle was a curious place. A land of peasants, feudalism and agriculture, it was also undergoing rapid industrialisation, fuelled by Western capital and technology and the genius of Count Sergei Witte the statesman and builder of the Trans-Siberian Railway. The picture often presented of a profoundly backward Russia is quite wrong. In many cases the ships designed to replace those lost to the Japanese in 1905 at the Battle of Tsushima were ahead of British and German equivalents. The Russians were also advanced in military aviation. One of their designs which performed well during the war, the Ilya Murometz, was powered by four engines, could carry sixteen passengers or half a ton of bombs and was similar in size to the Flying Fortresses of World War II. This advanced aircraft was designed by Igor Sikorsky who later emigrated to the US and perfected the first practical helicopter.

Russia may have been a land ruled by despotic monarchy, but it was also a nation where the despot walked in fear of his subjects. The revolution of 1905 had been brutally put down but it had frightened the Tsar and brought about the formation of the Duma which, for all its faults, was, nevertheless, a national parliament. As the memories of 1905 receded, however, so the Tsar came to take less and less notice of the Duma even though it was mainly composed of landowners and the new industrialists. But this served only to heat the forces of revolution bubbling beneath the crust of autocracy. It is argued that so strong were these revolutionary forces that the mobilisation of the Army and war served to delay rather than advance the Revolution; certainly there was a great upsurge of patriotism when the war started, but when the Revolution did batter at the gates of the Tsar's Palace it did so with the force of hunger and defeat and two million dead men behind it.

The Army, which was eventually to number nine million, fought with all the dogged bravery for which the ordinary Russian soldier is justly renowned. For the most part, the Tsar's soldiers were poorly equipped and even more poorly led at the highest levels of command. They were often without shells for their guns and in the early days some of them – still with their peasant's foot-cloths wrapped round their legs – faced the brutally efficient German machine-gunners armed only with a cross and a portrait of the Tsar, waiting to inherit a rifle from a fallen comrade. But although the quality of their commanders did not improve, by 1916 the deficiencies in rifles, ammunition and boots had been made up despite the crippling effect of mobilisation and the shortage of raw materials on Russia's newly established industries. Efforts had also been made to ensure that the peasant recruits were given proper training before being sent to the front.

26

The importance to Britain and France of this huge unwieldy army was simple: it held eighty German divisions on the Eastern Front. As the military historian B. H. Liddell Hart was to write: "Let us not forget how many times Russia had sacrificed herself to save her allies, preparing the way for their ultimate victory as surely as for her own downfall."

The greatest of those sacrifices came in June 1916. In answer to desperate pleas from the Allies to take the pressure off the French Army (which was bleeding to death in the man-mincing machine of Verdun), and off the Italians after their defeat by the Austrians at Trentini, General Alexai Brusilov launched an offensive against the Austro-German Front in the Carpathians.

Initially, it was a surprising success. Brusilov defeated the Austrians, forcing them to halt their advance into Italy, and rescuing the French by making the Germans put an end to the bloodbath at Verdun in order to rush thirty-five divisions to the Eastern Front. Brusilov lacked the support of his fellow generals and his success was not followed through, but his offensive probably prevented the Allies from losing the war. Later to become one of the professional soldiers who fought for the Red Army against the White Russians, he was to argue that if his victory had been properly exploited he could have knocked Austria out of the war and thereby forced Germany to sue for peace by the end of the year.

Although the Russian Army performed nobly, Brusilov's victory cost over a million men, possibly half the total of Russians lost during the war as a whole (records were poorly kept – in some regiments not at all). The available figures show that some two million died, five million were wounded and two and a half million were taken prisoner; casualties far greater than any of the other warring nations and as many as the rest of the Allies put together. It is also estimated that something like another million men decided "I will soldier no more" and walked home to reap the harvest.

The war had to be paid for in money as well as in blood and the Russian economy was a shambles. And so, in order to keep the army in the field in the hope that even if the Russian "steam-roller" had stopped rolling at least it would prevent the Germans concentrating all their strength on the Western Front, the British advanced nearly £600 million in loans and the French some £160 million.

Writing about these subventions Konstantin Nabokov, Russian Chargé d'Affaires in London, said in his book, *The Ordeal of a Diplomat*, "Russia became entirely dependent on Great Britain for the prosecution of the war. [She] was unable to repay by material means for the sacrifices in war, material, tonnage, and capital which

Great Britain made to supply our armies. Russia paid only with the rivers of blood of her sons who died in battle. Russia was always asking. Britain was always giving. This condition of affairs undoubtedly had an overwhelming influence upon the psychology of British public opinion and of the government."

But by the beginning of 1917 neither blood nor money could keep Russia in the war. The factories, starved of men and material, were closing. Food shortages and the soaring cost of living brought unrest and strikes to Petrograd and Moscow. The soldiers and the land hungry peasantry of which they were part had had enough. Discontent spread through the middle classes and into the Tsar's entourage. The murder of Rasputin, the Tsarina's evil genius, by Prince Yusupov, worked to give encouragement to the malcontents.

Early in March disorders broke out in Petrograd – renamed from the Germanic St Petersburg at the beginning of the war. One eye-witness, Captain Francis Cromie (the British naval officer who was later to play a tragic part in this story) reported: "The lady tram conductors struck for bread, left their cars in the streets, and threw the starting handles into the canals. The garrison refused to fire on the demonstrators and by Sunday, March 11th, the troops were joining in the protests. Some regiments shot their officers and took to the streets with their rifles. The sailors of the Baltic Fleet mutinied and attacked their officers." Cromie reported that at the Kronstadt naval base, "Viren, the Commander-in-Chief, was cut up in small pieces and burnt in a wooden box in the public square. His wife died, the daughter killed herself and the son, a lieutenant, was shot. One hundred officers have been killed, two hundred are in prison and only eight remain at liberty . . ."

On March 12th, the Duma elected a "Provisional Committee" which assumed the task of restoring order. On March 15th, Tsar Nicholas lost his nerve and abdicated, thereby ending the rule of the Romanov dynasty. There was a ripeness about its fall which made it seem almost inevitable.

Eight months of indecisive rule by the Provisional government followed. A leading role was played by the Constitutional Democrats, confusingly known as the Kadets. This government (a coalition based on existing parties in the Duma), underwent a number of changes during its short life, being led first by Prince George Lvov and then by Alexander Kerensky. It survived an attempt by the Chief of Staff, General Lavr Kornilov, to set up a military dictatorship, and a premature Bolshevik attempt at a coup in July which failed through lack of support and determination. The hard men of

Bolshevism had returned to Russia from exile after the March revolution, Lenin by sealed train from Switzerland, Trotsky by ship from New York, Stalin and other second rank leaders from exile in Siberia.

The revolutionaries had all been caught by surprise. They had not expected the revolution and they had certainly not expected the Tsar to abdicate. The March revolution was not of their doing. The Bolsheviks did not overthrow the Tsar. Only two months before, Lenin had told a group of students in Zurich: "We older men will not live to see the international Socialist revolution . . ." The fabric of Bolshevism in Russia had become threadbare.

But once the Germans, plotting to get Russia out of the war, had helped Lenin and his party of Bolsheviks to return to Russia he began to weave his oratorical magic and the Bolshevik pattern started to emerge.

The Provisional government had to rule in uneasy concert with the Petrograd Soviet of Workers' and Soldiers' Deputies, who were mainly Mensheviks★ who had broken with the Bolsheviks to form their own party, and Socialist Revolutionaries. Nevertheless, despite its less than firm grip on the country, it was recognised by the Allies as the government of Russia because Britain and France desperately needed to keep the country's 8,000,000 soldiers in the war.

This need to maintain the war on the Eastern Front was the overriding motive behind the Allies' dealings with Russia and their attitudes towards the revolution. Nothing else mattered. From the moment the Provisional government took over, the Allied representatives in Petrograd urged on the new rulers the absolute necessity of keeping the German divisions occupied so that they could not be transferred to the Western Front. The new government assured the Allies that Russia would "fight to the last drop of her blood" and "sacredly" swore by the alliances binding her to the other fighting nations.

Kerensky was in dire need of money and Somerset Maugham, an experienced British intelligence agent whose *Ashenden* stories bear all the hallmarks of autobiographical authenticity, was given the job of getting it to him. Then working at the New York "station", Maugham made his way to Vladivostock and then across Siberia to Petrograd – a journey not without adventure – with a large

★ The Mensheviks were a political party set up in August 1917 at a Congress of several Social Democratic groups. Before 1917 the word denoted the non-Leninist faction of the Russian Social Democratic Workers' Party.

amount of cash for the Russian leader. "I went as a private agent," Maugham wrote in his autobiography, "who could be disavowed if necessary, with instructions to get in touch with parties hostile to the government and devise a scheme that would keep Russia in the war and prevent the Bolsheviks, supported by the Central Powers, from seizing power."

However, the Allies wanted more than just protestations of loyalty in exchange for their money, and their ambassadors and military representatives urged Kerensky to break the semi-truce which had settled over the front line – Germany was preoccupied with the Western Front and Russia with her own revolution. So the unwilling soldiers, once subject to the discipline of the knout, the heavy leather whips so freely wielded by Tsarist NCOs, but who now debated every command, were ordered into a summer offensive. It opened on July 1st and achieved some initial success. But the Germans counter-attacked and by late July the offensive had turned into a catastrophe. The men of the Eleventh Army shot their officers and went home looting and burning villages in their path. Some loyal regiments held the line but the Russian Army's role in the war was finished, a fact which took the Allies a long time to accept. Once again wishful thinking prevailed over reason.

This final military disaster gave rise to a wave of violence which became known as "The July Days". At first the demonstrations seemed to be spontaneous and sporadic but there was one common cry: "Down with the Government – all power to the Soviets." These Soviets – committees – were by no means all Bolshevik, being composed of members of a number of different political groups. The Bolsheviks had indeed been active in stirring up trouble but when the time came the leadership of the party hesitated and failed to take the final step. Even Lenin, who had returned in haste from Finland where he had been plotting, advised caution. The demonstrations fizzled out and when the government released evidence which appeared to show that Lenin had been working for the Germans the people's anger turned against the Bolsheviks. A group of armed men wrecked the offices of *Pravda*, the party newspaper, and another group burst into the ornate palace of the ballet dancer Mathilda Kshesinskaya which the Bolsheviks had taken over for their headquarters. But the Bolshevik leaders had gone underground. Kerensky, who had been at the front, returned to Petrograd and on July 19th ordered Lenin's arrest. The Bolshevik leader was on the run, hiding in a haystack in a forest a few miles north of Petrograd, before seeking refuge with sympathisers in Finland. Many years later Kerensky, in exile, was asked why he had not ordered Lenin to be shot while he had had the chance. He replied that he had not, at the time, thought that the Bolshevik leader was important enough for such a drastic act.

By the end of July the Bolsheviks were in disarray. Trotsky was in prison and Lenin was forced to write letters and pamphlets from Finland denying he had worked for the Germans. It has become an article of faith in the Soviet Union that he was innocent of these charges, even though German official records of the time show that he was in contact with the Germans and accepted help from them. But then Lenin would have supped with the devil himself to bring Communism to Russia.

However, if the Bolsheviks were in disarray so was the government. Kerensky's economic policies had collapsed. There were strikes, mass unemployment and hunger. All confidence in his ability to govern was lost.

Then on September 6th, 1917 General Kornilov, the commander-in-chief of the Army, marched on Petrograd in an attempt to take over the government. He failed, largely because his troops had little stomach for the enterprise. But he caused such alarm in the city that the government issued weapons to any organisation willing to fight him. And that included the Bolsheviks, many of whom were released from prison to fight Kornilov. When the scare was over Kerensky asked them to return these weapons. They laughed at him. The Bolsheviks were back in business.

Kornilov was used by the Bolsheviks as a reactionary bogeyman to frighten the people. They exploited the strikes and hunger and general discontent. Lenin wrote from Finland on September 13th urging the Bolshevik Party's Central Committee to prepare for an armed uprising. Plans must be made, he demanded, for the seizure of Petrograd. The Central Committee, appalled by his violence and his indiscretion, burnt the letter. But nothing would now stop Lenin. He harangued his colleagues from the safety of Finland, demanding action.

On October 22nd, Lenin shaved off his beard and, wearing a wig, travelled from Finland, and so disguised slipped into Petrograd. The next day the Central Committee convened a meeting. In a night-long debate Lenin convinced Trotsky, who had been released from prison, Stalin and Dzerzhinsky, the man who was to run the Red Terror, that "an armed uprising has become inevitable and acute."

It seemed that everyone knew the Bolsheviks were about to attempt a coup. The Petrograd Soviet met continuously. The Delegates to the All-Russian Congress of Soviets assembled.

Everywhere there was speech-making and uproar with Trotsky whipping the Congress's meetings into Revolutionary frenzy with the power of his oratory.

The time was unquestionably ripe for another revolution: even the fact that elections arranged by the Provisional government to form a democratic Constituent Assembly were about to be held did not prevent it. But when the uprising came, it was a rather weak, badly organised affair, despite all Lenin's exhortations. It could have been put down with resolution and two regiments of loyal troops – for all the Bolsheviks had were their Red Guards, armed civilians with little discipline, and even more unruly sailors from the Baltic Fleet. But when Kerensky left the city to rally the Army's support he could find only seven hundred Cossacks willing to fight for him.

By the evening of November 7th, with Kerensky still out of the city trying to convince the Army to march, his leaderless government had gathered in the Tsar's Winter Palace (everywhere else was in the hands of the Bolsheviks and the mob). As most of the Winter Palace's garrison had fled, demoralised by Bolshevik propaganda, the Ministers were guarded only by a party of officer cadets and 130 women soldiers from a battalion of women led by a redoubtable woman called Maria Bochkareva. They had sworn to fight to the death against the Germans. But that was a different war, and when the cruiser *Aurora* fired a blank shot at the Palace and field artillery opened up a sporadic bombardment, the women surrendered. The cadets, who were willing to fight, but were forbidden to open fire by the fearful Ministers, followed suit. Thus when the Bolsheviks stormed the Palace there was virtually no resistance. Their death-toll was minimal: six Red Guards were killed, four of them by bullets fired by their own comrades.

The next day the British Ambassador, Sir George Buchanan, made the following entry in his diary:

> I walked out this afternoon to see the damage that had been done to the Winter Palace by the prolonged bombardment of the previous evening.
>
> In the evening two officer instructors of the women's battalion came to my wife and beseeched her to try and save the women-defenders of the Winter Palace, who, after they had surrendered, had been sent to one of the barracks where they were being most brutally treated by the soldiers. General Knox [Military Attaché] at once drove to the Bolshevik headquarters at the Smolny Institute. His demands for their immediate release were at first

refused on the ground that they had resisted desperately, fighting to the last with bombs and revolvers. Thanks however, to his firmness and persistence, the order for their release was eventually signed, and the women were saved from the fate that would have inevitably befallen them had they spent the night at the barracks.

In the evening Lenin was thunderously cheered into the Congress of Soviets, where he read his *Decree of Peace* proposing "to all belligerent peoples and their governments the immediate opening of negotiations for a just and democratic peace." The resolution was passed unanimously. John Reed, the American journalist, recorded the scene in his *Ten Days that Shook the World*: " 'The war is ended,' said a young workman near me, his face shining. And when it was over, as we stood there in a kind of awkward hush, someone in the back of the room shouted, 'Comrades, let us remember those who have died for liberty.' So we began to sing the Funeral March, that slow, melancholy, and yet triumphant chant, so Russian and so moving."

However, the triumph was not yet complete nor was the fighting over. The Bolsheviks waited apprehensively for Kerensky who was marching on the city with his Cossacks. In the city there was some fighting and a strike of civil servants against the new masters. Red Guards went to meet the Cossacks.

The battle, when it was joined at Tsarskoe Selo, was short and, once again, little blood was spilt. The Cossacks quickly gave up the fight, having listened to the speeches of Bolshevist agitators who had crept into their camp. Kerensky fled into exile. Through lack of resolution he had lost Petrograd, lost his government and lost Russia. It had been a revolution of words. Even the *Aurora*'s historic opening shell had been a blank. The bloodshed was still to come.

There had been no outpouring of grief in the West when the Tsar abdicated. Certainly King George V was deeply saddened by the downfall of "Cousin Nicky" for whom he had a great affection and arrangements were suggested whereby the Tsar and his family would be put on a British cruiser and taken to exile in Britain. The Provisional government was happy to agree to this but political realities obviously triumphed over Royal sentiments. According to evidence given later by Kerensky the Provisional government received a message by way of Ambassador Buchanan which said: "The [British] government does not consider it possible to extend its hospitality to the former Tsar while the war continues."

33

The Tsar's presence would certainly have been an embarrassment to the government at a time of great danger on the Western Front and the threat of civil disorder at home, especially on the Clyde where Russian sailors marched alongside British socialists in the May Day parade of 1917. To most Englishmen the Tsar represented a system of feudal tyranny which was anathema to the British system of democracy.

As for the Americans, most of them were delighted by the downfall of the Romanovs. The Russian monarchy represented everything to which the Americans, aggressive in their traditions of individual liberty, were opposed. What is more, shipload after shipload of refugees from Russia and its subject nations, fleeing from the pogroms, the knout and the Cossacks' sabres had been arriving in the United States in a wave of immigration since the 1890s. Not one of the immigrants would shed a single tear for the Tsar.

Even France, which had entered into an alliance with Russia in 1892, expressed no sorrow over his fall.★ The principles of France's own revolution, Liberty, Equality and Fraternity, remained the very antithesis of Tsarist autocracy.

Internationally there had been indeed something of a rush to recognise the Provisional government. The United States did so on March 22nd, just one week after the Tsar's abdication. Britain and France followed two days later. The House of Commons and the French Chamber of Deputies sent messages of sympathy and encouragement to the new government. In a despatch to Prince Lvov, David Lloyd George welcomed Russia into the ranks of those nations "which base their institutions upon responsible government." And when President Wilson led the United States into the war on April 2nd, 1917, he welcomed "the heartening things that have been happening within the last few weeks in Russia" and he praised "the great, generous Russian people [who] have been added in all their native majesty and might to the forces that are fighting for freedom in the world, for justice and for peace. Here is a fit partner for a League of Honor."

These official messages undoubtedly reflected the feeling of the people of Britain, France and the United States. But, in truth, the military and political leaders of the countries who for nearly three years had been fighting the most dreadful war which they were

---

★ This alliance was designed to safeguard both countries against Prussia's expansionist designs. The French Ambassador, Maurice Paléologue, was so deeply committed to the Tsar that he had to be recalled immediately after the revolution.

fearful of losing did not care who controlled Russia as long as they fought the Germans.

This preoccupation with keeping Russia in the war became an obsession which led to the wildest of military fantasies: the re-establishment of an Eastern Front by an Allied army transported seven thousand miles across Siberia and then supplied by non-existent roads and a railway in a chaotic state of disrepair. The French general, Ferdinand Foch, who, in 1918 became Commander-in-Chief of the Allied Forces in France, urged this plan in an interview with the *New York Times.* "Germany is walking through Russia," he argued. "America and Japan who are in a position to do so should go to meet her in Siberia."

The need to prevent the Germans – and the Turks – "walking through Russia" led to Britain and France giving support to various nationalist groups which sprang up in Southern Russia: Cossacks, Ukrainians, Georgians and others who saw the break up of the Tsarist empire as an ideal opportunity to assert their independence. This was a dangerous game for the Provisional government and, later, the Bolshevik government, were determined to maintain as much of the empire as possible and reacted strongly to the British and French support of these groups, some of whom were little better than bandits.

The British Ambassador, Sir George Buchanan, and General Alfred Knox, the Military Attaché, both warned that these bands were ineffectual and that to support them would serve no useful purpose. Furthermore, as Knox cabled to London: "to ask us to intrigue with Cossacks while we are in the power of the rebel government is merely to get our throats cut to no purpose." But even that warning – and Buchanan and Knox came close to being arrested after the Bolshevik takeover – was ignored in the belief that if these forces in the south were provided with money and weapons they would continue to fight the Germans and the Turks.

There were other factors involved, too. There was also the need to prevent wheat from the Ukraine and oil from Baku being used to break the British naval blockade which was strangling Germany. And, with the Russian Army giving up the fight, there was a revival of the "Great Game" fear of an invasion of India, Britain's "jewel in the crown", through Persia and Afghanistan; not now by Russia but by the Germans and their Turkish allies who were trying to raise the flag of Islam throughout Central Asia.

The British, who had a number of intelligence officers operating in the south, and the French, who had a military mission established in Rumania trying to preserve the remnants of that country's defeated army, then made a move which the Russians claim was the first indication that the Allies intended to intervene in Russia. On December 23rd, 1917, they signed a convention dividing Southern Russia into zones of influence. The French assumed responsibility for Bessarabia, the Ukraine and the Crimea, and Britain was assigned the Cossack territories, Caucasus, Armenia, Georgia and Kurdistan. We shall later examine the results of this convention but what should be pointed out now is that by the end of 1917 both Britain and France were very heavily involved in the confusion of events in South Russia.

It seems astonishing today that the Allies still hoped that they could persuade the Russians back into the war. After the débâcle of the summer offensive the Russian Army had ceased to exist as a cohesive body; according to General Knox it had been "irretrievably ruined". And once Lenin seized power there was never any question but that he would sue for peace with the Germans on almost any terms, for he needed peace in order to consolidate Bolshevik control over Russia.

Lenin had spelt it out in his *Decree of Peace* in which he demanded an immediate end to World War I on "just and democratic peace terms"; and on November 22nd, the Bolshevik government ordered the troops in the front line to fraternise with the Germans and start truce talks wherever they could. General Dukhonin, Commander-in-Chief of the Army, was told to open immediate negotiations with the Germans. Poor Dukhonin. He was in an impossible situation. Kerensky had vanished, and Dukhonin was on his own though still nominally in command of millions of soldiers. Eventually he refused to obey the order, only to be replaced on Moscow's direction by an ensign called Krylenko who turned up at army headquarters at Mogilev with a bodyguard of fifty Red sailors. Dukhonin was seized and then lynched by his own soldiers, being thrown into the air to land on their bayonets. It was thus that the Russian soldiers celebrated the decision to make peace with the Germans.

On November 24th, Trotsky told the Army: "Your Soviet government will not allow the foreign bourgeoisie to wield a club over your head and drive you into the slaughter again." On November 29th, the Allied Embassies received a message from the Bolshevik government informing them that military operations on the Russian front had ended and that negotiations with the Germans would start on December 2nd. The following day Lenin and Stalin combined to issue an appeal to the people of India to liquidate

British rule, "overthrow these robbers and enslavers", and urged them to "struggle for the freedom that the coming of Soviet power had given the eastern peoples of Russia." It was a call to action hardly likely to please the British government and further worked to make British moves in Southern Russia to defend India's frontiers seem both timely and apposite. Then, on December 22nd, the German and Bolshevik emissaries met at Brest-Litovsk in the first plenary session of the peace talks which were finally to take Russia out of the war.

Ever since the failure of General Brusilov's summer offensive the Allies had disregarded Russia as a functioning member of the war effort. Additionally British and American newspapers had begun to snipe at the Russian leaders. And when the humiliating peace terms were eventually accepted by Lenin on March 3rd, 1918, the Bolsheviks were attacked as traitors in the pay of the Germans.

The Times had already responded to delegates at the Soviet Congress who had spoken of "the coming world revolution" with an editorial arguing that "the remedy for Bolshevism is bullets". Now the *New York Times* ran stories about Bolshevik treachery under headlines reading: "Russians Sell Out to the Germans" and "Bolsheviki Yield Russia's Riches to Berlin". Winston Churchill later summed up British feelings: "Every British and French soldier killed last year," he said in a speech at the Connaught Rooms on April 11th, 1919, "was really done to death by Lenin and Trotsky, not in fair war, but by the treacherous desertion of an ally without parallel in the history of the world."

He later returned to this theme in his book *The World Crisis*. The Germans, he wrote, "had employed poison gas on the largest scale and had invented the '*Flammenwerfer*' (flame-thrower). Nevertheless it was with a sense of awe that they turned upon Russia the most grisly of all weapons. They transported Lenin in a sealed truck like a plague bacillus from Switzerland into Russia."

Churchill and the Allies, however, were not the only critics of the Treaty of Brest-Litovsk. Its terms were harsh: Russia surrendered Poland-Lithuania, Courland, Riga and part of Belorussia to Germany. In the Caucasus, Kars, Batum and Ardahan were ceded to Turkey. Russia also acknowledged the independence of the German-protected government of the Ukraine. The loss of this territory amounted to 27% of the sown area of Russia, 26% of the population – 46 million people – 26% of the railways and 75% of the iron and steel. In addition the Bolsheviks agreed to pay three thousand million roubles in gold as reparations. So brutal were these demands that many Bolsheviks were in favour of taking up the fight against Germany again and waging a "revolutionary war".

It was Lenin who bullied and cajoled and manoeuvred them into accepting the terms, not because he was a German agent but because he knew that if Russia went to war again the Bolshevik Revolution would be finished; the Germans could not be stopped. And to him nothing mattered except the survival of Bolshevism. He was sure that as long as it did survive, then world revolution would eventually follow as sure as night follows day.

But there were few with his vision and his faith. Russia appeared to be on the point of disintegration. The Tsar's empire was crumbling with its peripheral states claiming independence; the German Army still menaced Petrograd and Moscow; the Tsar was still alive and his supporters were building their forces; the Bolsheviks were by no means the strongest party in Russia and they were riven with dissension. There was hunger in the land, unrest in the factories, mutiny in the forces. Every day was full of danger.

It was now in the spring of 1918 that the Allies decided to intervene.

CHAPTER 3

Intervention by Invitation
Murmansk, March–June 1918

By the end of 1917 there was an astonishing number of foreign soldiers on Russian soil, men caught up in the restless tides of war. An army of Czechs marched about the Ukraine, having been recruited as prisoners of war. They now turned against their erstwhile masters, the Austro-Hungarians. Serbs trudged north from Odessa where they had been stranded when the Russians gave up the fight. British agents, professing Islam, spied throughout Central Asia. A Royal Navy armoured car squadron, commanded by the dashing Commander Oliver Locker Lampson, a Conservative Member of Parliament, had been operating with skill and panache on the Galician front. A French Military Mission was making its way north from Rumania, following the defeat of the Rumanian Army by the Germans, and a British Military Mission served in Petrograd where there was also an Anglo-Russian hospital. At sea, a squadron of British warships based on Murmansk and Archangel patrolled the far north, with British, Japanese and American warships far to the east at Vladivostok. And a flotilla of British submarines operated out of Russian bases in Finland.

All these forces would eventually play their part in the Allied intervention, but the distinction of carrying out what is generally recognised as the first overt military act fell to 130 men of the Royal Marines.

On March 6th, 1918 they disembarked from the old battleship, HMS *Glory*, flagship of the British squadron in the far north, and marched through the dank, cold, refuse-strewn streets of Murmansk to a verminous log-hut previously occupied by Russian sailors. There, they set up their guns and remained for the next few weeks doing little else but clean up their malodorous living quarters. They were part of an extra-strong detachment of 176 men plus their officers embarked on the *Glory* specifically to quell any disturbances which threatened the safety of the stores and harbour at Murmansk. In fact the *Glory* was carrying so many marines that

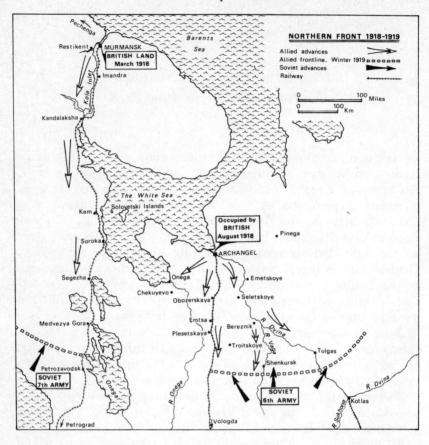

she had to disembark some of her seamen to make room for the soldier-sailors known in the navy as "The Turkeys".

The landing was considered so routine by the Royal Marines that it is only briefly mentioned in their official records. But it is seen in the Soviet Union as the initial act of a worldwide conspiracy by the forces of capitalism and imperialism to strangle the newborn Communist state. The fact that the marines landed with the full agreement of the local soviet, or council, acting under the express instructions of Trotsky in order to save the port falling into the hands of the Germans is simply regarded as another example of Trotsky's perfidy.

It happened that the leader of the Murmansk Soviet, a former sailor called Yurev, convinced like everyone else in Murmansk that a fifty thousand strong army of Germans and White Finns was about to attack, telegraphed Trotsky in Petrograd asking for permission to accept Allied help. This telegram arrived when it seemed that the Brest-Litovsk peace talks were breaking down and that the Germans would resume their march into Russia. In these circumstances Trotsky telegraphed back: ". . . You must accept any and all assistance from the Allied missions and use every means to obstruct the advance of the plunderers . . ."

Indeed the landing was marked by an unusual courtesy from the mutinous Russian sailors who had taken over their 11,000 ton battleship *Chesma*. As the Royal Marines marched into barracks, the *Glory* fired a salute to the Red Flag and it was answered by the guns of the *Chesma* – named after a Russian naval victory won, thanks to British help, over the Turks in 1769.

That the White Finns (who under Marshal Mannerheim had fought and won a three-month-long civil war against the Red Finns), were equipped with German uniforms and were therefore mistaken for Germans thus giving an exaggerated picture of German strength in Finland, is of no consequence in the argument because the danger was perceived to be real. With the Russians obviously unable to defend the port in the anarchic situation which prevailed – the Bolsheviks were clinging to power by their fingernails and the Germans were threatening to resume their march eastwards – it was seen by Britain and her allies as imperative that they should intervene to beat off the threat to Murmansk.

Ironically, Murmansk, which today is the main base of the Soviet Northern Fleet of some six hundred ships including nuclear powered and armed submarines (some of which are targeted on Britain) was built at the insistence of the British with British financial and technical help.

The Allies had to have such an ice-free port in order to land the supplies needed to maintain Russia's war effort. Archangel, the only established port in North-West Russia not blockaded by the Germans, was open for only five months of the year. The figures show the importance of this northern route: in 1916 more than 600 ships, most of them British, landed a million tons of coal and a million and a half tons of weapons and food for the loss of thirty-six ships to German U-boats. Nearly five million tons of war supplies were delivered to Russia by the Arctic route in the First World War, one million tons more than in the Second.

Archangel could not cope with this flood of supplies in the short time it was open each year. Neither the men, the handling facilities nor the railways were available, and by the end of 1917 some 12,000 tons of explosives and 200,000 tons of other military supplies for which the armies were crying out in France were rusting and rotting in the open around this post.

Work on building Murmansk on the River Kola was started in September 1915 on the site of a run-down fishing village redolent with the stench of rotting codsheads. It had the soon to be embarrassing name of Romanov and lay on the east bank of the Kola under the side of a hill about 600 feet high. Korean and Chinese labourers were brought in to do the heavy work and, as there were no means of communication except along the rivers and through forest paths, a single track railway was started across the 600 miles of pine forest and marsh which separated this primitive fishing village from the glories of Petrograd.

It was a task of the utmost difficulty. Neither the port nor railway was finished until the end of 1916, just a few months before the Tsar abdicated. The building of the railway was a desperate affair, the First World War's equivalent of the Burma–Siam Railway in the second. The Russians used German prisoners of war to gouge the railbed out of the wilderness and these half-starved men, living in appalling conditions, frozen in winter and plagued by clouds of mosquitoes in summer, were struck down by malnutrition, typhus and cholera. So many died that German Army lore says that there is a man buried under each sleeper of the line. On completion it was so crude that trains swayed alarmingly in the summer as the rails sank into the thawing marsh. Hundreds of wooden bridges spanned swift rivers and the track roller-coasted up and down steep inclines, but the line was effective and provided the vital link from Murmansk to Petrograd, from the Arctic to the then capital of Russia.

At the grand opening ceremony trains loaded with officials steamed through triumphant arches. Allied officers were shown the workmen's dwellings, the hospital and the new station buildings and they remarked how they were mostly built of logs with moss rammed into the crevices to keep out the wind. But though there was much speechmaking nobody referred to the German prisoners who had died during its construction.

With its fine harbour Murmansk served another purpose. It was used as the base for a British squadron of ships under the command of Rear-Admiral Thomas Kemp whose task was to keep the sealanes free from German U-boats and minelayers. This was properly the Russians' responsibility but they were either unable or unwilling to do the job and so it fell to the British to undertake most of the anti-submarine and minesweeping patrols.

Kemp used the Kola inlet where the river ran into the Barents Sea in the winters before Murmansk was built, leaving a large staff frozen in at Archangel to handle the stores landed during the summer. However, simply by building Murmansk the Allies had created a new, even graver problem for themselves: if the Germans could succeed in capturing the port, they would have a ready made U-boat base from which they would have a free run out into the North Atlantic past Iceland without having to run the gauntlet in the densely mined and closely patrolled North Sea.

The Americans, helped by the British, had laid a barrage of 70,000 mines across the North Sea to bottle up the U-boats and prevent them from getting among the troopships carrying the fresh, eager armies of America on which Britain and France, drained of men and weary of war, were relying to defeat the Germans. By capturing Murmansk the Germans would have stretched Allied naval resources to breaking point. And it was the naval blockade which was bringing Germany to her knees.

The political and military consequences of the Kaiser's U-boats sinking troopships full of young Americans heading for the battle-fields of France would have been disastrous and it was mainly for this reason that the Royal Marines landed at Murmansk. Even so, it was only a token gesture, for in late February Admiral Kemp had asked for 6,000 men to defend the port against the threat of attack from Finland.

His request was refused because every man was needed for the Western Front where General Erich Ludendorff, the German quartermaster-general, was preparing his critical series of attacks designed to defeat Britain and France before the Americans could bring their full strength to bear. He had massed 62 divisions, 35 of which he had been able to switch from the Eastern Front when Russia opted out of the war. At the same time Britain was so short of infantrymen that its army divisions had been cut from 12 to 9 battalions and the tank and aircraft factories were being raided for able bodied men. Another factor in British thinking was the knowledge that Admiral Kemp was an excitable man: possibly his superiors thought he was getting a touch over-anxious.

However, the unfounded reports of thousands of Germans pouring across the Finnish border and heading for Murmansk caused such concern among the Allies that plans were made to use the Czech forces remaining in European Russia to defend the northern ports. The Admiralty also detached the cruiser *Cochrane* from the Grand Fleet, the French sent the heavy cruiser *Amiral Aube* and the Americans, with the reluctance which was the hallmark of their behaviour throughout the intervention, sent the cruiser *Olympia* –

but not until April. These ships provided much needed support for Kemp whose Squadron had shrunk to the *Glory* and eight trawlers armed with 12-pounder guns and converted into minesweepers. Kemp also had his personal steam yacht which had been given to the Imperial Russian Navy by Sir Gordon Bennett, the wealthy racing driver, and which was still manned by Russian sailors.

Moored near his ships were the *Chesma*, which was now aground and unseaworthy, and the cruiser *Askold* which, because of her five tall slim funnels, was known to the British Navy as the "packet of Woodbines". The *Askold* had led a curious existence. She had narrowly escaped the Japanese destruction of the Russian fleet in 1905 and then in 1915 the Tsar sent her to Gallipoli to take part in what he anticipated would be a great Allied victory. When that victory turned to ashes she spent nearly a year refitting in Toulon before sailing to Devonport in February 1917 to complete her refit. The crew, subverted by Russian communists living in exile in France, were ripe for mutiny. When the Revolution broke out they formed a ship's committee and sent two delegates to call on Ivan Maisky, then one of the émigré leaders in London. Maisky, later Soviet Ambassador to Britain, was to recall his feelings in his book *Journey into the Past*: "I had been reading and thinking so much of the Russian Revolution and was so passionately yearning to take my part in the distant, splendid events unrolling in Petrograd, in Moscow . . . so far away . . . And now the Revolution had suddenly come to me on my own doorstep, here in London, and calling me to service under the Red flag. It was something out of a fairy story."

Maisky told Ramsay MacDonald about his callers and the Labour leader insisted on giving them lunch in the House of Commons where, posing beside the framed sentence of death passed on King Charles, he declaimed: "We have been a revolutionary nation before and we will be a revolutionary nation again."

Maisky then went to Devonport and spent three days on the *Askold* with the crew endlessly debating what to do with their officers. Maisky, fearful of British reaction if the crew mutinied in a British port, persuaded them to sail for Murmansk. Once there, the captain was taken on shore and shot. The other officers were arrested.

The *Chesma*'s crew mutinied at the same time along with those of four destroyers and a number of minesweepers and steam yachts. The breakdown in discipline was complete. Once they got rid of their officers the sailors spent their time holding political meetings.

Lieutenant Augustus Agar (who is to figure further in events) was in Murmansk on HMS *Iphigenia* when the mutiny broke out. He was especially affected by it because the *Askold* had been "chummy ship" to HMS *Hibernia* when he served in her at Gallipoli. "We never," he wrote "saw any of our officer friends again."

But although rust bloomed on the Russian warships, as the mutineers neglected their upkeep, the guns – the *Chesma* mounted four 12-inch and twelve 6-inch and the *Askold* twelve 6-inch – could still be brought into action. Additionally there were nearly 2,000 sailors in Murmansk, all of them committed to revolution. Obviously they presented a threat to Kemp's meagre squadron.

Given this background to the landing of the Royal Marines it can hardly be seen as the opening move of a great conspiracy. But as the story of the intervention unfolds we shall see how its character changed. What began as a series of self-contained expeditions thousands of miles apart, each with its own aims and dynamics, connected only by the over-riding need to defeat Germany would turn inexorably into a crusade against Bolshevism. Lenin, driven by fear and ambition, made that crusade inevitable. His fear stemmed from German threats to resume the war in Russia if he did not get rid of the Allied forces operating on Russian soil; and his ambition lay in his dream of world revolution and the downfall of capitalism.

That was still to come, however, and in the weeks following the landing of the marines the Murmansk Soviet, the Red Guards and Admiral Kemp's men continued to co-operate. In the middle of April the British undertook their first operation of the intervention. Far from being an attack on the Bolsheviks, they went into action at the request of the Murmansk Soviet, going to the aid of a party of Red Finns who had been chased over the border by the White Finns and were being harried along the line of the now completed Murmansk to Petrograd railway.

HMS *Cochrane*, which had sailed into Murmansk the day after *Glory*'s marines had marched ashore, landed a party of its own marines who, reinforced by members of the French Military Mission to Rumania who had at last arrived at Murmansk, set out by armoured train for the village of Kandalaksha. Their wood-burning train puffed eighty miles through the pine forests with 3-pounder cannons and machine-guns poking out of the sides of flat cars crenellated with sandbags like a castle on wheels. But those among them who were spoiling for a fight were disappointed. Having frightened off the White Finns without any serious altercation, they got on the train and steamed back to Murmansk marvelling at this vast, strange land and its even stranger people. Further south down the railway line the White Finns did capture the town of Kem but they were driven out by Russian Red Guards.

A couple of weeks later *Cochrane*'s marines were sent into action again and this time they fired their guns in anger. These shots were of some historical importance because they were the first fired in the intervention and they were fired by the British in aid of the Bolsheviks.

On May 2nd, 1918, the Murmansk Soviet told Admiral Kemp that it had received reports that the White Finns, then allied with the Germans, had reached Pechenga (the Finnish Petsamo) which in those days was a tiny fishing village remarkable only for an imposing monastery. There were no wharves, no communications, no facilities, just acres and acres of mud at low tide, but it was feared that its landlocked harbour could provide a base from which German U-boats could sail to attack Allied shipping in the North Atlantic.

In those terrible days when Ludendorff's armies were raining blow after blow on the reeling, exhausted, British and French armies on the Western Front any new threat to the allies, especially to the troopships taking fresh, eager American soldiers to France, added to the mounting panic in Paris and London. So Admiral Kemp readily agreed to send a force to tackle the White Finns.

HMS *Cochrane* re-embarked her marines and steamed off to Pechenga, thirty sea miles away. She landed forty marines under the command of Captain V. Brown of the Royal Marine Artillery, forty Red Guards, and a hundred British seamen. They recruited fifteen sympathetic locals who knew the ground and engaged in a series of brisk running fights with the White Finns.

Like most Finns they proved to be skilful and courageous soldiers. Dressed in white, they were admirably camouflaged and used skis to move swiftly over the deep snow. In the initial encounters they forced the marines to retreat. But on May 6th another thirty-five marines from HMS *Glory* arrived with five Lewis guns; a naval 12-pounder was also dragged over the ice from the *Cochrane*. But what really gave the marines an advantage was the Finns' use of the only telephone line in the district. The marines plugged in and using one of their local recruits as a translator were able to learn the details of their opponents' plans.

When the marines went into action again on May 8th, they were able to give a much better account of themselves and after more fighting on May 10th established themselves with their headquarters in the monastery from which they controlled the village and the harbour, such as it was. Two days later they were able to head off a determined attack by over 150 White Finns. That was the last of the fighting at Pechenga. Among the few British casualties was Captain Brown, who was wounded in the shoulder and subsequently awarded the DSO.

The importance of these skirmishes was emphasised by the appearance of a U-boat off the coast near Pechenga which proceeded to sink a number of small Russian steamers and Norwegian fishing boats. However, the U-boat disappeared and the Finnish threat to Pechenga was removed by the coming thaw and the establishment of a substantial garrison which included some 200 Serbs who had finally struggled through to Murmansk. Many of them were unfit but the addition of 200 riflemen who were good soldiers was a great bonus for Kemp. They were, said one of the marines, "most excellent fellows".

In fact, the threat from Pechenga did not materialise until twenty-three years later when the Germans used it as the base for their unsuccessful drive on Murmansk during World War II. Their objective then was still what had been feared in 1918: the cutting of the supply lines by which the Allies were sustaining Russia and the establishment of a U-boat den from which the wolf packs could sail against the Allied convoys.

All the same this strange passage of arms in May 1918, conducted around a monastery in the remote snowfields of the northernmost tip of Europe saw the first shots, the first medal and the first bloodshed in a procession of events which has still not been resolved today.

While Captain Brown and his men were conducting their small but significant battles, the business of reinforcing Murmansk had moved into top gear. A Royal Marine Field Force was hurriedly put together under Lieutenant-Colonel R. C. Paterson, consisting of a field battery, a company of the Royal Marine Light Infantry and a machine-gun section. Formed on May 5th, it left Eastney Barracks on May 20th, embarked on the SS *Porto* at Newcastle and arrived at Murmansk on May 29th. The field force took over the wooden barracks previously occupied by the marines from *Glory* and were deeply thankful that they had done such a thorough job of attacking the lice and fleas. A detachment of Royal Engineers had also arrived for "demolition purposes", presumably to blow up the port if the Germans arrived.

On May 23rd the British government ordered the despatch of a small expeditionary force and training mission to North Russia. The following day Major-General Frederick Poole arrived in Murmansk on board the American cruiser *Olympia* which had been Admiral Dewey's flagship in the American-Spanish war. Poole had been sent out under the guise of "British Military Representative in Russia"; in fact he was Commander-in-Chief of Allied forces. A gunner, a fine soldier with an enviable fighting record who had been chief of the British Artillery Mission with the Russian Army, he knew Archangel – British guns had been landed there – and he knew about the Russian winter. He seemed in all respects to be ideal for the job. But, alas, he was a soldier's soldier, bluff and forthright, and what was needed in North Russia was a politician with the mind of a Machiavelli.

The man chosen to lead the expeditionary force was a much more subtle character, Major-General Sir Charles Maynard who had served in Burma, South Africa and throughout the Great War. As he recounts in his book, *The Murmansk Venture*, he was recruited for the job in typically British style, being accosted by an old friend serving in the War Office while he was lunching at his club.

Having accepted the job, Maynard found himself in some difficulty because he had been invalided home from Salonika and a medical board refused to pass him as fit for active service. He had to wangle his way past the board with the aid of a senior officer who insisted that he could not divulge the nature of his new appointment but guaranteed that it would be of a purely sedentary nature.

The board need not have been so fussy: when Maynard came to examine the men he was to command he found that nearly all of them were unfit for active service. They were either B2 (Base duty abroad) or B3 (Sedentary duty abroad) and most had been wounded at least once. Every fit man was needed for the trenches in France to withstand the German offensive. Maynard got only the rejects.

He was told that there would be 600 of them and that the 400 Royal Marines, and the Royal Engineers, Serbs and French artillery already in Murmansk would also come under his command. In addition there would be a military mission of 570, mainly officers and non-commissioned officers, whose task would be to re-equip and train the 25,000 Czechs who were supposedly making their way north.

Maynard's expeditionary force set sail from Newcastle on June 16th on board the heavily camouflaged *City of Marseilles*. It was a remarkable voyage.

Among the men who sailed that day was Lieutenant Peter Crawford, a regular soldier in the Royal Scots who had been commissioned in the field in France and was attached to the

48

Machine Gun Corps. In his graphic diary he tells how they set out on June 15th from their training camp:

> Alexandra Day, which the troops had been celebrating in good style, left Colchester about 9 p.m. Men had almost without exception flags attached to the end of their rifles. The band of the Queens Regiment played us to the station via Abbey Fields. Had a glorious send off. Colonel 'Two No Trumps' in a very merry mood or perhaps 'just nicely thank you'. The train moved off about an hour later, the band played 'Auld Lang Syne' and 'Will Ye No Come Back Again' and although we have at this time experienced nearly four years of war and thousands of men must have left this station for various parts of the Empire, the enthusiastic send off which was given to these men was indeed worthy of the inhabitants of the City . . .

The only problem was that nobody knew where they were going. On the train to Newcastle bets were struck on their destination. The favourites were Vladivostok, Archangel and Egypt. (Vladivostok and Egypt are of course about equidistant from Archangel.) It was not until the *City of Marseilles* was under way that Maynard called the officers together and told them where they were going and why. Crawford wrote: "At about 8.30 all officers attended a lecture by the GOC on the object and part we were to play in the Expedition, i.e. to prevent the Bosche from forming a submarine base at Murmansk, to make him withdraw troops from the Western Front (where we were being badly hit) and send them to Finland. As most people on board had been to, and come back from a considerable amount of service in France, the Expedition was looked upon as being a picnic."

But the fact that it was not going to be so soon became evident. The stokers on the *City of Marseilles*, all Lascars, were swept by a fever which killed twenty-two and left the rest too weak to stoke. Volunteers were called for from the soldiers who were so taken with the novelty of the idea and the desire not to loiter around the North Sea as an easy target for U-boats that there were more than enough volunteers. Two of the officers sharing Crawford's cabin were among them: "Mackie and Best arranged to go down and stoke the following morning," said Crawford, adding cynically, "guess one morning will be sufficient."

Another officer on board, Major Ambrose Sturdy, later suggested that because the Lascars were all Moslem and it was the time of an Islamic period of fasting between sunrise and sunset – Ramadan – the stokers succumbed because in the high northern latitudes at that time of year the sun never set and therefore they were unable to eat or drink. The truth was that the Lascars were suffering from that great killer of 1918, the Spanish Flu, which was eventually to do as much damage to the Expeditionary Force as the Bolsheviks. Although it would inevitably have reached Russia by other routes, it was the troopships from Britain which first carried the flu to the north.

Crawford played no part in the stoking. He had other duties. Because several of his Vickers guns had Russian barrels he had to stretch the pockets of the ammunition belts to take Russian ammunition, a tedious job "damned hard on the hands". He also had to set up and man four machine-guns in case of submarine attack. Two destroyers fussed about the troopship and the boom of depth charges was heard in the distance indicating the presence of at least one U-boat. Major Sturdy reported in his diary: "Tuesday 18, 12 noon. Saw and heard submarine sunk by depth bombs on port bow horizon."

They sailed north on a calm sea into the Arctic Circle with whales playing about them throughout the endless day. The men studied the little Russian phrase books they had been given, wrote and censored letters and attended lectures and concerts at which they listened to a Russian officer, "the proud possessor of many decorations" who sang Russian songs and accompanied himself on the piano. Crawford remained sanguine about the expedition: "I personally looked upon the stunt as a good chance compared with what we had at that time on the Western Front." He was undoubtedly correct. In the four months following the opening of Ludendorff's campaign, the Allies were to suffer nearly one million casualties on the Western Front. Nevertheless, there was hard fighting to be done and Crawford himself was to be awarded the Military Cross for his part in it.

They arrived off the Murman Coast on June 22nd, "an ugly barren surface, rising to several hundreds of feet with no sign of habitation to break the monotony of the scene", and pulled into the harbour at midnight.

"About two hours later, the alarm was given and on enquiring the cause it was discovered that there was a large body of Russian civilians marching towards the quay and supposed to be under arms. This however proved to be incorrect. Everybody was immediately ordered to stand by. Staff officers rushed on deck with field glasses in all sorts of dress, pyjamas, trousers, gum boots, staff caps. Mounted an extra machine-gun at barrier on quay but soon afterwards this proved to be a false alarm. It was only men returning from a meeting of the railway employees who I afterwards found out work for the Allies. Things gradually became normal . . ."

CHAPTER 4

The Fighting Starts
Murmansk–Archangel, June–August 1918

Normal would not be the word most people would have chosen to describe the situation at Murmansk. By the time the expeditionary force had landed it had become obvious that, although the Allies might be locally welcome as insurance against attack by the Germans and Finns, the Bolshevik government, under pressure from the Germans, was determined to force them to leave. Consequently Major-General Maynard had to face the prospect of attack by the Bolsheviks as well as the Germans and the Finns. With the small force at his command – many of them sick – he had to cover the right flank of the force from German and Finn infiltration from Finland and stop Bolshevik reinforcements coming up from the south. To do this he had to push small groups down the railway line to Kandalaksha and Kem on the White Sea, at the same time losing part of his force to General Poole's seaborne expedition from Murmansk to Archangel. There the Bolsheviks had been busy removing the war stores supplied by the Allies, sending them south where, it was feared, they would fall into the hands of the Germans. Archangel had also been chosen as the base for the military mission to retrain and re-equip the Czechs to carry on the fight against Germany.

He knew that more troops would be arriving for, three weeks previously on June 2nd, the Allied Supreme War Council meeting at Versailles had decided on a joint intervention at the northern ports. The case for intervention was argued by the British on the grounds given by General Sir Henry Wilson, Chief of the Imperial General Staff, that it was necessary to prevent the transference of further enemy troops from East to West and to deny the resources of Russia and Siberia to the enemy. His subsidiary reasons were: the desire to retain access to all anti-German elements in Russia; the counter-action of German attempts to reach possible submarine bases in the North Sea; the protection of Allied stores at the northern ports and at Vladivostok; the utilisation and protection of the Czecho-Slovak forces in Russia and Siberia; and finally the restoration of Russia by economic measures.

These arguments won over the reluctant Americans with General Tasker Bliss, the United States representative telling the War Council: "The President is in sympathy with any practical military effort which can be made at and from Murmansk and Archangel, but such efforts should proceed, if at all, upon the sure sympathy of the Russian people and should not have as the ultimate objects any restoration of the ancient regime or any interference with the political liberty of the Russian people." This was hardly the language of an imperialist power determined on the overthrow of the Bolsheviks.

The War Council decided that the total force in the north should be six to eight battalions and that the Inter-Allied Supreme Command would be entrusted to the British who were also to be responsible for co-ordination. "Negotiations were immediately set on foot," reported Wilson, "as a result of which the Americans eventually supplied three battalions and three companies of engineers." The French and Italians agreed to send a battalion each and the Serbian government said that its battalion which had made its way to Murmansk from Odessa could be retained as long as it was required.

However, as Wilson pointed out in his War Office report, "Short History of Events in Russia from November 1917 – February 1919", the arrival of these troops was much delayed, and he commented bitterly: "This tardiness cramped the whole campaign and helped rob it of the expected results."

For the moment, Maynard had to make do with what he had, and that was not enough to be comfortable. In his diary Peter Crawford records his disgust at not being nominated for the Archangel expedition. He was detailed to oversee the unloading of the cargo ship *Asturian* which had arrived with the force's supplies. His only consolation was the promise of promotion. The *Asturian* had sailed from England in such a hurry that she had not been loaded properly and the quayside soon resembled a military junk-yard with everything coming off the ship out of order. The situation was not helped by the fact that only Crawford and one other officer in the Machine Gun sections remained on their feet. Everybody else was down with the flu. Another Lascar had died and Crawford was himself running a fever. The sick men added to yet another of the problems, the lack of accommodation. Murmansk with its limited supply of log huts and its sudden influx of soldiers and refugees could not cope. The sick men were put into tents on the quayside and in disused box cars on the dockside railway. Maynard had to use a railway carriage as his headquarters.

On June 27th Crawford received orders to move his men out of the town:

Damned unfortunate move. Means sick will have a rotten time travelling in open trucks, quite warm. Baggage to be loaded up. Sick men made half comfortable amongst kitbags. Left about 2 p.m., arrived at the camp at 4.30 p.m. (reckless speed, 3 versts, 2 miles, in 2¾ hours). The camping ground was just like so many sand hills covered with short heather and absolutely infested with mosquitoes and flies. Unloaded all baggage, main stores and placed by the railway, simply thrown off anyhow, as the Express had to return immediately.

With the few fit men we commenced to pitch tents, which amounted to one being put up on each mound. By 8.30 we had 50 tents up. Had a meal which consisted of pressed meat, tea, biscuits. Quartermaster-Sergeant must have made a blunder for which he was duly "blessed". Mosquito nets issued by the RAMC but no means of fixing them inside the tents, so most people pegged their tents down and fixed the net over the door, which eventually proved very successful. Captain Harrison RAMC worked amongst the sick men day and night, with hardly any food. Really wonderful. Fixed up a stretcher on two ammunition boxes and turned in about midnight.

On the next day he recorded:

Moved some of the tents to a better tactical position, as information had been received that the Bolos [the British nickname for the Bolsheviks] may attempt to rush the camp. One section to quay for additional precautions. Hope to give the Bolo a hearty reception if he does come along. All guns in beautiful working order. Another day on biscuits and bully, what a change after the excellent food on board. Never mind, it is not too bad when you know you can get nothing better. All the officers collected in Cregan's tent in the evening and passed away a few hours assisted by his Decca.

That same day General Maynard set out by train to visit the isolated garrisons established to the south at Kandalaksha and Kem. However, he found his train being mysteriously held up at Imandra, some fifty miles north of Kandalaksha, by a station master who refused to give them permission to go on. Maynard solved that problem by putting a revolver to the station master's head, forcing him to clear the line and then setting out at full steam for Kandalak-sha. He arrived there to find another train filled with Red Guards on their way north to throw him and his men out of Murmansk. The Bolshevik leaders in Petrograd had learnt how woefully weak were the forces landed at Murmansk – they had expected several divisions – and gathered together a force to attack the British positions. Largely by bluff, Maynard convinced the Red Guard commander that he should stay in Kandalaksha under the none too friendly care of the Serbs and steamed off to Kem which he found filled with two trainloads of Red Guards. However, he had a garrison of some 500 men stationed there along with an armoured train and a naval 12-pounder which commanded the railway bridge over the river. Thus he convinced the Russians that they should stay where they were.

Maynard spent some days in Kem studying the lie of the land and getting the feel of the political situation. However, on his return to Kandalaksha from Kem he received news that the Red Guards he had stopped were only the vanguard of a sizeable force. He thereupon ordered his troops to disarm them, put them back on their trains, adequately supply them with rations and send them off south again, with that single 12-pounder gun pointing down the line to make sure they did not return.

So far his exploits had read like something out of a boy's adventure comic and, as he pointed out with some pride: "Without a single life having been lost, some 700 to 800 of the advanced troops of what was intended to be an attacking force had been turned back to their base minus machine-guns, rifles and ammunition; and an additional 300 to 400 who had been quartered on the railway, along my line of communication, had joined them."

All very satisfactory; but this operation did mark the turning point in the intervention. From this moment on Russia was no longer an ally. She was an enemy. Maynard realised the implications of his action and took the next step, one which seemed not only sensible but was also dictated by military necessity: he ordered the confiscation of all arms along the line to Kem. The cruiser *Attentive* sailed to Kem's port to lend the persuasion of her guns to the action. The searches of confiscation went smoothly in most places. Sixty machine-guns, nearly ten thousand rifles and a large amount of ammunition were seized. But on July 5th the local Soviet at Kem refused to co-operate.

The Soviet was disbanded. Seven of its members were arrested and its leading members, President Massorin, Vice-President Kamenev and Secretary Yezhov were shot dead. The exact circumstances of their deaths have since been clouded by a mixture of propaganda and military secrecy. Maynard himself has given three versions. In his book he was dismissive: "At Kem some slight opposition was offered and fighting resulted in which one or two Red officials lost their lives." But in a cable to the War Office he gave more detail: "While the Bolsheviks at Kem were being disarmed, three prominent citizens offered armed resistance with bombs and revolver, and during the struggle [they] were unfortunately killed. We hold about 100 Bolsheviks who plotted against the Allies or the (Murmansk) Soviet detained under guard." He gave yet more detail in a report to Poole: "I ordered the disarming of the Red Guards at Kem on July 2 and a search for arms. During the search a house was entered in which the local Soviet was sitting. The members leapt to their feet. Two of them drew out their revolvers and one fired on the Serbians who were carrying out the search. Another threw a bomb which did not explode. During the struggle which ensued three members were shot."

The Bolshevik version was somewhat different. The *Archangel Pravda* of July 17th accused the Serbs of leading the three men out of the town where "a volley was fired at them." Later, a Serb deserter was produced who said that after they had been arrested he had seen them being taken to the beach and shot.

The shootings caused consternation in Archangel where there was still an Allied presence, including a trainload of diplomatic refugees. Admiral Kemp was in the city when the news broke. According to the unpublished memoir of Douglas Young, the British Consul in Archangel, as revealed by Andrew Rothstein in his book, *When Britain Invaded Russia: The Consul who Rebelled*, "The Senior Naval Officer [Kemp] seemed to be as taken aback as I was. He immediately offered to take representatives of the Archangel Soviet across to Kem on his yacht in order to make an investigation. The invitation was declined, the Soviet representatives preferring to go on their own ship. The two vessels left the following day . . ."

Young, who was totally opposed to the intervention, later wrote how he had "told the Executive Committee of the Soviet that he entirely agreed with their description of it as an unwarrantable outrage." The Archangel representatives were treated with suspicion when they arrived in Kem, being kept on board a train and guarded by Serbian soldiers. Not unnaturally their report, published in Archangel on July 24th, supported the charges levelled against Maynard and his men. It is unlikely that the whole truth of the incident will ever be known now.

In the meantime Maynard, still with *Attentive* guarding his sea flank, had pressed on down the line and thrown the Bolsheviks out of Soroka, nearly halfway to Petrograd from Murmansk. Leaving behind a garrison of Serbs, he steamed back to Murmansk well satisfied with his work.

Maynard's actions were governed by the belief that the Germans were becoming increasingly powerful in Russia. Under the terms of the "Bread Treaty", Germany's separate treaty with the Ukraine, at least one million bushels of grain were to go to Germany, in order to break the Allied blockade; a forceful German Ambassador, Count Wilhelm Von Mirback, was behaving like a viceroy in Moscow, threatening military action if the Russians did not throw out the Allies; and the German Army was consolidating the territory it had occupied under the Treaty of Brest-Litovsk. Russia, vowed Ludendorff, was to be bled until she was "forced to bind herself to Germany". Maynard, however, did not intend to allow that to take place where he was in command.

In the face of such momentous events and with some two million Russians already dead, the killing of three men in a minor incident in the northern wilderness of Russia would seem to be of little importance. Maybe so. But it marked the point at which the erstwhile Allies began to shoot at one another, and it was from such small, bitter seeds that the suspicion and hatred grew into the great struggle which so deeply rules our lives today.

In Murmansk, the Allies had celebrated America's Independence Day, the Fourth of July. The ships in the harbour had "dressed overall" with their flags making a brave show against the dismal background of the harbour. Crawford was invited to dinner by the American marine officers from the USS *Olympia*. He was tired, having worked in the hold of the *Asturian* since five in the morning. The dinner consisted of bully and biscuits and it was served in a railway wagon. Nevertheless, he found the Americans "quite a nice lot of fellows" and had "a jolly evening".

They met again on July 12th when fifty Royal Marines from HMS *Glory*, fifty American marines from the *Olympia* and fifty French marines from the *Amiral Aube*, supported by Crawford's machine-guns, captured the Russian cruiser *Askold* whose mutinous sailors had become a centre of resistance to the alliance between the Murmansk Soviet and the expeditionary force. According to the Royal Marines' records a major part of the *Askold*'s crew was inveigled ashore – tantalisingly, the records do not say how – and a boarding party put the rest of the ship's company under lock and key. The breech-blocks and the sights of the cruiser's twelve six-inch guns were removed. It was all over in two and a half hours and after being cleaned the ship was commissioned as HMS *Glory IV*. Crawford, however, wrote a somewhat different account of the incident:

> Alarm sounded at 5 a.m. Turned out very hurriedly. Wet and cold. Mounted one gun on the shore and one halfway up the hill and laid on the *Askold*. Two guns to go with the infantry. [Lieutenant] Gheike took over the 2 guns on shore. Damned disappointed, went with the infantry and took over the 12 store huts and captured two sentries on the way, very amusing. During the raid we collected 700 rifles, 12 Boche machine guns, 15 swords and a colossal amount of ammunition and food supplies . . . In the meantime the guns under Gheike did some excellent shooting at some of the crew of the Askold who were trying to land. Sgt. Bowen reported that the teams worked splendidly, each man taking a turn as No. 1. Felt fearfully disappointed at missing such a splendid opportunity. Owing to the rain and mist, one of the guns fixed on a small motor boat which had been sent from HMS *Glory* in which was the Aide-de-Camp to the General. I saw the ADC later who said he had a very exciting time, the motor boat being riddled with bullets.

The following day Crawford took two guns to cover the pier on which the crew of the *Askold* were lined up to be addressed by General Poole. He spoke to them in his usual bluff manner, offering them the choice, either to stay and join his forces or to be put on a train and sent south. The sailors unanimously chose to join their Bolshevik comrades. On July 18th, they were given two days' rations and sent on their way.

The departure of the *Askold*'s crew eased the security problem in Murmansk but it did little to improve the accommodation shortage. Until hostilities broke out on the railway British and other refugees had been steadily making their way from all over Russia into this bleak arctic town. They were business people, saw-mill owners, industrialists, factory managers, a few "aristos" and a number of nannies. Crawford visited them and was appalled by what he discovered. On their journey north

> Men and women, married and single and children all travelled in the same truck, no sanitary arrangements made of any description. They slept on boards placed across the truck, just like

narrow shelves, piling them up in a corner during the day, so that they could have as much room as possible. No arrangements made about halting stations where one might get out for hot water . . . Their appearance was pitiful to behold. Tommies gave them a share of their Bully Beef and Biscuits for which they were extremely grateful . . .

The refugees were accommodated in the roughest part of the town. Crawford found

about 150 people of both sexes and all ages in a hut about 25 yards long and 8 yards wide, a partition about 7 feet high running down the centre and two rows of wooden shelves for beds, one row about 2 feet from the ground and another row about 3 feet above that.

Further efforts had been made to subdivide the beds two's and four's and thereby afford a little privacy. This was done in some case by piling up boxes, suitcases etc., but mostly a woman's underskirt and coat or perhaps a piece of cotton material suspended from a piece of string. The sight one met on entering this hut was simply astounding and yet I was assured that it was luxury compared with what they had experienced in Moscow and on the journey. I very reluctantly agreed to go a few yards along the hut that I might fully realise their conditions. Here I was confronted with people of both sexes in the act of undressing in the most casual way, absolutely indifferent to the presence of strangers, let alone the other occupants, yet in spite of this unpleasantness everyone appeared to be quite happy in their new abode, and feeling confident that whilst they were in a place where British troops were quartered, their trials and difficulties must surely be at an end . . .

Crawford recorded that one of the refugees was the sister of Sir Eric Geddes, the First Lord of the Admiralty. Geddes himself had turned up at Murmansk on a cruiser to inspect the situation, but it seems that he sailed for home before his sister arrived.

What an extraordinary place Murmansk was at that time! This small town of 350 buildings, built of fresh cut logs cunningly morticed by skilful Russian woodsmen using only axes, had been planned in districts each one with its own function. But the Revolution had overtaken the planners and it was rapidly becoming an overcrowded slum with no paved streets and little sanitation.

One British officer described it as having the appearance "of a temporary town, erected by a cinematograph company for some

Wild Western drama complete with its cowboys and Indians." The actors were in fact soldiers from Britain, America, France, Serbia and Poland. The ships of half a dozen navies swung at anchor in the harbour where supplies were being unloaded round the clock in the 24 hours of daylight. Finns and Karelians from the Finnish–Russian border rubbed shoulders with Korean and Chinese labourers. There were refugees of many nations, Russians who had fled from their estates to escape the Bolsheviks, Tsarist officers happy to serve as private soldiers under the British to strike back at the mutineers who had killed their fellow officers. There were British and French families who had enjoyed the rewards of Russia's industrial revolution and those who had known the Tsar's court at its most glittering. And there were the men who had come to run the town after the Revolution and, because of their alliance with the Allies, were now branded as traitors by the Bolsheviks, men who knew they had to prevail or die.

They were all thrown together in a great town of Babel, with different tongues, different objectives, different roles, but all shared the same growing fear of Bolshevism. No doubt the news of the murder of the Tsar and his family at Ekaterinburg confirmed them in their horror of the new government. But the killing of the Tsar seems to have made little impact on the men of the expeditionary force. Neither Maynard nor Crawford mentions it. Perhaps the news did not filter through to them. Or perhaps they were too busy. Crawford was made "King of Restikent" a village on the River Tuloma thirty miles south-west of Murmansk so small that it did not appear on the map. His task was to act as a tripwire if the Finns moved on Murmansk along the river route which led from the Finnish border. To do so he was allowed to take one NCO and six men.

"The task of selecting these men," he wrote, "was not an easy one for the company was, with the exception of the officers, of low medical category, only considered fit for home duties. Half of the section had already been used to replace the sick men of another section and this left about 12 men to choose from. The men selected would in all probability have many difficulties to overcome, as the river was reported to be extremely difficult to navigate. Out of the men selected, one had been wounded three times, three had been wounded twice and two, once. One of these men had a son, a Sergeant, serving the RAF."

Maynard was busy securing the town and the south and western approaches to Murmansk. He was also engaged in planning an audacious diversionary attack towards Archangel whose occupation had become General Poole's first priority. Archangel was important for a number of reasons. The Allied war material which had been stored there was being shipped south at the rate of 3,000 tons a week by the Bolsheviks. It was a long-established seat of regional government that had been founded in 1583 after a party of English merchants had landed to trade in timber and furs. And its communications by railway to Vologda and by the River Dvina to Kotlas made it a vital base for connecting with the Czechs who were supposed to be making their way north, and for reaching south into the heart of Russia.

But Archangel was not like Murmansk. It was run by a pro-Bolshevik Soviet and heavily defended by Red Guards. It was also a difficult place to attack, lying twenty-five miles up a narrow channel through thick pine forest from which hidden defenders could rake any ships trying to force a passage. In addition there were permanent batteries mounted on Modyugski, an island fort guarding the entrance to the channel. Poole was not prepared to mount an attack until he had sufficient forces. He was perhaps lucky that the ice did not break until late this year and was able to wait for the arrival of the 21st French Colonial Infantry Battalion consisting of twenty-two officers and 849 other ranks which landed at Murmansk on July 26th.

It was no secret that Poole was about to undertake the occupation of Archangel. It was simply a question of when he would arrive and if the Bolsheviks would stand and fight. The city was full of his agents. Some were arrested and a few were shot. A Commander Thomson of the British Naval Mission arrived from Petrograd and revealed himself to Douglas Young as a former captain in the Imperial Navy whose real name was Georgi Chaplin. He had served with the British Navy, admired the British and had been given the task of organising a coup d'état in Archangel to coincide with Poole's landing. He outraged Young when he applied for a new passport to replace the false one issued to him by the Embassy in Petrograd which he had lost. "The amazing indiscretions of the amateur Russian and Allied conspirators," wrote Young, "proclaimed almost from the housetops what was in the wind."

Chaplin had the Bolshevik police sniffing at his heels but had prepared his coup well enough. However, he needed the military muscle of the Allies to ensure his success and Poole seemed to be taking altogether too long to get his invasion force together.

There now took place the curious episode of the diplomats. At the end of February, with the Germans apparently marching on Petrograd, the various Allied embassies had shut up shop and left first for Vologda, due east of Petrograd, and then for the Finnish frontier. But once in Finland the diplomats, from thirteen assorted nations, found themselves caught up in the civil war between the Red and White Finns. Much to everybody else's chagrin only the British got through and eventually arrived home. The rest had to go back to Vologda where they stayed until July 25th, living an uncomfortable existence on board their train parked in a siding and quarrelling among themselves. They then got steam up and chugged north to Archangel, apparently fearing that the Bolsheviks would either hand them over to the Germans or lock them up in retaliation for the killings at Kem and the forthcoming invasion at Archangel. There were 132 diplomats and about seventy British and French citizens who had tacked themselves on to the diplomatic party. Once in Archangel they immediately opened negotiations with the local Soviet to be shipped across the White Sea to Kandalaksha which was now garrisoned by French artillerymen, Serbian infantry, and a few Finns all under British command.

The United States Ambassador, David Francis, a poker playing businessman who had arrived in Petrograd with a negro valet and a portable cuspidor, was a leading member of the party. He later explained to a Senate Committee why they were in such a hurry to leave the comparative comfort of Archangel: "We had determined to leave for Kandalaksha because there was an anti-Bolshevik revolution to be pulled off at Archangel, and we knew it, and we did not want to be there when it occurred, and they knew it."

The Archangel Soviet agreed to let the diplomats have two small steamers. It seems that they were just as eager for the diplomats to depart as the diplomats were to go. Among the passengers was Francis Lindley who had been Counsellor at the British Embassy in Petrograd. It was he who had spirited the British Embassy group out of Finland but he had returned to Russia with the intervention forces as Britain's "Co-ordinating Diplomatic Authority" and had made his way to Vologda with the intention of resuming diplomatic work in Moscow. Once in Vologda he realised that the situation had changed so much that it was pointless for him to press on to Moscow. Thus he arrived in Kandalaksha with the others on July 30th.

Once there, he hurried to the telephone to bully General Poole into advancing the date for his invasion. In a report to the Foreign Secretary he claimed to have told Poole that "a rising had been arranged at Archangel to take place at 3 a.m. on July 31 and the Allied military officers acquainted with the plan were absolutely confident that the town would be in the hands of our friends without bloodshed, and in the course of a few hours after the first move had been made. This move had already been postponed several times; and the result was that many people connected with it had been arrested by the Bolsheviks, and not a few shot. It was impossible for this to continue."

Poole at first demurred, saying that everything had been arranged for the operation to take place on August 6th, and it was absolutely impossible for him to advance it. Lindley then consulted with the senior Allied diplomats and they felt the matter could turn out so disastrously they agreed to leave for Murmansk that night to bring their combined pressure to bear on Poole. However, later that afternoon Poole sent another message, saying that in the light of Lindley's information he had reconsidered the situation and was proposing to set out for Archangel immediately with all the men he could muster.

Poole was eventually able to scrape together a force of just under 1,500 men, comprised of the officers and men of his mission – many of them specialists rather than infantrymen – the French battalion, some Poles who had been recruited in Murmansk, a detachment of United States Marines from the *Olympia*, about one hundred Royal Marines and a section of the machine-gun company. The marines and machine-gunners were part of Maynard's little army and he resented having to give them up to Poole.

They all set sail from Murmansk in the ever-busy *Attentive* which had been scouting the entrance to the channel leading to Archangel, the seaplane carrier HMS *Nairana*, the French cruiser *Amiral Aube*, and the fleet of minesweeper-trawlers. Admiral Kemp's yacht and two former Russian destroyers now manned by Royal Navy crews were also involved.

Fog and skilful navigation by *Attentive* under Captain Altham saw the fleet safely into the mouth of the Dvina on the morning of August 1st. They were then seen by the batteries on Modyugski which opened fire, hitting the *Attentive* in the forward funnel. If the shell had been a few feet lower it would have wrecked the cruiser's bridge. But that was the Bolsheviks' only success. Under the weight of fire from the armada they fled from their guns and in what was possibly the world's first fully combined operation, the ships, Fairey Campania seaplanes from the *Nairana*, and British and French soldiers joined together to clear the island of Bolsheviks. The only casualties were two wounded French soldiers.

The fleet then sailed on up the channel with one of *Nairana*'s seaplanes scouting for opposition. According to Young it was when this aircraft flew over Archangel that panic set in among the

Bolshevik leaders. In the words of Poole's subsequent despatch to the War Office: "During the night the Bolshevik government decided to evacuate the town, after having ordered two icebreakers to be sunk in the fairway to block the passage up the channel. On August 2nd the revolution planned by our supporters broke out at 4 a.m., and was completely successful. The Bolshevik Government was overthrown. The new Government cordially invited our aid, and declared itself pro-Ally, anti-German and determined not to recognise the Brest-Litovsk treaty. After some delay caused by exploring a passage between the sunken icebreakers, we were fortunate enough to find that there was just sufficient room to allow a passage for the ships. We then made a triumphal procession up the channel to Archangel being greeted everywhere with enormous enthusiasm."

Not everybody was as pleased as Poole. It was noted that the cheering crowds consisted entirely of the bourgeoisie and that there was not a workman to be seen. And both Young and Lindley pointed out from their opposing sides of the fence that Chaplin's coup did not take place until after Poole's show of force had frightened off the Bolsheviks. Young, who had argued so vehemently against intervention, returned to England within a fortnight, his health and career in tatters. Lindley became British High Commissioner in Archangel. Chaplin assumed the title of Commander of the Armed Forces of the Supreme government of the Northern Region. Political power was given to a Right Social-Revolutionary government under Nikolai Tchaikovsky, a respected former member of the Constituent Assembly. Poole proclaimed martial law, reintroduced courts martial and the death penalty for sedition, abrogated various Bolshevik edicts giving power to the workers, and proceeded to run Archangel as an occupied city.

While all this had been taking place at Archangel itself, Colonel C. J. M. Thornhill, a fluent Russian speaker who had been Britain's chief of military intelligence in Tsarist Russia under the guise of Assistant Military Attaché, led a raid from Kem with the aim of cutting the Archangel–Vologda Railway at Obozerskaya and capturing leading Bolsheviks fleeing from Archangel.

He gathered eighty-nine officers and men, among them forty-seven of the ubiquitous Serbs, six Tsarist officers now serving as privates in the Slavo-British Legion, two peasants who joined as recruits and several British officers and NCOs. Just when the raiding party was about to move off a scarecrow of a man appeared. He was Captain Denys Garstin of the 10th Hussars who in March, when it was still thought that the new Russia would fight alongside the Allies, was Britain's representative on a committee of Allied officers advising Trotsky on the training of the new Red Army. He then worked with Robert Bruce Lockhart, British representative and agent in Moscow, at various nefarious exercises before being ordered to join General Poole. Lockhart wrote of him: "He had to leave clandestinely owing to the difficulty in securing a Bolshevik pass for him. He went with a sad heart . . ."

Garstin proceeded to walk most of the way to Kem from Petrograd and arrived there famished, with his uniform in tatters. But he insisted on joining the raid. The *Times* Special Correspondent describing the events which followed wrote:

The party embarked on the *Michael Archangel*, a boat belonging to the monks of Solovetsky, and were accompanied by the trawler *Sarpedon*. In the bay the flag was taken down and the red one of revolution hoisted. On board the monks' boat there was suspicion of the Russian pilot. Colonel Thornhill, who speaks Russian like a native, never left the man's side; if there was to be treachery the pilot would be the first to pay the price.

Onega was reached, and here the real drama began. The town was in the hands of the Bolshevists. The boat made fast to the pier; on shore, a Bolshevist guard of three or four men awaited her. The Colonel, disguised as a Russian soldier, ordered the whole of his party to stay below, and, leaning carelessly over the rail, answered the questions of the guard. Was this the Monks' boat bringing food? It was. They laughed and jested, the Colonel stepped back into the alleyway, dropped his disguise, and, in the uniform of a British Staff Officer, leaped ashore. The attack was so sudden that the guard lost its head. One lunged at Thornhill with his bayonet, but the Colonel parried the blow with his arm and shot the man through the head.

Aroused by the firing, the party below deck disobeyed orders and came up. The Colonel was engaged, single-handed, with three Bolshevists. One of them raised his rifle and fired, but an ex-Russian Officer, Oluchakov leaped between Thornhill and the rifle; he took the bullet in the arm. Quickly, the gallant little party formed its plan of campaign; one or two of the guard had escaped to give the alarm, and by six a.m. street fighting was in progress and machine-guns were rattling. Four cardinal points were selected by Thornhill and by 11 a.m. resistance was over. There had been a force of 90 Bolshevists in the town under the leadership of Popoff, an ex-sailor. Our losses were one killed and one wounded; the Bolshevists lost one killed and two wounded. Thornhill's party took 60 prisoners, three machine-guns, 300 rifles and a large quantity of ammunition. Popoff escaped.

In the town there was much jubilation among the inhabitants. Seventeen Poles were released from prison where they were awaiting execution and they joined the expedition. At 2 p.m. the inhabitants gathered in the square and Colonel Thornhill explained the situation and reassured them.

That was the way *The Times* reported in those days.

The party pressed on. Ten more Poles joined. They raised sixty horses and carts with peasant women as drivers. They shot a Bolshevik who had confessed to killing a Polish lieutenant on his way to join Poole. At Korelskaya they were able to telephone Archangel to learn that the expedition had not yet landed. They fought their way out of an ambush in a forest, then after marching all night clashed with a force of 350 Bolsheviks and fought them for six hours. They killed ten and lost five of their own number. Soon after this fight the scouts learnt that a force of some 2,000 Bolsheviks with field artillery had entrenched themselves across the raiding party's route. Thornhill decided that enough was enough. They now had no chance of cutting the railway line, but they had succeeded in diverting a major force of Bolshevik soldiers from the defence of Archangel. So they returned to Onega, burning bridges as they went, boarded the ship *Kolo* and arrived back at Kem safely.

Thornhill's expedition had lasted for twenty days and between August 1st and August 6th they had marched some 140 miles. Thornhill won a bar to his DSO and Garstin was awarded the MC. But he never lived to receive it. He made his way to Archangel and on August 20th took part in another action, only to be killed after capturing an armoured car single handed. Photographs show him as a big, laughing young man mounted on a shaggy pony. He was one of the very first British soldiers to fall in the intervention. Bruce Lockhart wrote of him: "Poor Denys Garstin, who had worked with all his boyish enthusiasm for an understanding with the Bolsheviks was taken from me by the War Office and sent to Archangel where he fell victim to a Bolshevik bullet." The irony of Garstin's death is that while he was working with Bruce Lockhart it was he who had proposed the plan for Britain to land troops at Archangel to link up with other forces advancing from Siberia and so form a new Eastern Front against the Germans. But his plan had called for two divisions of fighting troops, not a mere 1,500 men of doubtful quality.

CHAPTER 5

Siberian Scenario
Vladivostok, December 1917–July 1918

Vladivostok, the "Lord of the East", was not settled until 1860 and only Chartered twenty years later, but in 1905 the loss of ice-free Port Arthur in Russia's war with Japan and the completion of the Trans-Siberian Railway combined to transform it into Russia's main military and naval base in the East. So, when World War I started it became the natural destination for supplies coming across the Pacific from Vancouver, San Francisco and Los Angeles. This time the Russians and the Japanese were on the same side and once the Japanese had mopped up the German base at Tsingtao in China and the Australian cruiser *Sydney* had accounted for the German commerce raider *Emden* the way was open for the supply ships. Like Archangel and, later, Murmansk Vladivostok became a funnel for the arms and raw materials destined for Russia's factories and soldiers.

Ship after ship steamed into the natural amphitheatre of its harbour on the peninsula between the Bay of Amur and the Bay of the Golden Horn. There, they queued to unload their cargoes of guns and ammunition, chemicals, metals, food, and, most crucial, the equipment to keep the railways running.

The Trans-Siberian, the longest railway in the world, was a momentous achievement. It took ten years from the time that Nicholas, then Tsarevich, drove in the first spike at Vladivostok in 1891 until the link was made between East and West, thus linking the Baltic and the Pacific coasts. Even then there was a section at Lake Baikal where ferries had to be used, a problem which was not solved until 1905 when a new section of line was opened round the southern shore of the lake.

The genius behind the construction of the railway was Count Sergei Witte, the man who did so much to bring about the industrial revolution in Russia. But he was bedevilled by the intrigues of jealous rivals and was forced to build his great enterprise on a shoestring. He could only afford to build a light road bed for the track which would only allow three trains a day to be run. Farm produce rotted in the sidings because the railway could not carry it away – a situation still not unknown in Russia today.

Some improvements had been made after Russia's disasters in the 1905 war with Japan, but the Tsar's officials, in the panic of combat, ordered vast quantities of matériel and when the flood of freighters started to build up in the early summer of 1916, the railway simply could not handle the traffic. The "godowns" (warehouses) in the port were filled. Piers and empty spaces in the city were commandeered and when these overflowed dumps were established in the open country round the Golden Horn. Like the farmers' produce, the supplies went bad, rotting and rusting in the open. This does not mean to say that nothing got through, however. Some extraordinary feats were performed including the transportation of twelve submarines each weighing 350 tons which were disassembled and carried on flat cars all the way across Siberia, five to the Baltic and seven to the Black Sea.

But as the war progressed the political situation in Siberia deteriorated. Roving bands of outlaws and deserters made life dangerous for the railway engineers, the railbed crumbled under the heavy traffic and the dumps of matériel grew even higher.

It was not only the Trans-Siberian which was in trouble. Railways throughout Russia were grinding to a halt. Even at the beginning of 1916, before the full weight of the war shipments had made itself felt, there were 150,000 railway trucks filled with supplies stranded on various lines. So many trucks blocked the lines that some were tipped down embankments to make way for those still arriving. There were 575 railway stations in such an advanced state of disrepair that they could no longer handle any goods. At Archangel as the shipments arrived and were piled on top of the dumps, so the crates at the bottom sank into the ground. And the rotting piles of grain, meat and butter at the stations along the Trans-Siberian now amounted to thousands of tons while people in the towns went hungry.

On January 1st, 1918, in a telegram to the British Embassy in Washington, Lord Robert Cecil, Britain's Minister of Blockade, estimated that there were 648,000 tons of supplies in dumps at Vladivostok. As with the supplies in Murmansk and Archangel they were sorely needed by the Allies who had spared them at great sacrifice to themselves. They feared, moreover, that if the Russians made a separate peace with the Germans, the German and Austro-Hungarian prisoners of war held in camps across Siberia – 250,000 near Vladivostok alone – would be organised to shift the stores west to be used by Germany.

The United States had recognised the difficulties in moving the supplies early on and had sent a Railway Advisory Commission to Russia under the chairmanship of John F. Stevens. He stayed on after the revolution to help the Provisional government sort out its railway problems. The Americans, who had advanced some 325 million dollars in credits to the new government, arranged to send 1,500 railway engines and 30,000 carriages of various kinds to replace the worn-out and damaged rolling stock.

Stevens also asked for teams of railwaymen, mechanics, works foremen, and shunters to be sent out. The US War Department was given responsibility for recruiting these men and soon the message was being tapped out on the railway telegraph across the United States. The prospect of good pay and adventure appealed: there were seventy-four volunteers from the Baldwin Locomotive Co., 215 from the Great Northern and Western lines at St Paul and others from the St Paul and Pacific Railroad. In the autumn of 1917 they were formed into the Russian Railway Service Corps, and were commanded by Colonel H. Emerson, General Manager of the Great Northern Railroad.

The volunteers travelled, appropriately enough, by special trains to San Francisco where they boarded the army transport ship *Thomas*. With the addition of some interpreters and Russian mechanics there were 329 of them. If everything had gone according to plan they would have been the first organised unit of American soldiers to land in Russia. It may be that they were civilians in military clothing but they were a unit of the American Army, and had been sent to Russia not to try to overthrow the Bolsheviks but to help the Provisional government.

However, when they steamed into Vladivostok harbour on December 14th, 1917, the unit found that Bolshevism had been carried along the 7,000 miles of the Trans-Siberian faster than the war supplies. The soldiers of the garrison and the sailors of the Pacific Fleet had been as ripe for revolution as their comrades in the West. Now the city was degenerating into anarchy. Ice was forming in the harbour and nobody had thought to provide accommodation for the railwaymen-soldiers. So the *Thomas* turned round and sailed off to Japan. Nevertheless, the very fact that they had to sail away without setting foot on Russian soil played its part in bringing about the intervention. John Stevens advised Washington that his commission would be unable to carry out any work on the railway unless his team was protected by regular units of the United States Army.

Stevens was undoubtedly right in his assessment, as Siberia was in turmoil throughout its vast expanse. A place of political exile since the early seventeenth century, it had its own revolutionary tradition established by the many intellectual, middle-class dissenters who lived out their lives and raised families in its rigorous climate. The Socialist Revolutionaries were particularly strong in cities such as Irkutsk which had a bubbling social, political and cultural life and was renowned for its red-headed, green-eyed women; the descendants of aristocratic rebels sent into exile by the Tsars.

The Bolsheviks were also well-established through latter-day exiles such as Stalin and Lenin who had spread their gospel during their forced sojourns in the villages assigned to them as places of exile. And there were other groups each with their own aims adding to the turbulence; the Cossacks who had won the East for the Tsar, and who treated the Siberian peoples in the same spirit of ruthless colonisation as the US Cavalry had treated the Siberians' cousins, the Red Indian tribes; the bands of deserters and outlaws; and the hundreds of thousands of German and Austro-Hungarian prisoners of war kept in camps strung out along the railway line, among whom the Bolsheviks were busy proselytising. The Cossacks were scenting independence from the Russians; the outlaws were after loot, the POWs wanted to go home, most of them to return to their families, but some, crucially, to spread the Bolshevik message of revolt.

The joker in this pack was the Czech Legion. It was the manifestation of a country which did not exist but a people who did. The Czechs, ruled by the hated Austro-Hungarians, had been conscripted to serve on the Russian and Italian fronts. Thousands took the opportunity to desert and offer their services to fight against the Austrians and the Germans. They were joined by thousands more who changed sides after they had been captured. Their inspiration was Thomas Masaryk, leader of the Czech national movement who went over to the Allied side in 1914 to work for Czech independence.

The basis of the Legion was a Brigade, formed of Czechs and Slovaks who had fled to Russia from Austro-Hungarian rule before the war. They were incorporated into the Russian Army and performed well, retaining their discipline when the Army began to collapse. The Tsar's generals were reluctant to increase the size of their force and it was not until after the Revolution that the Provisional government allowed the prisoners of war, most of whom had been captured on the Austrian front in 1915, to form the Legion.

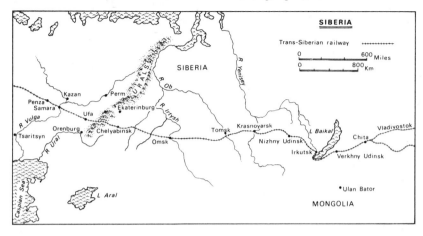

Soon there were some 60,000 serving in the Legion; tough, skilled soldiers dedicated to winning their independence by way of the battlefield. They fought well alongside the Russians and won a brilliant victory at Zborov in Galicia in July 1917. As we shall see, it was concern for the fate of the Czech Legion which finally brought President Woodrow Wilson to agree to the Allied intervention in Siberia.

Intervention had been discussed among the Allies in the spring of 1917 as soon as it became clear that the Russians had shot their bolt and could no longer make an effective contribution to the war. The discussions centred round the possibility of Japan sending an expeditionary force to Vladivostok to protect the stores. There was even the far-fetched notion, especially in French minds, that the Japanese Army could somehow be transported seven thousand miles across Russia to open up a new front against the Germans in the Carpathians.

Only Japan among the Allies could undertake a Siberian expedition. Apart from mopping up the German colonies in the Pacific, her large and well-trained armies had not been engaged. Britain and France needed every one of their men on the Western Front, and America's untrained, ill-equipped, new army was destined for France. But there were serious objections to the Japanese being given a free hand in Siberia, not least from the Russians.

All factions remembered the humiliation of 1905 when the Imperial Russian Fleet sailed round the world to be sunk by the Japanese at the Battle of Tsushima, and they feared Japan's expansionist ambitions. It was felt among the Allies that Russian distrust of Japanese motives was so great that a Japanese landing would lead

71

to the Bolsheviks asking for German help to drive them out – with disastrous consequences for the Allied cause. America too, was suspicious of Japan's intentions towards the maritime provinces of Siberia and Manchuria while Japan herself refused to undertake any action without first being given a free hand.

It fell to the French, clutching at any straw that would help defeat Germany, to make the first official proposal for a multi-nation intervention in Siberia. It got nowhere. The Japanese wanted to do it on their own while the Americans reasoned it would do more harm than good. The British, meanwhile, played their cards close to their chest.

In the end the British resorted to the action which had served them so well throughout their history; they sent a warship. The six-inch gun cruiser HMS *Suffolk* was despatched from Hong Kong to Vladivostok to protect the stores and British nationals in the increasingly anarchic streets of the port. The *Suffolk* arrived on January 15th, 1918. The Japanese did not take too kindly to what they saw as British poaching on their preserves and when they heard of the *Suffolk*'s mission, they sent two cruisers, the *Iwami* and the *Asahi*, the *Iwami* arriving on January 12th and the *Asahi* six days later. Each ship carried a complement of marines who were to be landed in case of trouble. On February 13th the United States despatched the cruiser *Brooklyn* from Yokohama, principally as a warning to the Japanese government that American interests were involved. And that for the moment was that. The ships remained in port and the marines stayed on board.

March came with its momentous happenings. HMS *Glory* landed her marines at Murmansk. The Bolsheviks signed the Treaty of Brest-Litovsk and abandoned the war. And Ludendorff, bolstered by the divisions he was able to withdraw from Russia, launched his attacks on the Western Front. But the Allies still bickered over Siberia.

The Japanese were now pressing hard for approval to take independent action. The British, French and Italians were in agreement that because of the dangers imposed by Russia's withdrawal from the war it had become essential for the Allies to occupy the whole length of the Trans-Siberian Railway. It was now recognised that there was little danger of the Germans being able to get their hands on the supplies at Vladivostok but action was needed to prevent them advancing through the Ukraine and making use of Russia's wheatfields and oil wells. President Wilson vacillated, at one time being about to sanction a unilateral Japanese landing but changing his mind at the last moment.

The British, meanwhile, were trying their own hand at unilateral intervention, but by surrogate. They had agreed to support a young Captain, Gregori Semenov, part Cossack and part Mongol, who, at the head of some 750 freebooters, had set out to carve an independent fiefdom for himself in the Trans-Baikal region in south-eastern Siberia by kicking out the Bolsheviks. As the British now regarded the Bolsheviks as traitors because of the Brest-Litovsk Treaty they agreed to supply Semenov and his horsemen with arms and money in the hope that he could raise a proper army and achieve the aims of intervention without the Allies having to intervene.

It was a mistake whose effects are still felt in Anglo-Soviet relations today. It was also an example of surrogate warfare whose lessons have never been forgotten by the Russians.

Vladivostok, because of the four Allied cruisers swinging at anchor in the bay, remained the only large Siberian city not now controlled by the Bolsheviks. But a process of gradual subversion in place of the usual armed coup had put them in the position of being able to take over whenever they chose to brave the guns of the warships. They were, moreover, moving out the war supplies for their own use in considerable quantities. There was violence in the air, with political scores being settled with the revolver and armed men taking what they wanted at pistol-point.

It came to a head on April 4th when a gang of men in Bolshevik uniforms brandishing revolvers burst into a Japanese shop and demanded money. The shopkeeper refused, whereupon the bandits opened fire and shot three of the Japanese.

The next morning, the Japanese commander, Admiral Kato, marched 500 of his marines ashore "to protect Japanese lives and property". Not to be outdone, Captain Payne of the *Suffolk* threw a cordon of fifty Royal Marines round the British consulate. Admiral A. Knight, commanding the US Asiatic Fleet, was more circumspect; he kept his marines on board because he saw no danger to American lives or property.

It was Admiral Knight who had backed the right horse. The Bolshevik government launched a swingeing propaganda attack on the British and Japanese governments, and they, taken by surprise by the landings and not yet ready to intervene, ordered their marines back to their ships. The British went first, followed on April 25th by the Japanese.

The effect of this withdrawal, apparently at Moscow's behest, convinced the local Bolsheviks that they could now take over the city without opposition from the Allies. And by May 2nd, Vladivostok was Bolshevik.

It was at this juncture that the Czech joker came into play. Three factors had combined to put the Czechs into the position where they, unwittingly, were to play a vital role in the Siberian game. First, the French were desperate for fighting men to boost their depleted and mutinous ranks. Second, the Czechs remained anxious to demonstrate that they were worthy of nationhood. And finally the Bolshevik government had no wish to have a large, well-armed and disciplined military force in Russia which owed allegiance to neither the country nor to Bolshevism, a force moreover largely led by former Tsarist officers.

A deal was struck with the Bolsheviks under which the Czechs would take the Trans-Siberian Railway from their base at Kiev to Vladivostok where they would embark on British and American ships and be carried all the way round the world to fight with the French Army on the Western Front. Their first task was to fight their way past the Germans who were advancing into the Ukraine. This they did alongside a force of Ukrainian Bolsheviks, but some who were caught by the Austrians were hanged as traitors. News of the hangings only strengthened the resolve of the Czechs to go east. They made their way to Penza on the Trans-Siberian where they started to board whatever trains were available. It was a laborious process. There were 60,000 of them and soon they were strung out all along the line, an army snaking its way across 6,000 miles to nationhood.

Their journey east had hardly started, however, before the Bolsheviks began to have second thoughts about the wisdom of allowing such a potent force to enter the volatile situation which now existed in Siberia. They began to make conditions: the Czechs would have to give up their Tsarist officers and would only be allowed 168 rifles and one machine-gun to guard each train. The Bolsheviks justified their claim for the Czechs to surrender their arms by pointing out that they had been supplied by the Russians who now needed them back. At the same time the Bolsheviks tried to subvert some of the Czech soldiers to Communism.

In this atmosphere of mounting distrust the Czechs held a secret meeting at Kirsanov and decided that they could put no faith in the Bolsheviks. They hid a considerable number of weapons on their trains and set out, determined not to be stopped.

However, while the French were still anxious for the Czechs to reach the Western Front as soon as possible, the British had other ideas. They argued that while the Czechs were numerous enough to severely strain British maritime resources in bringing them all the way to France, there were not enough of them to make any significant impact on the fighting on the Western Front. Instead, said the British, those already in Siberia proper should link up with Semenov and create the basis of a new Russian army to resume the fight against the Germans in the East, while those still west of the Urals should make their way to Archangel where a British training mission would arm and organise them to protect the northern ports.

While the Czech leader, Eduard Beneš, agreed to the latter proposal, the French insisted that wherever the Czechs went in Russia their ultimate destination had to be the Western Front. Eventually, on May 2nd, the day the Bolsheviks took control of Vladivostok, the Supreme War Council agreed that: (a) the British government should undertake to do their best to arrange the transportation of those Czech troops at Vladivostok or on their way to that port; (b) the French government should undertake the responsibility for those troops until embarkation; (c) the British government should undertake to approach Trotsky, the Bolshevik war commissar, with a view to the concentration at Murmansk and Archangel of those Czech troops not belonging to the Army Corps which had left Omsk for Vladivostok.

Thus the French thought they had won their point and believed that the British were committed to shipping the Czechs to France. But the British thought the agreement sufficiently loosely worded for them to pursue their own plans, and on May 23rd they ordered the despatch of General Poole's training mission to Archangel, to arm, clothe and train the Czechs for their new mission. The British hoped that some 60,000 Czechs would eventually join them in the north.

As is so often the case in war a minor event a long way away destroyed a well-laid plan; not a single Czech reached Archangel because of a fracas in a railway siding at Chelyabinsk, the southern gateway through the Urals to Siberia. There, on May 14th, a trainload of Czechs going east encountered a trainload of Hungarian prisoners of war who were being repatriated under the Brest-Litovsk agreement. Historically, there had never been any love lost between the Czechs and the Hungarians and an argument broke out: the Hungarians called the Czechs traitors, the Czechs referred in soldier's language to the Hungarians' parentage. One of the prisoners of war picked up a piece of iron, threw it and killed a Czech soldier, whereupon the Czechs, roaring with rage, threatened to shoot everyone on the train if the murderer was not handed over. Convinced that the Czechs meant business, the Hungarians gave him up. A Czech renegade called Malik, he was lynched by his countrymen on the spot.

Events began to run out of control. The Bolshevik authorities decided to try to enforce order and detained several Czechs so that they could give evidence about the incidents. The Czechs then took up their rifles, disarmed the local Red Guards and set the prisoners free.

Strangely enough, the affair was then settled by the local Bolsheviks and the Czechs who saw no reason to quarrel. But the news had already reached Moscow and the Bolshevik government reacted fiercely. Two leading members of the Czech National Council were arrested in the capital and forced to sign a message to the Legion ordering them to lay down all their weapons. Trotsky sent out orders for the Czechs to be disarmed: they were to be stopped from continuing their journey east and would be formed into labour battalions or incorporated into the new Red Army.

During these events representatives of all the Czech units had met at Chelyabinsk as the "Congress of the Czechoslovak Revolutionary Army" and had decided that whatever the Allies planned or the Bolsheviks ordered they were going to Vladivostok, shooting their way there "if we have to". They made the decision on the same day that the British decided to send their training mission to Archangel. Trotsky responded by telegraphing to the Soviets along the Trans-Siberian informing them that "every armed Czechoslovak found on the railway is to be shot on the spot".

Fighting immediately broke out. Because the Czechs were strung out like a snake with its head already in Vladivostok but the tail still in Penza, the fighting was localised in the railway towns. Soon the Czechs, better disciplined than the Red Guards and outnumbering them at the crucial points, had gained control of large sections of the Trans-Siberian, and several of the largest towns.

On June 29th, they occupied Vladivostok, arresting the Bolshevik leaders, pulling down the Red Flag from the Soviet headquarters and running up the blue and white flag of the Tsar. Albert Rhys Williams, an American Presbyterian minister with a radical turn of politics, who was the *New York Evening Post*'s correspondent in Russia, recorded the scene: the Czechs had moved swiftly and quietly. The first Williams knew of the takeover was when he met a Soviet Commissar having his shoes cleaned near the Red Fleet building. "In a few minutes I may be dangling from a lamp-post," said the commissar, "and I want to be as nice looking a corpse as possible . . . our days are done for. The Czechs are taking over the city." When the Red Flag was pulled down someone shouted "The Soviet has fallen" and it rang round the city. People rushed into the streets, flinging their hats into the air. The first Soviet occupation of Vladivostok had lasted 58 days.

The marines came ashore again from the British and Japanese cruisers and this time the Americans joined them. The British occupied the railway station, the Japanese seized the arsenal and the Americans guarded their consulate. A week later a notice signed by the Czechs and the British, American, Japanese, French and Chinese representatives in the port proclaimed that the Vladivostok area had been taken "under the temporary protection of the Allied Powers . . . for its defense against dangers both external and internal."

The Czechs however, were still not safe. They were yet to gain control of Irkutsk, the important railway centre 2,570 miles from Vladivostok, through which some forty thousand of their comrades still had to pass. They feared attack not only by the Bolsheviks but by German and Austro-Hungarian prisoners of war who had been armed by the Bolsheviks and enlisted in the Red Army. It later became apparent that these armed prisoners numbered only a few thousand but at the time were thought to amount to a formidable fighting force which, positioned along the strategic barrier of Lake Baikal, could cut off the main body of the Legion, confined as it was to its trains and the railway towns.

The Czechs in Vladivostok therefore proposed to turn about and deal with Irkutsk, but they needed help from the Allies. According to the despatches of Captain Payne of the *Suffolk* they asked for a 100,000 strong expeditionary force and enough weapons to equip them as a proper army.

"Save the Czechs" now became the cry among the Allies while the British added "and keep them in Russia."

In his biography of Winston Churchill, Martin Gilbert records that Churchill, then Minister of Munitions, had written to the Prime Minister, Lloyd George, on June 17th arguing that "It is certainly against your instinct and convictions to shift the Czecho-Slovak Corps from Russia to France." Then, on June 22nd he warned his Cabinet colleagues:

If we cannot reconstitute the fighting front against Germany in the East, no end can be discerned to the war. Vain will be all our sacrifices of the peoples and the armies. They will only tend to prolong the conflict into depths which cannot be plumbed. We must not take "No" for an answer whether from America or from Japan. We must compel events instead of acquiescing in their drift. Surely now when Czech divisions are in possession of large sections of the Siberian Railway and in danger of being done to death by the treacherous Bolsheviks, some effort to rescue them can be made? Every man should ask himself each day whether he is not too readily accepting negative solutions.

Lloyd George needed no convincing. Neither did the French leader Georges Clemenceau. On June 2nd they appealed jointly to President Wilson to intervene in Siberia because failure to do so immediately "must inevitably cause effects which can only be described as disastrous to the Allied cause". They also pleaded with him to come to the aid of the Czechs who would be placed in dire peril unless the Allies acted immediately.

There was widespread sympathy for the Czechs in America, and Wilson, who had resisted intervention for so long, finally gave in to British and French pressure because he was convinced that the Czechs were in danger. On June 6th he called a meeting at the White House and announced that America was going to their aid. Seven thousand American troops would be sent along with an equal number of Japanese to guard the Czechs' lines of communication as they proceeded towards Irkutsk. Since America, fully stretched to provide men for the Western Front, could not provide such a force for some time, the Japanese would supply the Czechs with arms and ammunition with the Americans sharing the cost and sending her own supplies when they became available. All this, said Wilson, was being undertaken solely to protect the Czechs against the German and Austrian prisoners of war and there was "no purpose to interfere with internal affairs of Russia" or to infringe on Russia's territorial sovereignty.

There was criticism, especially from Lloyd George, that the American military commitment would be insufficient to accomplish anything useful in Siberia, so President Wilson sent a formal note to his allies making his position clear. Military intervention, he insisted, "would add to the present sad confusion in Russia rather than cure it, injure her rather than help her." Moreover, he added, that intervention would be "of no use in the war against Germany". The United States therefore, could not "take part in such intervention or sanction it in principle".

He reiterated that America would only send troops to Siberia in order to protect the Czechs and stipulated that the only legitimate object for which American or Allied troops could be employed was to "guard military stores which may subsequently be needed by

Russian forces and to render such aid as may be acceptable to the Russians in the organisation of their own self defence". This was not at all what Wilson's allies had in mind. But they took comfort in other paragraphs in his aide-mémoire where he explained that his conclusions applied only to the American forces and were not "meant to wear the least color of criticism of what other governments associated against Germany may think it wise to undertake" . . . The United States government wished "in no way to embarrass their choices of policy" and did "not wish it to be understood that in so restricting its own activities it was seeking, even by implication, to set limits to the action or to define the policies of its associates."

It was during the early hours of that same day, July 17th, that Tsar Nicholas and his family were murdered by the Cheka (Extraordinary Commission for the Struggle against Counter-Revolution, Speculation and Sabotage), at Ekaterinburg. This is not the place to tell the story of the murders in the house of Ipatiev the engineer, or recount the subsequent disposal of the bodies at the mine of the Four Brothers but we must in passing record our conviction that every member of the Tsar's family died that dreadful night. Those who want to believe otherwise should read the report of Nicholas Sokolov, the legal investigator appointed by the White Russian leader Admiral Kolchak to clarify the circumstances of the deaths.

During the year-long occupation of Ekaterinburg by Kolchak's forces after it fell to the Czechs in July 1918, Sokolov took statements from witnesses, recovered a mass of evidence from the mine shaft and proved beyond reasonable doubt that all the Tsar's immediate family, including the Grand Duchess Anastasia, had been murdered. Accounts of Lenin's behaviour during the meeting of the Central Executive Committee at which the Tsar's death was announced suggest that he knew that the killings had been ordered. He certainly gave no indication that he disapproved of them. Telegrams left behind by the local Bolsheviks when they fled from Ekaterinburg indicate that Lenin's close collaborator Jacob Sverdlov, Chairman of the Executive Committee, was the man who gave the orders. It must have been somebody with a macabre sense of humour who in 1924 gave the ancient city of Ekaterinburg its new name of Sverdlovsk.

There was one survivor of the massacre. It was the Tsarevich's spaniel, Joy, whose story was told by the late Pail Chavchavadze as a note in his novel *Because the Night was Dark*. He wrote:

A few days after the murder in Ekaterinburg the town was taken by anti-Bolshevist forces. With them, attached as Liaison Officer to a British Military Mission, came one of my mother's brothers, Colonel Paul Rodzianko. At a corner of the street not far from the Ipatiev House he saw the Tsarevich's spaniel running in circles. Recognising him, he called him by name. The spaniel came, wagging his tail uncertainly, stumbling a little, finally bumping into Rodzianko's leg. He was totally blind. Eventually my uncle brought him to England where Joy lived on for a number of years on the Rodzianko farm near Windsor. There in the early twenties I often saw the Tsarevitch's little blind dog.

The Tsar had been marked for death from the moment the Bolsheviks came to power – not only in revenge for the past but in fear for the future, as Lenin knew that he was the one man under whom the Bolsheviks' quarrelling enemies could unite. And, to make sure that no other Romanov could take his place, the whole family was cold-bloodedly wiped out. It was the first of the deliberate political killings by the Bolshevik government which eventually culminated in Stalin's purges.

What, in the end, made the murder of the royal family a matter of both urgency and secrecy was the swift advance of the Czechs from Chelyabinsk to Ekaterinburg, sweeping the Bolshevik troops before them, and threatening to free the Tsar.

These were those same Czechs whose "dire peril" had led President Wilson, despite all his misgivings, to agree to the intervention.

The British were unhappy at the political and military limits Wilson had set to the United States' role but decided to protest no further, confident that once the Americans arrived in Siberia, the pressures of war would lead inevitably to the widening of their role and the escalation of their commitment. Wilson had limited his original involvement to an arbitrary 7,000 men. With its commitments to the Western Front the United States had no more to spare but Wilson also hoped that by restricting the size of the American force he could secure the agreement of the Japanese to limit their force to a similar number.

In fact the Japanese government was bitterly divided between the liberals who wanted to work with the United States and the hawkish generals who saw Wilson's refusal to "set limits to the action or to define the policies of its associates", as the green light for their own occupation of the maritime provinces of Russia and China. The generals wanted to send 150,000 men immediately, a force which would have led to President Wilson backing out of the expedition. So the Japanese compromised and submitted a proposal that they should send a full division of 12,000 men and promised that no more troops would be sent than was necessary "to prevent the slaughter of the Czechs". Reluctantly Wilson agreed and his worst fears were realised within weeks as troopships crossed the Sea of Japan to land 70,000 Japanese soldiers, fresh, well-trained and well-armed; not enough to carry to the war with Germany but sufficient for the occupation of Russia's eastern seaboard.

Britain had already taken its own steps to ensure a presence in Siberia. It was only a presence, for as a military force it was laughable: one battalion of C3 medical class garrison soldiers from Hong Kong, the 25th Battalion of the Middlesex Regiment. They sailed for Vladivostok on July 27th, 1918 on board the SS *Ping Suey*, commanded by a Member of Parliament, Lieutenant-Colonel John Ward, known as the "Navvies' MP", a remarkable man who had started his working life as a navvy at the age of twelve. Ward joined the Army and, at the age of twenty, fought in the attempt to relieve Gordon at Khartoum. He returned to England and politics and founded the Navvies' Union before entering Parliament for the Labour Party in 1906. When the Great War broke out he raised no fewer than five labour battalions, then served on the Western Front with the Middlesex Regiment. Now he was to be commander of British forces in the field in Siberia, all one thousand of them.

The British also sent a military mission under Major-General Alfred Knox to Vladivostok. Previously Military Attaché in Petrograd, he spoke fluent Russian and had played a vital part in shaping Britain's policy towards Russia. The French also sent a military mission – but no fighting troops – headed by General Maurice Janin who had been France's representative with the Russian High Command before the Revolution, had commanded Czech troops fighting in France and was to assume command of the Czech Legion. In addition there were 4,186 unwilling Canadians sent to Siberia only after intense pressure from the British government. Their main function was to equip the Middlesex battalion with Arctic clothing and maintain the supply system; they were soon withdrawn. And, because they were Allies, there were small contingents of Italians and Poles attached to the mission.

So the stage was set. The players gathered in the huge theatre of Siberia, sheltering behind the ambiguities of the lines of President Wilson's script. Each nation had its own motives for being there, motives which were often contradictory. And it is not surprising that jealousy and misunderstanding flourished in the midst of political and military dangers which were only dimly compre-hended by those taking part in this tragic farce.

CHAPTER 6

Oil and the Twenty-Six Commissars
Baku, January–September 1918

At Baku, oil-town on the Caspian, the Great War met the Great Game. There was very much a North-West Frontier expedition feel about the first British intervention – a thousand men wearing solar topees and shorts sent up from Persia to try to stop the Turkish-German forces capturing the oil-wells and to block their advance towards Afghanistan and India.

Like the other intervention ports, Archangel, Murmansk and Vladivostok, Baku's dusty streets were filled with an extraordinary mixture of humanity: Georgians, Azerbaijanis, Armenians, Cossacks, Tartars, Jews, Persians and European Russians – a rough lot, most of them looking for an opportunity to cut the throats of the others. But unlike Archangel, Murmansk and Vladivostok, Baku could lay claim to an ancient existence, independent of Russia. First mentioned in the fifth century AD, it became a place of veneration among the Zoroastrians who worshipped at shrines built where fire sprang spontaneously from the ground as oil and gas burst from its huge underground reservoirs.

When the oil boom started in the late nineteenth century – for lamps and lubrication before the internal combustion engine was invented – Baku's inhabitants revived their worship of the "eternal fires", only now its shrines were wooden derricks. Baku became a rich, vulgar, brawling place where overnight millionaires built tawdry Italianate palaces among the minarets and imported harems of beautiful women from all over the world. Poor peasants were brought in from Persia to work in the oilfields. But while their masters gambled fortunes on the turn of a card, they slept in miserable barracks, and were too poor to afford wives.

The mixture of nationalities, religions and rich and poor made it a turbulent place. Riots, fights and murder were commonplace. Everyone was armed with knife or gun, and usually both. The millionaires had funk-holes built into their palaces, cellars protected behind steel doors and provisioned with wine and food and women in which they could sit out the riots while their bodyguards, usually

Circassian mercenaries or Georgians with faces as sharp as their long knives, battled it out with the rioters.

The richest of them all, a huge Armenian called Mantashev, consolidated his fortune by doing a deal with the Nobels, who were developing the fields, and the Rothchilds, who were marketing the oil, building a railway from Baku to Batumi on the Black Sea to export it.

In such a climate trouble was inevitable; powerful capitalist concerns in league with hell-raising local entrepreneurs making their fortunes off the sweat of a half-starved labour force in the midst of warring communal and religious factions. There could hardly have been a better breeding ground for revolution.

Not surprisingly, Marxism flourished. One of its underground moles was a "spoilt priest" called Dzhugashvili, son of a Tiflis cobbler, who later adopted the *nom de guerre* of Stalin, "man of steel". He ran an underground newspaper, *The Proletarian of Baku*, was reported to have robbed a bank in Tiflis to provide funds for the party and was arrested five times by the Tsarist police before being sent to exile in Siberia.

Trouble broke out with the mini-revolution of 1905. Old scores were settled. Several thousand died and the oilfields were set on fire. But by now Europe's industries depended on Baku oil. The motor car had arrived. The Royal Navy was moving towards the adoption of oil-fired engines to meet the threat of German naval rearmament. The 1905 riots therefore alarmed the foreign investors and European governments so much that they demanded that the Tsar station a military force at Baku to keep order and protect their investments.

Twelve years later, Baku was even more important. When the Russian Army gave up fighting after the November Revolution, the Russian commander in the Caucasus made his own armistice with the Turks who, of course, regarded the armistice as simply an invitation to keep marching forward. They had two objectives: the capture of the oilfields, thus enabling Germany to break the economic stranglehold of the British Navy, and to gather the Moslems of the Caucasus, Transcaspia and Turkestan into its "Army of Islam" and march on India. At that time Baku was said to be a Bolshevik island in a non-Bolshevik sea. It was to foil these plans, not to overthrow Bolshevism, that the British sent "Dunsterforce" to Baku.

The British force was not at first envisaged as a fighting unit, but as a mission composed of a group of officers and a section of armoured cars from what had been Commander Oliver Locker

Lampson's RN Armoured Car Squadron. This had been withdrawn through Archangel, transferred to the Army, re-equipped with Austin armoured cars and then sent back to Russia through the Persian Gulf.

Commanded by one of the army's "modern Major-Generals", L. C. Dunsterville, the mission's orders were to co-operate with Colonel Lazar Bicherakhov, a Tsarist officer who was determined to keep fighting, with the objective "to prevent the passage through the Caucasus of Turkish armies".

It set out from Baghdad, which had been captured by the British in 1917, in a convoy of 41 Ford Model T cars at the end of January 1918. But with roads virtually non-existent and whole areas of their route in the hands of brigands it was unable to reach the Caspian until June. In the meantime events had galloped ahead.

The Turks had demanded great chunks of Armenia from Russia, including the strategic fortified city of Kars under the terms of the Treaty of Brest-Litovsk. Armenia, Georgia and Azerbaijan, the three states south of the Caucasus mountains, and outside Russia proper, had formed the single state of Transcaucasia. Despite the hatred they felt for one another, they tried to maintain a united but independent existence. Transcaucasia lasted only a few months, however, collapsing under German pressure, the advance of the Turkish Army and its own inbuilt stresses. The Armenians gained breathing space in late May by defeating the Turks at the battle of Sardarab but at that very moment the Georgians broke away from the Transcaucasian republic, declared independence and signed a treaty with the Germans. The Azerbaijanis swiftly followed their example and allied themselves with the Turks. On June 4th the Armenians were forced to make peace with the Turks who for many years had committed the vilest of atrocities against the Armenian inhabitants of Eastern Turkey.

The Turks then pressed on towards Baku, its oil and the dream of a new Turkic Empire stretching to Afghanistan drawing them forward. There had already been violence in Baku in March of 1919 which had started as a struggle for power between the Bolsheviks and their left wing allies and the bourgeois Musavat party but which had degenerated into a race riot with the Christian Armenians and Moslem Azerbaijanis murdering each other as they had done for centuries.

The Bolsheviks, supported by the Socialist Democrats, held on to power under the guidance of Stepan Shaumian. This charismatic man, born in Tiflis in 1878, had been expelled from the Riga Polytechnic Institute in Latvia in 1900 for revolutionary activity.

He had worked for the cause in Germany and France, led an oil strike in Baku in 1914, been exiled, and in December 1917 had been appointed by Lenin as Extraordinary Commissar for Caucasian affairs. He was a dedicated Bolshevik, determined to carry out the party's orders despite the precarious position in which he found himself.

By now it was apparent that Dunsterville's military mission would not be strong enough to deter the Turks. Dunsterville asked for British infantrymen from Mesopotamia as reinforcements. He planned to use this augmented force as a nucleus round which the various local units – including the Bolsheviks – could build an army to hold Baku.

London, however, felt that the plan had little chance of success and would be a waste of men sorely needed to defend north Persia against the threat of a combined Turkish-German incursion. Lloyd George, at a Cabinet meeting on June 24th, went as far as to suggest that it might be better for the Turks to hold Baku as it was unlikely they would ever be dangerous to British interests in the East. This, however, was not true of Russia, if in the future she became regenerated.

At the same time Stepan Shaumian told the British Vice-Consul in Baku, Ronald McDonell, that he had received orders from Moscow telling him that he was not to allow a single British soldier to set foot on Russian soil. Dunsterville was stymied on both sides and spent June and July kicking his heels in the dust and unforgiving summer heat of north Persia. And all the time the Turks drew closer and closer to Baku. The Armenian majority in the city began to panic: they had no illusions about their fate if the Turks captured Baku.

Support for the Bolsheviks began to slip away. It had remained strong not because the Armenians believed in Communism but because the Bolsheviks kept the Azerbaijanis more or less under control and the Armenians knew that once that control was lifted the Azerbaijanis would carry off their women, burn their houses and slit their throats. It was not a question of politics, but a matter of survival.

As the Bolshevik forces tended to be strong only in debate and not in fighting the Turks, the Armenians began to look for someone else to save them. They had only one choice – the British. At the same time, the authorities in London, alarmed by the Turkish advance and the German occupation of Georgia, also had a change of heart and Dunsterville was given permission to go ahead with his expedition, albeit on a strictly limited basis.

On July 16th, the Armenians and the Socialist Revolutionary members of the Baku Soviet proposed inviting the British to defend them – just as the Murmansk Soviet had done four months before. But they were narrowly defeated. Nevertheless the vote was so close that Shaumian felt obligated to have his orders restated by the Bolshevik leaders. He got them in no uncertain terms from Stalin who had his headquarters in Tsaritsyn, later to become Stalingrad, and who refused to allow the Soviet to ask for help from the "Anglo-French Imperialists". The next day Lenin cabled from Moscow ordering Shaumian to follow Stalin's instructions. Shaumian, however, was in no position to do so. Stalin and Lenin may have had their own troubles but they were not surrounded by an army of Turkish regulars supported by bloodthirsty Azerbaijanis.

Neither did they have the cosmopolitan, frightened population of Baku to deal with. Shaumian spelt it all out to Lenin in another telegram on July 27th, and then four days later, with the grey figures of the Turks appearing on the hills surrounding the city, he and the other Bolshevik leaders steamed out of Baku harbour on a ship heading for the Red stronghold of Astrakhan which commanded the Caspian's Volga delta. They had only gone a few miles when they were turned back by gunboats manned by sailors sympathetic to the Mensheviks. In the meantime the government of Baku had been taken over by Socialist Revolutionary Armenians and Mensheviks under the name of the Central-Caspian Dictatorship.

The "Dictators" immediately did two things. They arrested Shaumian and his commissars. And in a formal note to Vice-Consul McDonell they invited the British to take part in the defence of Baku. It seemed at first that the invitation had come too late. But the Armenians, fighting with a courage that comes from desperation, stopped the Turks in their tracks with a fierce counter-attack. It forced the Turks to abandon their plans for simply walking into Baku, and instead to bring up supplies and prepare a proper siege of the city.

Dunsterville, his force augmented by infantry and guns released by the War Office, had now received permission both from the new Baku government and the British government to undertake his expedition. His task, as spelled out by the War Office, was not to try to occupy Baku on a permanent basis, but to close the Caspian to the Turks and to sabotage the oilfields to the extent that the Turks and Germans would get no oil.

For Dunsterville to fight his way into Baku by land was impossible, as the Turks had already reached the Caspian at Alyat, south of the city. Instead he mounted a naval operation, commandeering three ships and transporting his force, men, horses, guns, armoured cars, his Fords, and some Martinsyde Scout aircraft from the port of Enzeli in Northern Persia directly to the Baku peninsula. His own ship was the *President Kruger*, named after the Boer leader whose portrait, complete with top hat, dominated the messroom. The *Kruger*, which normally traded along the Caspian coastline, had become a "revolutionary ship" and was flying the Red Flag. Dunsterville had it hauled down and replaced by the Tsarist flag: he was immediately in trouble with the ship's revolutionary committee. But after much argument they reached a compromise: the flag would be flown upside down. In this way it resembled the flag of Serbia.

Dunsterville then set sail for Baku remarking on the "glorious tangle of it all. A British general on the Caspian, the only sea unploughed before by British keels, on board a ship named after a South African Dutch president and former enemy, sailing from a Persian port under a Serbian flag, to relieve from the Turks a body of Armenians in a revolutionary Russian town."

The arrival on August 4th, 1918 of the British Tommies at the wharf belonging to the Caucasus-Mercury Steam Shipping Company caused a great deal of excitement amongst the city's 300,000 inhabitants who watched them disembark and march through the streets to a ceremonial welcome by the new government. The soldiers of the Midland Brigade found themselves in a curious place, dirty and rubbish-strewn with camels wandering the streets. Everything was covered in a fine layer of sand-dust carried on strong north winds. Horse-drawn trams provided the main means of transport and when the horses, starved of fodder, could not get up the hills the passengers were harnessed to the traces. There were mosques and minarets and an obviously prosperous business quarter. And over it all hung the smell of oil from the derricks standing in the shallow waters of the Caspian.

The soldiers themselves, with their long shorts and rifles making them look like dangerous schoolboys, were equally objects of curiosity to the various nationalities who watched them march past. They hoped that these young men were going to save them from the Turks while they pursued their age-old feuds overlaid with the new one which cut across the old divisions, that of being for or against Bolshevism.

Among those taking a keen and highly critical interest in the British soldiers was a small, darkly handsome Armenian, twenty-three-year-old Anastas Mikoyan. Formerly Commissar of the 3rd

Brigade of the Red Army, then working underground in Baku, he was later to become one of the great pillars of Stalin's Russia. What his real thoughts were we shall never know but later he wrote a sanitised version of the events:

> On the first day some 200 troops arrived. But in order to make an impression on the local people they were marched down the same street twice. More arrived over the next few days, but only a few. In the end there were only about 1,000 of the 16,000 that the anti-Bolshevik Social Revolutionaries had promised would be there to hold off the Germans and the Turks. And even then the British did not send all their men up into the front line. A large number were held back in Baku itself. Clearly they wanted to keep control over the local government, as well as avoid losses at the front.

Mikoyan was being less than generous. In fact the British troops were rushed up to the front line as they arrived and those left in the city were needed for organisational purposes and to make sure they were not stabbed in the back by local malcontents. He was correct about the numbers however – "Dunsterforce" comprised only 900 men. It was the same story as Archangel, but in reverse. There the Bolsheviks feared a major invasion which could have overwhelmed them, but which failed to materialise. In Baku, the Central Caspian Dictatorship had hoped the British would send a large force and knew they were doomed when Dunsterville arrived with only two battalions.

The situation was not helped by the Bolshevik agitators like Mikoyan who circulated a news-sheet attacking the arrival of the British. Addressed to comrades, workers, sailors, Red Army and all Baku citizens, it said:

> The agents of the English Imperialists are carrying on counter-revolutionary work; they sow discord among you, they intend to put up the sailors against the workman, the workman against the revolutionary government.
>
> We have news that the English Capitalists have concluded a close agreement with our local counter-revolutionaries. They wish to destroy our power and put up in its place the power of the English and the Bourgeois.
>
> The Bourgeois and their despicable dependents are in favour of the English. The Workmen and Sailors are in favour of the Russian Revolution.
>
> The Bourgeois and their dependents are in favour of cutting

adrift from Russia. The Workmen and Sailors are in favour of the unity of the Russian Socialist Federalist Republic.

The Bourgeois pledged to the English, bartered souls, pitiful cowards, and all counter-revolutionaries, are in favour of cutting adrift from Russia, for English might, for a new war with Germany. They are against the independence of Russia:

> Away with the English Imperialists;
> Away with their paid agents;
> Away with the Bourgeois Counter-Revolutionaries;
> Hurrah for the People's Committees;
> Hurrah for independent Russia;
> Hurrah for the Russian Social Revolution;
> What can the English give you? Nothing;
> What can they take from you? Everything;
> Away with the English Imperialists;
> All to the front; to arms; All to the saving of Baku.

Dunsterville, a no-nonsense soldier, was not put off by such propaganda: he said he had never supposed that local reaction to the British would be "entirely friendly".

Far more worrying to him were the signs that the Turks were preparing their long-awaited offensive against the city, and the poor morale of the Armenian and Russian soldiers who provided the bulk of his defensive forces. He tried to bolster them with uniforms and rifles and quick training courses but the Tsarist loyalist Colonel Bicherakhov and his disciplined soldiers had gone off to fight in the north and Dunsterville had little to work with. He was fast running out of time. Shortly after he arrived Dunsterville watched a Turkish attack on a hill outside the city and saw the Russian soldiers walking away from the fight. The British detachment of seventy officers and men left holding the position called for a counter-attack. Nothing happened.

Established in two of Baku's best hotels, all crimson plush curtains and gilt furniture, Dunsterville and his staff worked out a plan of campaign with British units holding strategic hills, backed by the field guns which had been shipped from Enzeli and the Austin Armoured cars with their machine-guns in twin turrets acting as mobile reserve to plug the gaps. The welfare of his men caused him great concern because this was high summer and Baku was stricken by disease. In order to improve his soldiers' diet he bought a consignment of fresh Caspian caviare. It was not a success. He concluded that caviare required "a trained palate, the men called it herring paste and had no great liking for it."

None of them, however, had any time to train their palates. By the end of the first week in September, the Turks had set themselves up for their final assault on the city, shelling the streets, picking off outposts and spreading fear among the Armenians who now showed little stomach for the fight. Inside the city the "Dictatorship" which refused to place its men under British command argued tactics in long voluble meetings which achieved nothing. Dunsterville, enraged at one such meeting, told them that his men had come to Baku to help fight the Turks, not to "do all the fighting with your men as onlookers. In no case have I seen your troops when ordered to attack do anything but retire, and it is hopeless continuing to fight alongside such men. You would be best advised to send out a party at once with a flag of truce to the enemy and see what terms you made with him . . . to enable your womenfolk to get away. I beg you will forego your usual custom of speechmaking and the passing of resolutions."

The end came on September 14th when the Turks broke through the city's last line of defence. Dunsterville had prepared for this and moved his men down to the wharves by night so that the local populace, enraged by what they regarded as desertion by the British, could not interfere with the embarkation of the British troops on the *President Kruger*.

It had been a costly operation for Britain. The surviving Austin armoured cars and thirty Ford Tin Lizzies were incapacitated and pushed off the end of the pier – a practice later followed at Novorossiysk and Archangel. Two aircraft which had been shot up were destroyed. And no less than 180 men of Dunsterforce were listed as killed, wounded or missing. Of those, 71 were killed and 21 of the 85 wounded died later.

It was a high price to pay, but in Dunsterville's opinion the young men of the new battalions, the Hampshires, North Staffs, Gloucestershires, Worcestershires and the incomparable Gurkhas, had covered themselves with glory. They had been in the firing line for six weeks and kept at bay a Turkish army of ten times their strength over a twenty-mile front. The Turks later acknowledged that they had suffered 2,000 casualties.

Dunsterville regretted that he was only able to provide his men with bread, biscuits and cups of tea as they sailed safely to Enzeli because "every man deserved a Lord Mayor's banquet." In fact, the loss of Baku no longer mattered to the outcome of the war. The Germans had suffered their "Black Day" on the Western Front and their defeat was now inevitable. But inside Baku dreadful things were happening. The Turks stayed outside the city for three days while their Azerbaijani irregulars looted and pillaged in medieval style. Every Armenian fear born of long experience of massacre was realised. Their women were raped, their homes destroyed and 9,000 men were murdered. The stench of the dead blotted out the usually pervasive smell of the oil.

The effects of the Baku massacre, like so many other incidents in this story, rumble on today. It was one of the atrocities which has spawned the modern-day Armenian terrorist groups who murder Turkish diplomats in the name of their dead, demanding an admission of guilt from the Turks and the restoration of their nation.

While Dunsterville was fighting on the western shore of the Caspian, another British Major-General, Wilfred Malleson, was fighting inland from the Caspian's eastern coast, in Central Asia proper. Under the command of the Indian Army, he had a mixed force of British and Indian soldiers whose task was to prevent the Turks and Germans landing an expedition on the east coast and following the railway line through Transcaspia from the port of Krasnovodsk to Merv and then down to the Afghan border.

Malleson, an Indian Army Intelligence officer, had originally been sent to Meshed in North Persia in June 1918, to keep an eye on what was going on across the border where the Bolsheviks were in almost complete control. He was also ordered to sabotage the Trans-Caspian Railway if the Turks broke through and to make sure they did not capture large stocks of cotton stored at depots along the line. But, as with most military affairs, the situation changed rapidly. Before he had started his work at Meshed dissatisfaction with Bolshevik rule in the Transcaspian area had boiled over and by the middle of July, a coalition of Mensheviks and Socialist Revolutionaries had established a government of sorts called the Ashkhabad Committee.

They were in a precarious position because the vengeful Bolsheviks had armed some German and Austro-Hungarian prisoners of war and were advancing along the railway from the River Oxus to Merv and Ashkhabad. They fought off the first attacks east of Merv, but doubted if they could hold the position much longer and so, like their compatriots at Murmansk and Baku, they asked the British for help, sending a delegation to Malleson in Meshed to ask for men, money and weapons.

Malleson, anticipating this plea, had requested instructions. His reply came not from London but from General Sir C. C. Munro, Commander-in-Chief of the Indian Army, who gave Malleson the soldierly advice to get on with it since he was the man on the spot and presumably knew what he was doing. Malleson then made an agreement with the Ashkhabad Committee in which he committed himself on behalf of the British government to "guarantee the continuance of military and financial help so long as the Transcaspian government remains in power and continues to place at the head of its political programme the restoration of order and the suppression of Bolshevik and Turk-German intrigue and plans for invasion."

Malleson backed his words with actions. His Indian machine-gunners saved the day in a brisk action when Bolshevik reinforcements defeated the Ashkhabad Committee's raw troops at the Merv Oasis. He then sent in 300 men of the 19th Punjabi Regiment who stopped the advancing Bolsheviks in fighting at Kaakha on August 28th. Later, reinforced by two squadrons of the Seventh Light Cavalry (the second oldest regiment in the Indian Army), a battery of British field artillery and a company of infantry from Dunsterville's base at Enzeli, he was able to muster a force of some thousand men. It could hardly be called a major force of intervention but, as the official history of the Mesopotamia Campaign records, on November 1st it was able to drive the Bolsheviks out of Merv, that ancient seat of Islamic learning once conquered by Alexander the Great. This hard-fought victory, and the establishment on the Caspian of a flotilla of five small ships armed with guns dragged overland through Persia, combined with the progress of the war in the West to remove the threat to Afghanistan from the Turkish Army and, for the time being, the Bolshevik forces.

These small battles fought in faraway places, more like Kipling-esque campaigns against rebellious tribesmen than part of the most important political upheaval of the twentieth century, are largely forgotten now but they included an incident which still colours the Soviet Union's attitude towards Britain: the execution of the twenty-six Commissars of Baku.

When Dunsterville sailed away from Baku the Dictatorship still had Shaumian and his Bolshevik colleagues under arrest. According to Mikoyan there were thirty-five of them, of whom he was one. What happened next remains vague, perhaps deliberately so. But Mikoyan asserts that due to his efforts they were all released. They then set out for Astrakhan, the only Caspian port still in Bolshevik hands, on board the steamer *Turkman*. The Mikoyan version says that there were two British officers on board and they ordered the *Turkman* to sail east instead of north and put into Krasnovodsk which was under the control of the Ashkhabad Committee. It is almost certain that this version is not true. There is no record of any British officers being on board the *Turkman* and the real version shorn of Bolshevik propaganda would seem to be that recounted by Firuz Kazemzadeh, in his book *The Struggle for Transcaucasia.*

According to Kazemzadeh it was the crew of the *Turkman* who decided to change course for Krasnovodsk for the telling reason that they feared arrest by the Bolsheviks in Astrakhan. On September 15th, they sailed into Krasnovodsk where all thirty-five commissars were immediately arrested and held on another boat by a Cossack called Kuhn who had been appointed commandant by the Ashkhabad Committee. Aware of the importance of his captives, he asked the Committee in Ashkhabad, some 350 miles away what he should do with them. It was not until three days later that Malleson, still at Meshed in Persia, was told about their capture by the Committee's representative at his headquarters. At this time negotiations were going on between the British government and the Soviet authorities over the exchange of diplomats and others being held as hostages in both countries. Malleson saw immediately that the capture of commissars would be a good card to add to the British hand and asked for them to be handed over to him, offering to send a detachment of British troops to escort them to India, where a prison camp was later established to hold Bolshevik prisoners taken in Central Asia.

Throughout the affair no British officer laid eyes on the commissars. Malleson, needing all his men to fight his battles further east, had nobody in Krasnovodsk and the only Briton in the area, one of Dunsterville's officers, was kept in the dark by the local authorities.

However, one British officer, Captain Reginald Teague-Jones, Malleson's liaison officer with the Committee in Ashkhabad, was in a position in which he might have affected the fate of the commissars. Malleson wirelessed Teague-Jones to urge the Committee to hand their captives to the British. On the same day, September 18th, Fyodor Funtikov, the Socialist Revolutionary President of the Committee asked Teague-Jones, a fluent Russian speaker, to go to a meeting of the Committee to decide what to do. The drama of that meeting comes through Teague-Jones' account of it in his letter of explanation to the Foreign Office. Funtikov was, as usual, drunk. The Committee was frightened that Bolshevik sympathisers in Krasnovodsk would free the commissars. The commandant wanted them off his hands; his jails were full.

The jails at Ashkhabad were also full. Funtikov argued that the commissars should be shot and reported that Malleson had refused to take responsibility for them. For some reason Teague-Jones did not tell the Committee that Malleson was not only willing but anxious to take charge of the commissars. The argument rambled on inconclusively into the night. Teague-Jones left, disgusted by Funtikov's alcoholic ramblings and, presumably, assuming that nothing would be settled.

The following day he went to see Funtikov, who was still drunk, and who, after being pressed by the Briton, said it had been decided to shoot the commissars. Appalled, Teague-Jones cabled Malleson who summoned the Committee's representative, and he confirmed that twenty-six of the commissars had been shot because of the "seriousness of the situation" and the difficulties involved in meeting the British request that they should be handed over to be used as hostages. Malleson then made the disgusted comment which must have been uttered by many other Britons during the intervention: "In my opinion you are all alike. Red or White."

He then asked Teague-Jones for confirmation of the killings and was told that Funtikov had taken the matter into his own hands. He had given the order for the execution to Kuhn and on the night of September 19th–20th, the doomed men were put on a train, taken seventy-five miles into the desert to a place which is now known as "26 Bakinskikh Kommissarov" and shot.

Mikoyan's version of what happened is quite different. According to him the whole affair was the responsibility of the British "interventionists". The commissars were supposed to have been put on trial in Baku, but this did not happen because of the fall of the city. Then the men were taken on British orders to Krasnovodsk and Funtikov ordered their deaths, "acting under pressure from British bosses".

Mikoyan and eight others were released, he claimed, because their names were not on a list which had been sent from Baku to Krasnovodsk. They were turned loose, he wrote, on September 19th, the day their comrades met their deaths. There is some corroboration of this part of the story because on September 25th, two days after Malleson was told of the executions he reported on the affair to the War Office in London. In his telegram he said that the Bolshevik commissars from Baku had been shot "with the exception of five or six unimportant ones". Malleson, still at Meshed, also fired off a furious telegram to the Ashkhabad Committee protesting about the execution of men the British wanted as hostages.

News of the executions did not become general knowledge until the following March when a Baku newspaper printed a story by a Socialist Revolutionary journalist called Vadim Chaikin who had interviewed Funtikov, then being held in prison in Ashkhabad. Funtikov heaped the blame for the affair on the British. The Bolshevik government accepted this line and protested to London while Stalin wrote an article which argued that the executions "shouted of the lawlessness and savage debauchery with which the English agents settled accounts with the 'natives' of Baku and Transcaspia just as they had with the blacks of Central Africa."

From that moment on the British became the villains of the affair. On the first anniversary of the death of the commissars their remains were cremated in Baku and at the memorial service one of their comrades said, "These stalwart, honest heroes fell at the hands of the British, those from a country which touts its humanitarian attitudes, there lies the result of this humanitarianism – 26 coffins. But the hour of retribution draws near." The local newspaper eulogised "our 26 comrades who were savagely shot to death by British executioners and White Guards."

Paintings of the execution always show two British officers in attendance although none were within a hundred miles of the scene. Mikoyan got round that problem by insisting that the two officers he claims ordered the *Turkman* to change course went ashore at Krasnovodsk where they were greeted by two columns of British soldiers, a battery of British artillery and a group of local officials. Could he have been referring to Malleson's reinforcements who were later to fight at Merv?

The other great protagonist of British guilt was Funtikov himself. Understandably because he was on trial for his life, he tried to put all the blame on Teague-Jones who, he said, ordered him to have the commissars shot, expressed satisfaction that his orders had been carried out, and promised to help cover up the crime.

The dead men have entered the pantheon of Bolshevik heroes. Streets and factories throughout the Soviet Union are named after them. Their statues stand in Baku and other cities. Meetings and rallies commemorate the anniversary of their deaths. And, according to Mikoyan, it was all the fault of the "British Imperialists. They will never be able to wash away the shame of their complicity in the deaths of the twenty-six Baku Commissars."

But Mikoyan, the great survivor, was not untouched by the affair. Years later his enemies within the Politburo mounted a whispering campaign against him, suggesting, untruthfully, that he was released when the others went to their deaths because he had betrayed them.

Similar accusations of working for the British in Baku were made against Beria, the monstrous head of the Soviet secret police who tried to succeed Stalin, and they helped to justify Beria's disgrace and execution. So Mikoyan may be thought lucky to have died in 1978 in his bed.

Another victim was Captain Teague-Jones. Could he have prevented the execution of the commissars? He might have attempted to stop the drunken Funtikov by threatening to cut off British financial and military aid. But did he have the authority? Or, more pertinent, did he think it was necessary? It now seems probable that Teague-Jones took no action because he thought the Socialist Revolutionaries had embarked on an argument which, typically, would last for days and end inconclusively.

The fact that it ended shortly after he left the meeting and the executions were carried out so swiftly shattered the young British officer. When he returned to Britain he sank into silent anonymity, refusing to discuss the affair. By a strange quirk of coincidence we learnt a little more about Teague-Jones from Vic Clow, who, demonstrating his formidable memory, was telling us about the first leg of his journey home on board the Turkish refugee ship *Kapul Thala* from Novorossiysk to Constantinople. Clow had never heard of Teague-Jones or the Baku commissars but, talking about the other people on board, he mentioned meeting a Russian woman travelling in the name of Miller. It was not her real name, she explained; she was married to a British major called Teague-Jones who had been forced to change his name because he was in danger from the Bolsheviks and was still working undercover in South Russia.

It is extraordinary that with so many millions of people killed in the Civil War, in Stalin's pogroms and Hitler's war, the affair of the Baku Commissars should have retained its emotional impact on the Soviet people; but it does and to this day it provides a propaganda weapon for the Soviets to belabour the West, proof that the interventionists – and that includes the United States – were ruthless murderers of Soviet heroes.

CHAPTER 7

The Bolo Liquidation Club
Moscow and Petrograd, December 1917–August 1918

While the British Army was about its business at the military extremities of Russia another campaign was being waged by a band of British adventurers in the political centres of Moscow and Petrograd. The leading members of this band were Robert Bruce Lockhart, Francis Cromie, Sidney Reilly, George Hill, Stephen Alley, Ernest Boyce, Denys Garstin and W. L. Hicks. Each one of them was an accomplished agent and each one of them could have stepped straight out of the pages of a John Buchan story.

An indication of the type of men they were may be gathered from the membership of those who survived this campaign in an exclusive luncheon club formed by Alley, head of the British Secret Service in Russia until April 1918. This club, which met at London's Café Royal, was restricted to members of the Secret Intelligence Service and MI5, the Security Service, who had been involved in the struggle against the Bolsheviks. And with that schoolboy sense of humour to which the Secret Service is prone they called it "The Bolo Liquidation Club".

Schoolboyish or not, the members took proper precautions because a number of them had been sentenced to death by the Bolsheviks and they had a proper respect for the long and ruthless arm of the Cheka, forerunner of the KGB. On luncheon days they would stop their taxis two or three streets away and walk discreetly to the Café Royal. But it was still a far cry from those desperate days in Moscow and Petrograd when every moment and every action carried the risk of arrest and execution.

The story centres round Bruce Lockhart, a "Scot of the Scots" who joined His Britannic Majesty's Consular Service in 1911 after rubber planting in Malaya where he caused a scandal by taking a Sultan's ward as his mistress.

Posted to the Moscow consulate a year later, he took to Russia's glittering social life with the enthusiasm of a boy set loose in a sweet shop. Nights at the ballet and the opera followed by parties at fashionable restaurants and the houses of rich Russian friends, on a diet of champagne, vodka and caviare, laid the basis for a night club pallor which was to stay with him for the rest of his life. But he was far from being a mere playboy. He became fluent in Russian and cultivated a number of influential Russians especially among the moderate opposition to the Tsar. Both Prince Lvov and Alexander Kerensky, successive leaders of the Provisional government before the Bolsheviks seized power, were among his friends. He worked hard and rose from the lowest rank of Vice-Consul to become acting Consul-General in 1915, dealing with all the complexities of Consular work brought about by the war. He did not, however, confine himself to coping with this work. Because the Embassy was in Petrograd he had the opportunity to report on political developments in Moscow and his friendship with Prince Lvov and Alexander Kerensky paid handsome dividends. His knowledgeable despatches were eagerly read in the government offices in Whitehall where the politicians, officials and soldiers were all hungry for news from Russia, especially about the new government's attitude towards continuing the war against Germany.

However, as he had shown earlier in Malaya, he was somewhat indiscreet in his choice of women. He started an affair with a French Jewess and was reported to the Ambassador, Sir George Buchanan by his colleague, the novelist Hugh Walpole. As Lockhart had a wife his affair would have been disapproved of on three counts: his marriage and the fact that his mistress was both French and Jewish. What seemed like a brilliant career in the making was now threatened and Sir George, who much admired the young Scot, posted him home for "reasons of health".

Thus, just over a month before Lenin seized power, Lockhart, somewhat chagrined, found himself kicking his heels back in London while great events were taking shape in Russia.

Like any other large enterprise the Foreign Office is a great gossip shop and the news of his peccadillos spread through the service. But he was saved by Sir George's health gambit – ironically, as it turned out, for Sir George was himself to be brought home on genuine health grounds – and by the interest shown in him by Lord Milner, a member of the War Cabinet. There was also another figure guiding Lockhart's destiny, that of Commander Mansfield Smith-Cumming, Chief of the Secret Service. A flamboyant character with, like Lockhart and Reilly, a taste for women, he became known as "C" and the head of the Secret Service, MI6, has been called "C" ever since. The extent of his involvement with Lockhart, who was always coy about this side of his work, will only be known when – if ever – the appropriate papers are released. But there is little doubt that when Lockhart returned to Moscow he

(went under the control of the Secret Service as well as the Foreign Office.

On December 19th, 1917, Lockhart was summoned to dine with Lord Milner who was shortly to become the Minister for War. Two days later Milner took him to No. 10 Downing Street where he introduced the young diplomat to the Prime Minister – Lloyd George had already been briefed on Lockhart's views of the situation in Russia. He looked Lockhart up and down then said: "Mr Lockhart, from the wisdom of your reports I expected to see an elderly gentleman with a grey beard." He asked a few questions about Lenin and Trotsky, referred briefly to the chaotic conditions in Russia, emphasised the need for tact, knowledge and understanding and, turning to his Cabinet colleagues who were listening to the conversation, said that Lockhart was a man whose place was obviously in Petrograd and not in London.

And so it was arranged. Lockhart was to return to Russia "to keep unofficially in touch" with the Bolsheviks. With three assistants, Captain Hicks, a Russian speaker formerly attached to the British Military Mission in Russia, Edward Birse, a civilian who had been in business in Moscow for a number of years, and Edward Phelan, a young man from the Ministry of Labour, he would operate under the cover of a Commercial Mission. His salary would be £2,000 a year and he could spend up to £5,000 without reference to London – but he had to keep careful accounts. No reference was made to his extra-marital activities. And the records of his briefing by Cumming are closed probably for ever – even supposing they have escaped the attentions of British Secret Service weeders.

Before setting out he had a number of conversations with the Russian emigré Maxim Litvinov over cups of tea at the Lyons Corner House in the Strand. Litvinov had settled in London, married into a British literary family and had worked for the Tsarist delegation's purchasing committee, buying arms and matériel for the Russian forces. At the same time he was also leader of the Bolsheviks in London and in January 1918 was appointed the Soviet representative in London. The Foreign Office refused to accept his appointment officially but it was agreed that he and Lockhart would be accepted as unofficial representatives with certain diplomatic privileges, not least being allowed to send messages in cypher. (These dispositions were important to both countries because the conventional diplomatic arrangements were breaking down under the impact of the Bolshevik Revolution and the growing threat of intervention.)

Lockhart arrived in Petrograd early in February. Sir George Buchanan had already gone home. Sir George was a diplomat of the old school and although opposed to the absolute monarchy of the Tsar he had built up a personal friendship and much trust with the Russian Royal Family. He had even taken it upon himself to warn the Tsar that unless he made sweeping changes in his government to bring in men who understood the aspirations and the sufferings of the people then a revolution was inevitable. The Tsar heard him out politely but took no action. Buchanan continued his good work with the Provisional government but once the Bolsheviks came to power he found he was dealing with men he neither knew nor understood. He returned to London, his health broken in the service of his country, after a final Christmas Night celebration in the great hall of the Embassy, a palace built by Catherine the Great for one of her favourites. The diplomats, soldiers, sailors and spies sang their Christmas carols of peace and hope but each one had a revolver in his pocket. Buchanan left the Embassy in charge of Francis Lindley, the Counsellor, but there was no longer any useful contact between the Allied embassies and the Bolsheviks.

Six weeks later, on February 18th, the German Army resumed its march into Russia to force the Russians to capitulate to the harsh terms of the Treaty of Brest-Litovsk. With Petrograd in danger of being captured, the Allied embassies fled, heading for Finland. As we have seen, Lindley was able to talk his party across the Finnish border to safety while the other nationalities ended up in Vologda. Two of Lockhart's assistants, Phelan and Birse, made a rapid exit with the diplomats, but the third, Captain Hicks, stayed and Lockhart recruited Garstin from the military mission. They did not move into the Embassy which was now under Dutch protection but took over an elegant apartment on the Palace Quay.

Lockhart found himself in a curious position. He had no real diplomatic standing and although British consuls still operated in Moscow, Petrograd and several other major cities, he remained responsible for a number of British officers and officials whose activities did not stand too close an examination. He later complained that he was completely in the dark about the work of these men "for whose presence in Russia and for whose protection my position with the Bolsheviks was the only guarantee".

There were, of course, professionals around who did not need Lockhart's protection. One was Major Stephen Alley MC, head of SIS in Russia. He stayed on until April 1918, but, like his successor, Commander Ernest Boyce, he was more concerned with intelligence operations against Germany than spying on the Bolsheviks.

Their objective at that time was the defeat of Germany rather than the overthrow of Bolshevism.

There was also Captain Francis Cromie, the devastatingly handsome submariner who, much against his will, had been made Naval Attaché and had stayed on in Petrograd as the senior British official there when the diplomats left. He was the genuine all-British hero. In September 1915 he broke the German naval blockade of Petrograd and its naval base of Kronstadt, sailing HM submarine *E19* through the minefields and destroyer patrols of the Baltic. He sank a German destroyer that same month and in November torpedoed and badly damaged the light cruiser *Undine*. Then, in December, he forced the Germans to halt their traffic to Sweden by sinking or capturing ten steamers sailing under the German flag. In May 1916 he was awarded the DSO followed by a chestful of Russian and French decorations and took command of a joint Russian and British submarine fleet. There were seven British submarines, some of which had been transferred from Archangel on grain lighters through the inland waterways, operating in the Baltic with their crews based on the depot ship *Dvina*. This ship, under the name of *Pamiat Azova*, had played a bloody role in the 1905 uprising and was crewed by sailors always on the verge of mutiny.

In a letter to Admiral Phillimore, affectionately known as Filthy Phil, who had been liaison officer to the Tsar's naval headquarters before taking command of the *Ark Royal* in the Aegean, Cromie described what happened when the Tsar was overthrown. All the foreign officers gathered in the vestibule of the Astoria (still Leningrad's best hotel) which was then a military hotel with a retired general in charge of each floor. General Poole, chief of the British Artillery Mission to the Russian Army, soon to be commander of the British expeditionary force in Archangel, took command and sent the Russian officers upstairs out of the way so that –

when the yelling mob came in they were quite put off their stroke on being calmly met by smiling faces. I think they were quite disappointed and so surprised they listened to reason and after searching one or two rooms they returned peacefully. The effect of this was to put us way up top with the crowd and with the (Russian) officers. Ladies were seven deep round each Englishman, clamouring for protection. Neither Gilbert nor Sullivan dreamed of such situations.

But the light operatic atmosphere soon faded. Cromie went on to describe the fate of Admiral Viren, the harsh Commander-in-Chief who was seized by mutinous sailors, "cut up in small pieces and burnt in a wooden box in the public square". Other unpopular officers were pushed through holes in the ice and drowned.

> This can't pass without marking the men [his British crews]. A quarrel may start an international rumpus . . . I find being indirectly under the orders of mutinous foreign seamen an intolerable position for any portion of the English fleet . . . The Russians refuse to assist in depot work and demand the curtailing of some of our privileges. If they succeed in stopping our spirit ration I cannot be responsible for collisions between the English and Russian crews.

He spent the early months of the Revolution trying to keep his flotilla in operational order and to prepare for a new campaign against German shipping once the ice had broken. There were all sorts of problems, apart from the bloodymindedness of the Russian sailors on board the depot ship. There were no spare parts for faulty engines, and the British crews had to do all their own maintenance. There was the continuing shortage of food – "our sailors got their pleasure for ten lumps of sugar". And there were constant attempts by the Bolsheviks to subvert the British sailors.

Nevertheless, when the ice broke in the spring of 1917 he was able to mount a number of patrols which met with some success. But they were British successes, not Russian for, as he recorded, "eight out of seventeen Russian submarines are ready to put to sea but they generally break down when asked to go." He moved his boats to Helsingfors (Helsinki) in an attempt to get away from the revolutionary hotbed of Kronstadt, but by October 1917 and the Bolshevik takeover, he was writing a series of despondent letters to Admiral Phillimore and, significantly, to Admiral Sir Reginald "Blinker" Hall, Director of Naval Intelligence. On October 10th he wrote to Hall: "Have you considered relieving me? I am not applying for it, but I am ready to go . . ." And later, "the whole thing is beyond belief and one's best efforts are paralysed. I feel sick of this and long for a clean chance instead of fighting in this muck. Please forgive this strain."

His request was granted in December but while he was waiting for the train to begin his journey home he received a wire telling him that he had been made temporary Naval Attaché. He wrote a bitter letter to Hall: "This is the very billet I asked you to protect me from . . . a position I cannot afford when I have to support a family and my mother out of my pay. Therefore I earnestly ask you not to abandon me for ever to the backwaters of diplomacy . . . Please don't forget I am still a submarine officer."

Ironically, he was soon doling out thousands of roubles to Russian agents in his efforts to stop the Russian fleet falling into German hands and to hold up supplies, particularly mines and guns, to the Red Guards opposing the British intervention forces in the north. At a time when he had £1,500,000 hidden in the British Embassy to pay for the destruction of the Russian ships he had just £720 in his Portsmouth bank. It seems likely that his appointment to the "diplomatic backwaters" marked his transition from "a submarine officer" to being one of Blinker Hall's agents.

His first major task was to scuttle his own submarines. Writing to Hall, he reported: "I have arranged two systems of destruction for the boats. One, explosive, working off an alarm clock so that all can go up together and one of just messing everything up and blowing through our 130 odd torpedoes with '1840' acid."

In March 1918, a division of German cruisers captured Revel (Tallinn) the capital of Estonia, just across the Gulf of Finland from Cromie's base. Then, in the first week of April the Germans started landing in South Finland and met no opposition whatsoever from the Russians. Cromie's boats, iced in, had to be destroyed before they were captured by the Germans. It was a desperate affair lasting three days. Each of the seven boats had to be inched out in the bitter cold with the crew breaking thick ice to get to deep water where the torpedoes and stores were thrown overboard and the submarines scuttled. At Cromie's urging the Russians also sank four of their submarines. Throughout the operation Cromie was plagued by looters. "One night I lost my temper and held a party of fifty looters with my toy pistol . . . I told them I would kill the first armed man that set foot aboard, backing my words with an absurd twenty-two pistol."

Afterwards he wrote to Hall: "A short note to let you know that our business is finally finished out here . . . I am afraid the Huns will obtain much valuable material, but devil a stitch of ours."

However, Cromie was mistaken in thinking that his work was finished. He was given another much more ambitious task – the scuttling of the Russian Baltic fleet in Kronstadt in order to prevent it falling into the hands of the Germans who were now threatening to capture Petrograd. At that time the fleet consisted of two battleships, several cruisers, a mine-laying cruiser, the submarine depot ship and a number of destroyers. Although a number of the ships were old and in poor condition they would nevertheless have proved an embarrassment to the Royal Navy if they had been co-opted into the German Navy.

In April Cromie wrote to Hall: "I consider the Fleet at Kronstadt far from safe, but destruction is out of the question unless Razvosov will accept office again." Vice-Admiral Razvosov took over as C-in-C Baltic after the murder of Viren but soon retired and although the Bolsheviks asked him several times to return to duty to reorganise the Fleet he always refused. He paid the price for his intransigence, being murdered at Helsingfors in September 1918. Cromie, it seems, was relying on this old Tsarist officer to help him with his scuttling schemes.

The best he could do without Razvosov was to bribe some saboteurs. On April 23rd, he wrote to Hall: "I have hopes (faint ones) of buying some nasty accidents at Kronstadt." It is worth noting that the Russians themselves scuttled ships of the Black Sea fleet in June 1918 to prevent them becoming prizes of the Germans.

It was at this time that the Gigolo-handsome figure of Sidney Reilly arrived in Russia, the land of his birth and the scene of a previous episode in his life: he had worked for the British Secret Service acquiring the secrets of German naval constructors building the ships to replace the Russian fleet defeated by the Japanese in 1905. His arrival was somewhat less than fortunate. Hired by "C" and armed with a pass from Litvinov, he had travelled to Murmansk by sea on his way to make contact with Lockhart. However, as his name on the pass had been misspelled and in the suspicious eyes of the Royal Navy he was an unlikely looking Irishman – not surprising because he was a Russian Jew from Odessa – the Navy arrested him and clapped him in the cells on HMS *Glory*.

Fortunately for Reilly, Major Stephen Alley was also passing through Murmansk, on his way home from his stint as chief of Britain's Secret Intelligence Service in Moscow. Admiral Kemp asked Alley to question Reilly and once Reilly was himself convinced that Alley was a fellow spy he produced a bottle of aspirins, took out the cork and extracted a tiny piece of paper on which was a message to Lockhart written in SIS code. There were rueful apologies and laughter all round – Alley and Reilly later became close friends – and Reilly was off across country to Petrograd where he stopped only long enough to report to the silver-haired Commander Boyce before heading for Moscow and a meeting with Lockhart.

Operating under the code designation of ST1 (ST stood for

Stockholm SIS station and he was the first of the agents) he thus started five months of high adventure. It may well be that Reilly's life as a spy has been over-dramatised but little could be more dramatic than the events of those five months. His first act on reaching Moscow was to put on his Royal Flying Corps uniform and march up to the Kremlin where he demanded to see Lenin. Not surprisingly, he was turned away.

But not even his enemies in the Cheka were without praise for Reilly. The following extract comes not from a paperback romance but a report in a Soviet secret police file released for a Soviet book about the Cheka:

> I looked up from drinking a cup of coffee and returned the brown-eyed gaze from across the room. For a fleeting moment he looked into my eyes and I felt a pleasant shiver. He was well-dressed and well-built. His lean tanned face spoke of a strong will and decisiveness. His eyes were quiet and kind and had a touch of sadness about them. All the same he had an expression which suggested that he had often come face to face with death.

The author who wrote that was none other than a woman agent of the Cheka. Her report on Reilly was passed to Artur Artuzov, the Cheka's head of counter intelligence who wrote in the margin: "An experienced lover who only a few strong-willed women can resist. So he can rely on women. Use their flats as hideouts."

The report gives no details of any further contact between Reilly and the woman Chekist but there is no dispute about his ability to charm women both into his bed and his plots. He married three times and two of his marriages were bigamously contracted – with the full knowledge of the SIS – while at least another seven women thought they were married to him. He had many mistresses – among them several prostitutes who fell in love with him – and were used, as Artuzov predicted, to provide him with safe houses.

After being turned away from the Kremlin, he went back to Petrograd, ostensibly to help Cromie in his plans to destroy the Russian Fleet. But Reilly had other ideas. A Soviet file says he lived with a "courtesan" named Yelena Mikailovna Boyuzhovskaya. As well as spending time in the city's best restaurants with a succession of beautiful women, he patronised the small, smoky, Balkov café, the haunt of anti-Bolsheviks of both left and right. There, he was known as Monsieur Massino, a Turkish merchant, and conducted business in whispered conversations with mysterious men and women. Reilly was tapping in to the opposition who had their own plans for overthrowing Lenin and his comrades and soon he was playing a leading part in their councils. He became especially involved with Boris Savinkov, the Socialist Revolutionary who had been Minister of War in the Provisional government and had become leader of a violent group called the "Union for the Defence of Fatherland and Freedom". Many of its members had been officers in the Tsar's army and it was now in contact with other left-wing and centre groups opposed to the Bolsheviks.

The Socialist Revolutionaries had good reason to hate the Bolsheviks: on January 18th, 1918 Lenin had cynically ended the Constituent Assembly, the only truly democratically elected body ever to exist in Russia, to which the SRs had won an overwhelming majority in the elections held immediately after the Bolsheviks seized power. The Assembly met only once and attempted to demonstrate its independence. However, Lenin sent his Lettish riflemen to threaten the delegates, and it was closed down forthwith. Trotsky later wrote: "The simple, open, brutal breaking up of the Constituent Assembly dealt formal democracy a finishing stroke from which it has never recovered."

Reilly and Savinkov became close friends and together pursued their hatred of Bolshevism. But Savinkov brought disaster to everything he touched and in the end it was he who led Reilly to his death.

Savinkov did not, however, "belong" to Reilly. Just about every country involved in the Great War had agents operating inside Russia. The French were particularly active. They gave Savinkov money for his movement and their principal agent, Colonel de Vertement, was deeply involved in the Czech uprising in Siberia. The Germans, who had sent their hard-nosed Ambassador, Count Wilhelm von Mirbach, to Moscow after the signing of the Treaty of Brest-Litovsk, had an efficient and aggressive network of agents. It was led by Colonel Rudolf Bauer whose men conducted personal vendettas against the British agents and exerted a great deal of influence among right-wing opposition groups. The Americans lagged badly in the spy business, relying for much of their information on the rich and eccentric Raymond Robins who commanded the American Red Cross Mission in Moscow. He was the only American with access to the Bolshevik leaders and he worked passionately to bring about an understanding between the United States and the Bolshevik government. The actual head of American espionage in Moscow was an American of Greek extraction, Xenophon Kalamatiano. The Japanese had a long-established network of agents in Siberia and, as we have seen, the British were busy in the Caucasus and Central Asia. Much of Russia's present suspicion of foreigners and paranoia about spies stem from those early days in 1918 for Russia was then a Tom Tiddler's ground for agents indulging in all kinds of activities – all of them detrimental to the Bolsheviks.

Perhaps the most accomplished of all these spies was a man whose reputation has been overshadowed by Reilly's notoriety but who was much more professional at his business than the more glamorous womaniser. He was George Hill, code number "L.K.8", who ran his own organisation reporting to the Director of Military Intelligence at the War Office and who saw his role as conducting his own private war against the Germans.

Hill's father had been a British businessman in Russia and he had been brought up there. He had travelled widely, spoke perfect Russian and knew the country well. He eventually went into business in Moscow, but when the Great War broke out he was fishing in British Columbia. He immediately joined the Canadian Light Infantry and found himself on intelligence work in France – lying out in no man's land listening to the German front line troops' conversation, the target for extreme hostility if discovered. Hill was eventually wounded by a grenade and brought back to the War Office in London. By 1916 he was in Salonika reporting on enemy troop movements. He then volunteered for the Royal Flying Corps and became one of the first pilots to land agents behind the enemy lines; on one occasion he was even chased by a cavalry patrol as he took off again. He got away but not before the cavalry had pumped half a dozen bullets through his primitive BE2 bomber.

On leave in July 1917, Hill was ordered to join the RFC mission in Russia but on arrival found that the mission had withdrawn to Moscow and the war on the Eastern Front was running down. He made his way to Mogilev, a provincial capital some 400 miles south-west of Petrograd which housed the General Headquarters of the Russian Army. Here were Britons, French, Americans, Serbs, Japanese, Belgians, Italians and Rumanians all advising the Provisional government's White Generals how to fight a war with troops who would no longer fight, as well as reporting the march of events to their own governments. There was also the German Secret Service, two of whose agents ambushed Hill, but as he described the incident in his memoirs, *Go Spy the Land*:

Just as they were about to close with me I swung round and flourished my walking stick. As I expected, one of my assailants seized hold of it. It was a sword-stick, which had been specially designed by Messrs Wilkinson, the swordmakers of Pall Mall and the moment my attacker had the scabbard in his fist I drew back the rapier-like blade with a jerk and with a forward lunge ran it through the gentleman's side. He gave a scream and collapsed to the pavement. His comrade seeing that I had put up a fight and was not unarmed, took to his heels while I withdrew and fumbled for my revolver. Meanwhile the man I had run through staggered off, leaving my scabbard on the pavement, and I went back and recovered it. That sword-stick thereafter had a value in my eyes . . .

Hill, officially under the command of General Poole, was ordered to work with a Canadian engineer, Colonel Joe "Klondyke Bill" Boyle in getting Russian railways running again. With the permission of the Bolshevik authorities they commandeered a railway carriage, No. 451, that had belonged to the Tsar's mother, Empress Maria Feodorovna. It was a conveyance of some opulence, consisting of an observation-dining salon, a combined state bedroom and sitting room, five coupés with double sleeping berths, a pantry with a stove and system for heating the carriage, and a lavatory. It could also generate its own electric light, and came with its own conductor.

No. 451 became Hill's home for the next seven months. He and Klondyke Bill steamed off to Petrograd in style, where they became the first Allied officers to get through the gates of the Smolny Institute, the Bolshevik headquarters. They obtained permission from Lenin himself to continue their operations on the basis that the British were ready to withdraw their support from the overthrown Provisional government and back the Bolsheviks instead.

Armed with Lenin's passes, they embarked on a remarkable adventure story. Acquiring a gang of navvies, they steamed around the congested railways clearing the way by tipping whole trains down embankments. Hill later claimed that as a result of clearing the lines, food reached the hungry people of Petrograd and, in the other direction, supplies and fodder got through to the southwestern army which was still trying to halt the German advance through the Ukraine.

They witnessed the murder of the Russian Commander-in-Chief General Dukhonin by his own men: "It was like watching a pack of wild wolves . . ." They were also persuaded to take on the job of returning to Rumania its gold bullion, crown jewels, Foreign Office archives and reserves of paper money which had been moved to the Kremlin for safe keeping when the Rumanian Army collapsed. Off set our heroes in the No. 451 for Jassy, temporary capital of Rumania. It took them nine days during which they never removed their clothes. During the journey they acquired coaches full of passengers who stopped the train to loot a burning vodka factory; they had hijacked an engine and driven it into Rumania themselves, and they had been shot at. But they delivered their precious cargo and in return were awarded the Order of the Star of Rumania.

In between his acts of derring-do Hill also won the confidence of Trotsky who was then the Bolshevik Commissar Minister of War. It must be remembered that the Allied intervention had not yet started and the Bolsheviks were desperate for expert military help with Trotsky more ready than any of the others to accept such help from the West.

Hill wrote: "Trotsky knew all about the work I had been doing and received me well . . . After our first talk he appointed me Inspector of Aviation and I was given extensive powers in that department. This brought me into close touch with the aviation personnel, gave me access to all aerodromes and also linked me up with the Evacuation Committee (formed to remove anything likely to be of value to the advancing Germans). I was to give Trotsky advice on the formation of a new air force. Two or three times a week I would spend half an hour with him discussing aviation. He had marvellous powers of concentration and the knack of putting his finger on the weak spot of anything and of scenting when information was not being freely given."

Through his connection with Trotsky Hill was able to build up a network of Bolsheviks to report on the movement of German units. He was thus able to warn London that certain German divisions had been pulled out of the Eastern Front to take part in Ludendorff's great spring offensive in 1918. Trotsky later created the "Third Section" of his new Red Army to incorporate Hill's network. In 1920 it was renamed the Registration Directorate, and later became the Chief Directorate of Intelligence, the GRU, which operates in every country of the world today, doing what its predecessor did: acquiring military information.

While Hill, Reilly, and Cromie were conducting their nefarious business Bruce Lockhart was struggling with the immensity of the task with which he had been saddled. The real problem he faced was that nobody in Whitehall knew what was going on or understood the nature of the men who were now running Russia. It was assumed in the capitals of the West that Lenin, Trotsky and their followers would soon be washed away in the tide of history and it did not really matter who was in charge at the moment as long as they agreed to keep on fighting the Germans.

Lockhart, who had moved with the government to Moscow, had a stormy first meeting with Trotsky on February 15th. The Russian attacked Britain for its support of anti-Bolshevik groups while Lockhart condemned Bolshevik agitation in Britain. There was justification in both arguments. Britain had been giving money to nationalist and Tsarist groups, especially in the south, while in England Litvinov was busy preaching Bolshevism and urging the workers to demand an end to the war.

Despite the high words, Lockhart was impressed with Trotsky and cabled the Foreign Office that "Trotsky will co-operate with us as long as it suits him. Our attitude should be the same." Arthur Balfour replied to Lockhart in words which summed up Britain's attitude towards the Bolsheviks. "Internal affairs in Russia are no concern of ours. We only consider them in so far as they affect the war." Where the Bolsheviks were actually in charge, said Balfour, Britain had no desire to interfere. However, he stressed, Britain had no intention of abandoning "our friends and Allies in those parts of Russia where Bolshevism cannot be regarded as the de facto Government".

It was a statement of policy which put Lockhart in an extremely difficult position. While it may have seemed perfectly logical in London, it made little sense in Moscow. If the British were to support the Bolsheviks' enemies then the Bolsheviks would regard the British as enemies. Moreover, in large parts of Russia it was impossible to decide if there was a de facto government or not, and even if there was, whether it would be in charge the following week. There were subtleties involved of which London had no understanding whatsoever.

While the Treaty of Brest-Litovsk was being hammered out and Lenin was forcing through its acceptance by a reluctant Bolshevik party, Lockhart was pleading with the Foreign Office not to allow the Japanese to carry out their threatened intervention in Siberia, but instead to give support to the Bolsheviks to carry on the fight against the Germans. "This is our last chance. In taking it we have everything to gain and nothing to lose which we have not already." There was of course no "last chance". Lenin was determined to make peace with the Germans in order to save Bolshevism in Russia. The thought must be considered that Lockhart and his friend Raymond Robins of the American Red Cross, were led by the nose during this period into pleading the Bolsheviks' cause.

Certainly Lockhart's pleas for co-operation won him few friends in Whitehall. Major-General Alfred Knox, the former Military Attaché who had gone home with Ambassador Buchanan and was soon to be appointed head of the military mission to Siberia, was the most formidable of his opponents. In a paper urging immediate intervention in Siberia he accused Lockhart of sending dispatches which were politically unsound and "in a military sense criminally misleading". Knox urged Lockhart's recall: "I am convinced that our cause in Russia is being more damaged by keeping a British official in communication with the Bolsheviks than it could possibly be by Japanese intervention, no matter how stupidly arranged. The policy of flirtation with the Bolsheviks is both wrong as a policy and immoral."

Lockhart replied in kind: "I must point out that since the Revolution his complete misunderstanding of the situation has been one of the chief reasons for our failure in this country . . ."

Typical of the lack of trust between Whitehall and Lockhart was the incident of Captain Hicks and Siberia's mythical German armies. Reports reaching London from Irkutsk and Vladivostok suggested that the Bolsheviks were releasing and arming thousands of German and Austro-Hungarian prisoners of war held there. Lockhart dismissed the stories as nonsense and was promptly rebuked by London. He thereupon went to Trotsky and asked him if he was indeed arming the Germans. Trotsky denied it but suggested that the Allies should go to Siberia to see for themselves. Lockhart sent Hicks and Raymond Robins sent Captain W. B. Webster of the American Red Cross Mission.

Hicks, curiously, an expert on poison gas, and Webster spent the next six weeks visiting POW camps. They came to the conclusion that some thousand POWs had been armed at Irkutsk to defend themselves against Semenov, the Trans-Baikal Cossacks' leader, while another thousand Hungarians had been formed into a Red Guard unit at Omsk. Their report to this effect infuriated the War Office and Hicks was recalled for apparently failing to carry out orders. But Lockhart dug in his heels and said that if Hicks returned to London, so would he. That was the end of the incident, but it made Lockhart more enemies.

While Hicks and Webster were in fact right in dismissing the story about German and Austrian armies being formed in Siberia, they were very wrong about the numbers of POWs being armed for service in the Red Army. Desperately short of trained men, the Bolsheviks looked to the POW camps for likely recruits. In January 1918 a Prisoner of War Congress held in Samara (now Kuibyshev) asked to be allowed to form Red Army units and this led to the establishment of "International Battalions". Among them were Czecho-Slovak, Hungarian, Rumanian and South Slav battalions which eventually numbered some 50,000. There was also a Chinese battalion drawn from some 10,000 men serving in labour units.

Up to this point it is difficult to discern the hand of the Secret Service in Lockhart's work. Everything he had done indicated a genuine desire to co-operate with the Bolsheviks, even endangering his career to do so. But as the events of the spring and summer of 1918 unfolded . . . the Treaty of Brest-Litovsk . . . the landing at Murmansk . . . the killing of the commissars at Kem . . . the revolt of the Czech Legion . . . the murder of the Tsar . . . so Lockhart changed his mind, turned at last towards advocating intervention and began to make contacts among anti-Bolshevist groups.

By the beginning of July he had become embroiled in the schemes of the men he had grumbled about when he arrived in Russia six months before. There is no evidence to show whether this was a natural evolution or whether it was part of his brief from "C" which only now began to emerge.

On July 6th Boris Savinkov led his Union for the Defence of Fatherland and Freedom in a full-scale rising against the Bolsheviks at Yaroslavl, strategically placed north-east of Moscow on the railway line to Archangel. It was a cruel battle with Savinkov's men holding out for two weeks, waiting for Allied help to come down the line from the northern port. They were, however, finally crushed by Bolshevik field guns brought up from Moscow a week before the Allies landed at Archangel.

By coincidence Savinkov's attempt to overthrow the Bolsheviks started on the same day that the German Ambassador, Count Wilhelm von Mirbach, was assassinated by a group of Left Socialist Revolutionaries. The murder signalled the start of an attempt by the left SRs to take over Moscow. They succeeded in capturing the Lubyanka, the secret police headquarters, along with Felix Dzerzhinsky, the much feared head of the Cheka. They also occupied the Central Telegraph Office and sent cables to a number of cities announcing that the SRs had assumed power and that all orders signed by Lenin and Sverdlov were invalid. But their success did not last long. The Bolsheviks rallied and, with their praetorian guard of Lettish Riflemen, one of the few disciplined units in Russia, they drove the SRs out of the Lubyanka. Artillery and machine-guns were then brought to bear on the SRs' remaining stronghold, the mansion where Dzerzhinsky and some other leaders were being held. It did not seem to matter that their fire could have wiped out almost the entire Cheka leadership. It was quickly over. Dzerzhinsky was released. And the executions started.

The British and French were immediately blamed by the Bolsheviks for the Savinkov and the Left SR uprisings. Certainly the French had financed Savinkov and encouraged him with stories of an immediate landing at Archangel by large Allied forces; and it was true that Yacov Blumkin, who killed von Mirbach, had lived for some months in the room next door to Lockhart at the Elite Hotel. But Lockhart had been specifically forbidden by Balfour to have anything to do with Savinkov's plans while Blumkin was later proved to have worked as a double agent for the Cheka, which was itself infiltrated by the Left SRs.

The Left SRs themselves denied that either the Allies or the Cheka were involved in their plot. With a long history of terrorism, they were perfectly capable of carrying out their own murders and their reason for killing von Mirbach was to provoke the Germans into restarting the war and so bring about the overthrow of the Bolsheviks.

A question remains about the British involvement with Savinkov. Reilly certainly knew about his plans, and Hill later wrote that he was "constantly in touch" with Savinkov's group and "was kept informed" of the plans for the rising of Yaroslavl. Given the involvement of Reilly and Hill it is possible that Balfour's order to Lockhart to have nothing to do with Savinkov was a blind to prevent Lockhart interfering in an affair already under the control of British agents. Lockhart himself later blamed the failure of the Savinkov rising on Joseph Noulens, the French Ambassador, for encouraging Savinkov to strike by telling him that a major Allied landing was about to take place at Archangel.

Without further evidence the only verdict we can reach about British involvement in both these incidents is not proven. What is certain is that life now became extremely difficult for the Britons working in Petrograd and Moscow. They no longer had easy access to the Bolshevik leaders. Trotsky himself tore up Hill's passes, commenting as he did so: "That is all over now." They could no longer travel around the country wearing their British uniforms. Reilly went underground, using a variety of identities, including that of Comrade Rilinsky of the Cheka – and he had the papers to prove it. Cromie was showing increasing signs of strain in Petrograd, sending embarrassing messages *en clair*. In one of his cables he reported that the Bolsheviks were losing power in Petrograd and were preparing to evacuate the city. In another, he said that Lenin had arrived at Peterhof, the Tsar's palace east of Petrograd, and was preparing to leave the country in a Swedish yacht.

Lockhart, cut off from the Bolshevik leaders, and no longer able to fulfil his brief from Lloyd George to "keep unofficially in touch" with them, recognised that his mission was coming to an end. Intervention was inevitable and the Bolsheviks would oppose it. The enemy for the Allies would henceforth be the Communist government of Russia, and as we shall see from George Hill's secret report to the Director of Military Intelligence, there was now put into operation a plot to overthrow that government and replace it with one more amenable to the Allies.

This time there could be no doubt about Britain's involvement. It was a British plot, planned and led by Reilly, financed by Lockhart and Cromie, with Boyce, the SIS station chief, acting as case officer and Hill providing safe houses and couriers. But, before the plot could be sprung the British, French and Americans at last landed at Archangel and the following day, August 3rd, the 25th Middlesex on board the *Ping Suey* were escorted into Vladivostok by a Japanese destroyer and marched to the Old Siberia Barracks behind the band of the Czech Legion.

CHAPTER 8

More Men, More Money, More Weapons
Murmansk, August–December 1918

On August 2nd, the day that General Poole took over Archangel, Lieutenant Peter Crawford set out from Murmansk with his seven-strong band of scarred warriors to take over his "Kingdom of Restikent" in the wilds of Lapland. He drew two months' rations, boarded a tug, sailed past the *Askold* and proceeded up river through clouds of mosquitoes. Steep hills rose on either side and the river grew narrower until they had to leave the tug and transfer to a small motor boat, crewed by local rivermen, and a canoe-shaped boat, the only type capable of getting through the rapids. He was forced to split his small force and send two men back to wait until the motor boat returned some ten days later.

At one set of rapids they almost lost both canoe and stores. They had to carry their cases of bully beef round the rapids and then haul the canoe over the rocks. "Took us two hours", he wrote in his diary. "Issued rum to all peasants who worked splendidly, continued journey after having had tea. Made a huge log fire to dry clothes." They arrived at a rest house at four in the morning where they found that –

> a party of peasants had preceded us on the journey by only a short time, as all were standing by a huge fire drying their clothes. Men and women all of whom were almost naked did not appear to pay much attention to our men when they arrived who in turn divested themselves of all their wet clothing and joined in. Had another meal – curds given by the owner of the house. About twenty people slept in the house. Too much. Decided to have a few hours sleep on the river bank, men as well. Woke up at 6 a.m. intending to start. Went to see how the occupants of the house were faring. The atmosphere was awful, everyone snoring peacefully. Woke up men. Had tea. Could not induce the motor boat skipper to proceed until 12 noon. He had advantage over me. Had I known what we had in front of us I should certainly have agreed with him and taken the opportunity of a few more hours sleep. Lovely sitting on the bank having breakfast just as

the sun was rising . . . dew glistening . . . river calm . . . pretty shadows on the water.

The small force reached Restikent on August 5th to be greeted warmly by the village headman, Pochenkov. Crawford organised the most suitable local men into patrols to scout the Lotta and Nota rivers, the only way through to the Finnish frontier. If there was going to be an attack from the south-west on Maynard's positions at Murmansk it would have to come along these rivers. The British occupation of Pechenga had already sealed off the northern route. What Crawford had to do was survive, get early warning of any Finnish–German attack and send the news back to Maynard in Murmansk before his force suffered the inevitable and was mopped up. There were several scares, reports of Finns being seen coming in over his network of patrols and scouts and through the forest grapevine. But on the whole he spent a very agreeable summer, swimming every morning, taking pot shots at duck and learning to admire the Lapps and their way of life. The main danger to his little force came from the vagaries of the weather while they were on the water. Tragedy struck when one of his men drowned in a rescue bid to save a colleague when they were swept over a fall while fishing – almost every unit in the north lost at least one man by drowning. "A very sad day," recorded Crawford. "Poor Mrs Mcleod, what-ever will she do. There are three small kiddies to look after. A braver act than Mcleod's is very difficult to imagine . . . what a sad task to have to write to Mrs Mcleod and tell her about this event."

As the year drew on, the weather turned colder and the lake froze. The Lapps, colourfully dressed, gathered their reindeer herds and moved into their winter village. Crawford and his men built a blockhouse in case the Finns arrived overland on their skis. Then on November 27th – two weeks after the event – a friendly Finn brought in a rumour that an armistice had been signed on the Western Front. A few days later the Antarctic explorer, Commander Victor Campbell arrived, having skied all the way from Murmansk. He was followed the next day by a reindeer convoy bringing winter clothing and provisions. With the convoy were three members of the renowned explorer Sir Ernest Shackleton's expedition to the Antarctic.

Shackleton had gone out to Murmansk to study the problem of fighting in the intense cold and snow and had designed a complete set of arctic kit which included "4 sets Wolsely [*sic*] underclothing . . . 1 Burberry suit. . . 1 Arctic cap . . . 1 pair blizzard goggles . . .

1 pair skis and sticks . . . 1 large woollen overcoat . . . 1 pair Shackleton boots."

Everything worked beautifully except the Shackleton boots. Few items of military clothing can ever have been so universally hated. The boot was made of canvas with a wooden sole up to size 14, wrote one victim of its awfulness, "and you had to take four or five sizes beyond your normal size so that you could put on socks, stockings (very thick), moccasins and then into the boot and pack in rags or hay in the vacant space and tie up." They were certainly warm but they were so cumbersome the men could hardly walk in them and certainly could not fight in them. The kit "proved excellent," said one official report, "with exception of the so-called Shackleton boot which was a dismal failure." And many years later Richard J. Zank of the US 338 Infantry recalled: "My memories are very vivid of how I lived through the Russian winter, the very poor rations, heavy clothing and the unforgettable Shackleton boots."

But Crawford's visitors had brought more than winter clothes. Among the stores were thirty-two gallons of rum.

Commander Campbell suggested that as we had not celebrated the Armistice we should do so, and invite the village to rum and coffee. Old Bradley the cook made three camp kettles of coffee adding more than a reasonable supply of rum, the result being that the men folk (Russian) were in a glorious state of intoxication in a very short time. No doubt this was accentuated by the vigorous dancing which had been going on in the meantime to the accompaniment of the Balalaika. The visitors from Murmansk then went to supper with Pochenkov taking a small jar of Navy rum which proved fatal to Pochenkov who drank deep and long until he slid off his chair onto the floor, there to remain for the rest of the night.

Crawford did his duty well above the Arctic Circle among the pine trees, the wolves and the Lapps, leading a rough but invigorating life totally different from his long service in India and that other war he had fought on the Somme. But events were marching in Murmansk and Archangel which would soon put an end to his idyll. Throughout the summer General Maynard had been pushing south down the railway line from Murmansk towards Petrograd.

In those first months of the intervention the British force's enemies were the Germans and their allies, the Finns. Maynard feared that they would sweep across from the Finnish border, in some places less than a hundred miles away, cut the railway line at

Kandalaksha, thus preventing the Royal Navy ships on the White Sea from coming to his assistance, and then advance on Murmansk from the south. Initially, he looked on the Bolsheviks as a sideshow. He did not like the Bolos and was always ready to fight them but, he insisted later, "our embroilment with Bolshevik Russia must be regarded as a thing apart." Not that the Bolsheviks regarded his advance down the railway line towards Petrograd as "a thing apart". To them his force appeared to be aimed at the capture of the city and its naval base of Kronstadt and the overthrow of Bolshevism. Inevitably, therefore, as he pushed south he met increasing Bolshevik resistance. And, as all the British commanders in Russia found, this resistance came not only from soldiers in the field but also from the Bolshevik underground in the towns and along the lines of communication.

He estimated that to cope with the 55,000 Germans believed to be in Finland allied to an equal number of White Finns and whatever Bolsheviks were moved against him he had an effective force of only some 2,500. Along with a company of the 29th London Regiment, the 253rd Machine Gun Company and two sections of the 384th Field Company of the Royal Engineers, these included a French Artillery Group, a Serbian Battalion, an embryo legion of Red Finns along with the beginning of the Slavo-British Legion raised from local Russians, and a Karelian Regiment of men living in the district which lay between the Murmansk railway and the Finnish border and who wanted independence from both the Russians and the Finns. These newly formed units were to provide Maynard with much needed manpower and a great many headaches. In addition to these forces he had a few agents run by the ubiquitous Colonel Thornhill, the Intelligence officer who had organised the last Christmas party in the British Embassy and had led the raid behind the Bolshevik lines in support of the Archangel landing. General Maynard commanded this mixture of forces, many of them stricken with flu and scurvy, first from a box car in the sidings at Murmansk and then from a newly built, substantial log house. His early expeditions along the railway took place in some discomfort but soon changed to luxury when, like George Hill, he acquired a palace on wheels belonging to one of the deposed Royal Family. Maynard's carriage had belonged to Grand Duke Nicholas. The Grand Duke had no further use for it. Dismissed as Commander-in-Chief by the Provisional government he fled to the Crimea, and from there left Russia for the last time.

Maynard considered himself so short of men that he went to Pechenga to see if he could withdraw some of the garrison and, concluding that the shallow harbour could never be used as a U-boat base even if it was captured by the Germans, he proposed pulling out the whole garrison and redeploying the troops. The Admiralty, however, was horrified and refused. It being one of the first laws of military life that as soon as a general is given command of troops he immediately asks for more, Maynard now followed that law to the limit. He used the Admiralty's refusal over Pechenga's troops to blackmail the War Office into sending him an infantry brigade, three batteries of field artillery, two machine-gun companies and a trench mortar battery.

He also got troops from the Italians, who sent an expeditionary force of 1,200, the Canadians who sent a company, and the French who sent an invaluable company of skiers. But these reinforcements did not start to arrive until September and in the meantime Thornhill's agents had reported a build-up along the border of White Finns with some German officers. Maynard decided he had to squash this potential threat to the railway line. First he sent off a small force composed of a platoon of British Infantry and 120 Serbs to push down the railway line to establish the strength of the Bolsheviks south of Sumski Posad and to prevent them from interfering with his proposed operations. Led by Captain Sheppard, this enterprise by what was no more than a strong raiding party, was a great success. It met a force of Bolsheviks consisting of an infantry battalion and two hundred cavalry, inflicted heavy casualties and drove it some thirty miles down the line.

Maynard had also sent off two columns to take on the White Finns and Germans, one from Kem composed of Karelians and the other, from Kandalaksha, drawn from the Finnish Legion. Maynard described them as "two small columns of semi-barbaric auxiliaries". It was rough going, too rough for transport vehicles and there were not enough pack animals to keep the column supplied. Everything had to be back-packed or, when the rivers permitted, carried by boat. Karelian women were hired to run the boats. Two of these women, unarmed and alone in one of the big canoes, were seen by a group of White Finns who opened fire but missed. Three of the Finns jumped into a boat and set off in pursuit. But the women, expert on the water, turned their boat around and rammed the Finns and then set about them with their oars. They put all three of their pursuers out of action and knocked two of them overboard. Maynard took great pleasure in awarding them the Military Medal.

Both columns met the usual sturdy opposition from the Finns but on September 11th, the Karelians under Lieutenant-Colonel Woods who raised and trained them, outflanked the Finnish White Guards and scored a small but decisive victory at Ukhtinskaya on the north bank of the River Kem. A great deal of war booty was captured and among the enemy dead were found several German officers and NCOs. The Red Finns, led by a Canadian officer, Major Burton, met with similar success and by early October the whole of Karelia had been cleared up to the Finnish frontier.

This brisk little campaign in fact signalled the end of the threat to Murmansk, but Maynard, a worrying man, looked at it in a different light. He assumed that because the Finns had been defeated, Baron Rudiger von der Goltz, the German commander in Finland, would retaliate by bringing up regular German troops to attack Murmansk. Thus he prepared for a winter war. Blockhouses were built, the Shackleton winter kit issued, Italian and French ski troops welcomed and attempts made to teach the British troops to ski.

All that changed of course on November 11th. But by then the Germans' role as enemy had been taken over by the Bolsheviks. There never was a clear cut order saying that as from today we are at war with the Bolsheviks. It happened as if by osmosis.

Maynard's worries remained the same: not enough men – although in reality he had more than enough – and hardly a penny to spend. To these were added the growing opposition of the Bolsheviks in Murmansk and in the towns along the railway line, and increasing disaffection among his locally recruited soldiers. The men of his Finnish Legion did not want to fight against their Bolshevik friends. The Karelians were demanding independence and that meant from any Russian government, not only the Bolsheviks, and the Slavo-Russian units, comprised mostly of conscripted men, were riddled with mutiny.

At times the bluff General Poole also appeared to be an enemy, for he was intent on seizing the 5,000 reinforcements Maynard had prised out of the War Office. Poole refused to give back the 100 Royal Marines Maynard had lent him for the Archangel landing. And, as Maynard wrote with some bitterness to General P. de B. Radcliffe, Director of Military Operations at the War Office, when he was forced to send a battalion of the Liverpool Regiment all the way round by sea to Kem because saboteurs had cut the railway line, Poole hijacked the whole battalion when the ship put into Archangel to deliver a battery of howitzers.

Poole was probably justified. He faced much stiffer opposition with fewer men than Maynard who now had some 15,000 under his command: 7,400 British, 1,350 Italians, 1,200 Serbs, 1,000 French and more than 4,000 Russians, Karelians and Finns. Even given the uncertain loyalty of the locally raised troops Maynard had enough men to cope with his military problems.

Ships arrived at Murmansk almost every day bringing stores, weapons and men. Among them were gunners, machine-gunners, sappers and infantrymen from the Royal Sussex Regiment, the King's Royal Rifle Corps, the Middlesex Regiment and the 6th and 13th Battalions of the Yorkshire Regiment.

The Yorkshires had a particularly harrowing time reaching Murmansk. Their voyage started with a near-mutiny. Private F. Hirst of the 6th Yorks recorded what happened in his Globe exercise book. They had gone by train from Aldershot to Grimsby where on October 15th, 1918 they boarded a decrepit former German ship, the *Traz-os-Montes*, whose sailing was delayed because of mechanical trouble. The troops expected to be allowed to go on shore and when permission was refused some 150 of them made for the dock gates where they were stopped by the Military Police and sentries with fixed bayonets. They then returned to the ship where they harangued their comrades who had remained on board, and called "for us to be men and rush the gates". The colonel drew his revolver and threatened that the next man to go over the side would be fired upon, whereupon he was told that "if he does the rifles will soon be fetched out. So he has to put his revolver away. In another place the brigadier-general has a crowd round him and the lads are telling him what they think of him."

The problem was solved when a tug towed the ship into midstream, where there was no chance of the men getting ashore. They then set out for Russia with Hirst noting with foreboding that the ship was sailing with a pronounced list. They were heading towards Norway, escorted by two destroyers when the engines broke down and they found themselves drifting towards a minefield, "an easy target for old Jerry's subs". One of the destroyers passed a tow rope but it snapped. Eventually a tug arrived and towed them to safety in the Shetlands. On November 4th they put to sea again – and broke down again. On the 6th they tried again, this time sailing into a storm. Everyone was sick and the ship took on even more of a list. The next day they sought shelter at anchor in a bay in the Orkneys.

On the 8th Hirst was woken by an unusual grating noise. The sea "was awful" and the ship was dragging her anchor and drifting on to the beach. Distress rockets burst in the sky and an SOS was sent out. Some men made the hazardous trip to the beach in the ship's boats. One man was seen to be taking his regimental cap badge off in the boat. When his sergeant asked him why he replied: "I don't want Kitchener to know what a mob I belong to." (Kitchener had been drowned in that area two years before when the cruiser *Hampshire*, taking him to Russia, struck a mine and sank.)

However, they all survived with a few minor injuries and they celebrated Armistice Day among the hospitable people of the Orkneys. But they still had to go to Russia and, eventually on December 3rd, seven weeks after they first set foot on the *Traz-os-Montes*, they landed at Murmansk with Hirst commenting, "I consider we are the luckiest 2,500 men who ever stepped on board a vessel."

They were put to work in the bitter darkness of the Arctic winter as a service battalion, helping the Royal Engineers build barracks. With hindsight, and given the history of the traumatic voyage it was inevitable that there would be trouble with these men.

We do not know if Maynard anticipated the problems in store. In any case there was little he could do about it. In the end as we shall see he was fortunate enough – or clever enough – to transfer the Yorkshires before the trouble broke.

The *Traz-os-Montes* arrived when he was in London seeking a solution to the monetary problems of his command. At the start of his enterprise he had gone to the Treasury to ask for a "modest sum in honest English currency" to pay for his force's necessities. He was refused. Instead the Treasury came up with the extraordinary scheme that he should take over a huge quantity of salted herrings which had been bought by Britain and were stored at Vardo in Norway and use them instead of cash.

Maynard pointed out that he had no way of shipping the herrings to Murmansk. He had no idea of their condition and doubted that a long continued diet of salted herrings would appeal to the Russian workman as a substitute for his wages. Maynard added that he had a "strong objection to adding the running of a glorified fish shop to my other duties." He was eventually allowed a minuscule amount of British currency but it was soon spent on accommodation for the troops, transport, fodder and wages.

Maynard's problem was made more difficult by the very success of the British campaign to woo the Murmansk Soviet away from the Bolsheviks and the increasing amount of territory which came under his control following his occupation of the railway towns. He became responsible for protecting and feeding about 100,000 people in the territory he had taken over. And since the railwaymen and dockers now worked solely for the British forces they expected to be paid by the British. But Maynard was sent little food and no money at all. In late August, the railwaymen went on strike. His communications with the south and his garrisons at Kandalaksha and Kem were threatened and the discontent was played upon by local Bolshevik sympathisers. Maynard was forced to search through the British troops in Murmansk to find men who could drive railway engines and eventually found five. These he sent south on a Ford car which had been fitted with railway wheels in a naval workshop and was driven by his ADC. They arrived safely after a hair-raising ride through the forest. Two of the men got off at Kandalaksha and the others went on to Kem. Maynard was now confident that in an emergency he could get his troops out of both towns by train if they came under attack. He also, humiliatingly, borrowed enough money from the French Ambassador, who was then at Archangel, to pay off the strikers.

There were a number of developments during the autumn: General Poole, whose lack of political subtlety had become embarrassing, went home to London for consultations and never returned, his place being taken by the formidable Major-General Edmund Ironside who was to become Field-Marshal Lord Ironside in the Second World War. The two military commands at Archangel were divided with Maynard being given his independence from Archangel. But at the same time Murmansk was brought under the political authority of the new Russian government which had been set up in Archangel. The Murmansk Soviet which had invited the British to intervene was dissolved and power was assumed by Deputy Governor Yermolov who wisely refused to take up his appointment until he was given enough money to pay at least a proportion of the wages due to government employees.

Maynard's problems with money grew worse. He was promised £150,000 but then the Treasury refused to allow him to spend it without special permission. The destroyer HMS *Dublin* which brought the English banknotes also brought out the first batch of the new issue of Russian banknotes which had been printed in England. Unfortunately they were engraved with the murdered Tsar's coat of arms and his monogram, N.II. Although never put into circulation in Murmansk, they were used in Archangel after every note had been laboriously overstamped. The situation now became so bad, with trains no longer being maintained because of strikes, that in December Maynard took passage on the *Dublin* on her return trip to Thurso. In London he had one of those icily polite discussions with the Treasury which are more deadly than any shouting match. But eventually he won his point. He was given permission to spend the £150,000 and assured that a new issue of currency was being sent out.

In one of those strange turnarounds that war provides, one of the men with whom he talked in London was the White Finnish leader, General Mannerheim, against whom he had been fighting all that spring and autumn. It was probably at this meeting that Maynard finally realised that the threat from Finland was ended and that his only enemies now were the Bolsheviks. The talk with Mannerheim was not entirely successful, however, for Maynard wanted him to take back the men of the Red Finn Legion who were demanding an amnesty and the right to return to their homes. But Mannerheim, after leading his country to freedom from the Russians, had no wish to accept men who had fought to reimpose a new sort of Russian rule.

His business in London finished, Maynard found himself back on the *Dublin* at Invergordon on Christmas Day which he celebrated with the explorer Shackleton, also returning to Murmansk – no doubt to listen to more complaints about his atrocious boots. The game had changed completely for Maynard. He had gone out to Murmansk to protect it from the Germans. Now, six months later, his task was to help provide the infant "government of North Russia" with space and time to establish itself before the Allied forces inevitably withdrew. And if he could strike some hard blow at the Bolos then so much the better. Maynard had no qualms about his role. "Russia's leaders," he argued, "had not been chosen by the people. Their rule was hated, and they owed their retention of power solely to the terror inspired by systematic bloodshed and massacre . . ."

As he steamed back through the narrow ice walls of the Kola Inlet a few days later he felt well satisfied. He now had enough men and enough money. His troops were settled into comfortable, well-heated blockhouses. The menace of the Germans and the Finns had been removed. He had secured his military independence and in Yermolov had a civilian administrator whom he respected. In Ironside he had a military colleague in whom he had confidence.

What he did not foresee, however, was ten months of hard fighting against an increasingly numerous and skilful Red Army. During this period the original small-scale engagements developed into a war involving battles between flotillas of armed ships, bombing raids by the RAF and duels between heavy guns mounted on armoured trains.

CHAPTER 9

General Ironside and Sergeant Parrish Go to War
Archangel, August–December 1918

Archangel had echoed to British voices ever since its foundation over three hundred years before HMS *Attentive* dropped anchor. Timber, virtually Archangel's only product, was exported mainly to Britain. British ships brought in food and coal. Britons came out to run the saw mills and in 1899 Lenin complained that "this region of European Russia has served in this respect as an external market for Britain without being an internal market for Russia." Indeed, until the railway to Vologda was built by Count Witte in 1897 it was easier in the summer months for the people of Archangel to take ships to Britain than to travel to Moscow. It was, as Consul Douglas Young described it, "A human backwater . . . nobody lived at Archangel except from accident of birth, banishment or business; and the banished included officials as well as political exiles of minor misdemeanour." No one would willingly live there but at the same time it was not sufficiently unpleasant to be a place of real exile.

Archangel had broad streets paved with wood. It had trams and electricity but no sewer system and water had to be drawn from pumps. Life centred round the magnificent cathedral of the Archangel Michael with its four domes of blue and white surmounted by golden spires, and the wharves where the debris of 300 years of seafaring trade lay rotting. The war had changed Archangel to the extent that it became very much busier, for until Murmansk was completed, it remained Russia's only European port not blockaded by the Germans or the Turks: on its quays were piled the supplies and armaments bought abroad by the Tsarist government on war credits from the Allies, especially Britain. So much had been ordered and delivered that, as at Vladivostok, the railway could not cope. Guns, shells, factory-fresh aircraft still lay in their crates, and whole cargoes of raw materials awaited the freight trains south: 14,000 tons of copper, 5,000 tons of lead, over 2,000 tons of aluminium, another 2,000 tons of antimony and 250,000 tons of coal.

Otherwise the war brought little radical change to the city. It was a bourgeois place and remained bourgeois after the March revolution with the Mensheviks and Socialist Revolutionaries forming a government and nothing particularly violent taking place. Some unpopular officers were rounded up, but instead of being killed were sent off to Petrograd. And when the Bolsheviks seized power there were no excesses. Bolshevism was slow in coming to the north. The banks still operated, priests still taught in the schools, the fashionable restaurants were thriving. It was business as usual, until, that is, the arrival in May 1918 of Mikhail Kedrov as head of a "Revising Mission".

Kedrov had a bourgeois background and had studied law at Moscow University but was expelled for revolutionary activities. He spent several periods of exile in Siberia before emigrating to Switzerland, where he met Lenin. An accomplished pianist, Kedrov used to play Beethoven to his leader. He made his way back to Russia in 1916, took part in the Revolution and had been put in charge of demobilising the Tsar's forces and, consequently, of expanding the Red Army. When the Royal Marines went ashore at Murmansk and the threat of intervention began to loom, Kedrov and his "Revising Mission" was sent to Archangel to bring it properly under the Bolshevik rule.

He arrived impressively on an armoured train bristling with guns accompanied by a retinue of forty Bolshevik officials and a bodyguard of thirty-three Lettish riflemen. His task, according to Soviet accounts, was to put down revolts, "discipline" the locals and "persuade" men to join the Red Army. While Kedrov attended to the political discipline of Archangel, its military defence was entrusted to General Alexander Samoilo, one of a number of Tsarist officers who had gone over to the Bolsheviks either out of conviction or because their families were threatened with death if they did not do so.

Samoilo was one of those who went over freely and he served his new masters faithfully. At the end of June he became commander of land and naval forces in the White Sea military area. His military commissar was R. Kulikov and his fleet commander was Rear-Admiral Ya. E. Vikorist.

Kedrov was not at Archangel when the British seaplanes flew over the town and panicked the Bolsheviks into fleeing. He was in Moscow making a report on the situation in the north. But he soon returned, stopping his armoured train at villages along the track to shoot any "traitors" he sniffed out and harangue the villagers.

The British and the French and the Americans need the poor as cannon fodder [he would tell them], they need reinforcements for their regiments. They have everything else, guns, ammunition, but they don't have the men. So they have come to Soviet Russia for men, a country that wants no more war and wants to live in peace with everyone, except the rich and the Kulaks [rich peasants]. So, they will try to bribe you with money. They will send you to fight against the Germans and the Turks and against your own brothers. We are temporarily retreating in the face of their cruisers and their guns. But we will return. There is no force which is able to crush the power of millions of workers and peasants.

[He would end his exhortation:] The decisive hour has come. Everyone whose soul has not been stilled and whose heart is not yet hardened must crush the intruders. Join our ranks. Form partisan detachments. Contact the Red Army. Unite. Catch and kill spies. Block the enemy's roads. Burn their bridges. Destroy the railway tracks they are using. Deny them everything. May thousands of our eyes watch their every movement. Set traps, sow death at every step they take. Turn into merciless revengers. Have no mercy on them.

In September Kedrov returned to Moscow to demonstrate how to show no mercy. He was given control of a special section of the Cheka whose task was to destroy "counter revolutionaries" in the Red Army. Later he dealt with what was regarded as "sabotage" by doctors who declined to join the Red Army and in May 1919 he was sent to Petrograd to purge the city of "counter-revolutionaries".

Twenty years later he and his son, also a secret policeman, fell foul of Beria, the secret police chief. His son was shot. Kedrov was tortured and later died in a labour camp.

While Kedrov was whipping up the civilian population, Samoilo was organising defences along the only two routes the invading force could take, the River Dvina and the railway to Vologda. Rear-Admiral Vikorist assembled a flotilla of shallow draft river boats and armed them with field guns to block the river while Samoilo halted the fleeing Red Guards who, although poorly trained and armed, were far superior in number to Poole's force. The Bolsheviks had feared that the Allies would land in overwhelming force and that their revolution would be crushed. It was this fear, turning into panic when HMS *Nairana*'s floatplanes flew over Archangel, which had sent the Red Guards fleeing through the forests and swamps. As we have seen, some two thousand of them had already been despatched with their artillery to meet Colonel Thornhill's raiding party and their absence also affected the morale of Red forces in Archangel. Samoilo collected his scattered men, called for reinforcements from Petrograd and waited to meet Poole's advance.

Meanwhile Poole took over Archangel, settled his mission into houses in the city – he had astonished Young by asking for 600 billets before the expedition sailed for Archangel – and sent patrols up the River Dvina towards Kotlas and along the railway line towards Vologda. But he did not have the men to undertake any serious military move into the interior. He also discovered that one of the aims of his enterprise had been pre-empted. Nearly all the war stores had been taken away by the Bolsheviks to a safe site near Vologda.

He remained in Archangel setting up what amounted to an occupation administration. Ostensibly, Nikolai Tchaikovsky ran the affairs of the city. A relative of the composer, he was a liberal, civilised man who had spent twenty-six years in exile in England and another six in America, and after Chaplin's coup of August 1st he formed a government consisting of six Socialist Revolutionaries. But it was a government without real power. Poole appointed a French Officer, Colonel Donop, as Military Governor of Archangel. Between them Poole and Donop ran the city and they did so with an unfeeling disregard for the wishes of its citizens.

The White Russians had so few and such poor troops that they feared an uprising by the Bolsheviks which they would not be able to withstand. It did not help their cause that both the British Consul, Douglas Young, and the American Consul, Felix Cole, were totally opposed to the intervention. Poole therefore insisted on imposing a strict military rule over Archangel. His attitude towards Russian sensibilities was such that when Maynard was having problems with railwaymen striking for the wages due to them, Poole suggested that Maynard should use force to get them back to work. Maynard, wisely, borrowed the money instead. Despite his bluff good humour, there was no chance that Poole, in the modern phrase, would win the hearts and minds of Archangelskis.

He set up his headquarters in a large stone building in the centre of the town. In a letter home, Major Ambrose Sturdy of the Leicestershire Regiment who was working in the cypher section of the headquarters wrote: "It is just like a young war office; we have a fine large cypher room, complete with telephone etc., We are billeted in a very comfortable house. Like most of the houses here, it is one storied and wooden but very fine and luxurious." The fact that the arrival of an army in a small town, especially one as overcrowded as Archangel will always cause problems seemed to escape the admittedly jaundiced eye of Consul Young. In a report to the Foreign Office he complained:

> One of General Poole's first acts was to requisition for himself and his personal staff the largest and finest residence in town, belonging to a sawmill owner who was a Russian subject. Even the Bolsheviks had allowed the owners to occupy part of this house, but it was only after the owner's wife had told General Poole that he was "worse than the Bolsheviks" that the British allowed her to retain four rooms. The same thing was evident in the innumerable departments of the Allied military organisation. Whole school buildings were requisitioned, and in large rooms capable of holding four or five people might be seen one officer and one table.

Young would seem to have been singularly ignorant of the way the military conducts its affairs but no doubt his report reflected the thinking of the citizens of Archangel.

The letters of Ambrose Sturdy to his family give some idea of what it was like to be on Poole's staff. To his father he wrote: "My life is made up entirely of work, hard work, roast mutton, incompetent staff and about 200 yards of slippery wooden pavement. If I don't get at least an OBE for it, I'll turn Bolshevik . . ."

Like every other soldier who has left a record of his sojourn in North Russia, Sturdy also complained bitterly about the failure of the authorities to get mail through. "The post here is an awful scandal." And he had other complaints. To his sister he wrote: "I have decided that the Russian girls aren't really at all pretty. I only thought they were at first after coming from a benighted spot like Murmansk." And, again to his sister: "I have come to the conclusion that all Russians are unpleasant savages, their eyes are close set, they have no noses and the manners of pigs. They are nearly as bad as Arabs. Our English soldier servant is a useless and senseless country lout. We have been too busy to go for a bath for 4 weeks, (12 roubles at the bath house) but we are hoping to manage one tomorrow."

However, it was not all hard work. Sturdy went to a party at the house of an English sawmill owner . . . "extremely bourgeois with two unprepossessing flapper daughters . . ." And he attended a "grand concert and dance given by all the Allied military – tickets 40 roubles, proceeds for Slavo-British-Allied Legion comforts fund."

Later, he was to mellow. On the eve of going up to the front he wrote again to his sister: "I've grown quite fond of Archangel; we've had some very decent dances lately, and there are some awfully nice girls here (for Russians) . . ."

It is possible that if Poole had been able to land a large force he could well have pushed far enough up the Dvina to take Kotlas. But it was not till August 26th that his first sizeable force of British infantry, the 2/10th Royal Scots, disembarked. Even they were all B2 Medical category and many were old soldiers full of wounds and war weariness. Nevertheless they were immediately embarked on barges and sent up the Dvina with the Poles while the French Colonial Infantry moved along the railway line. The railway ran due south while the river ran off to the south-east so that the two forces were fighting some eighty miles apart from one another. They fought an uncomfortable, hard little campaign. Samuolo had rallied his men and received a batch of Red Guards, armed factory workers, from Petrograd. He set up blocking parties in the villages of which there were a surprising number tucked away in the forests along the river and its tributaries. The barges, in constant danger of being stranded on sandbanks in the shallow river, and of being blown up by mines floated down the river, were sniped at from the banks while the box cars carrying the French were shot at from the dense forest through which the railway line was carved. The line was cut often, easily done when it passed over so many bridges, beautifully built of wood but vulnerable to saboteurs armed with a bale of hay and a gallon of paraffin.

Progress was slow. Once off the boat the soldiers had to cope with the bewildering forest and deep swamps in which men disappeared without trace. And around each man buzzed his own personal cloud of extremely hostile mosquitoes. One man wrote in his diary: "I had bought some anti-mosquito cream from Boots. It seemed to attract great swarms of them from miles around to dine on it and me." The local men, some fighting for the Bolsheviks and others acting as guides to the Allies, seemed inured to the mosquitoes and blazed trails through the forest, marking trees so that they could move as if along streets. But the Petrograd Red Guards, city-dwellers to a man, were even worse off than the British and French who at least were professional soldiers accustomed to a hard life in the open.

131

Despite all the difficulties, the Royal Scots took the river town of Bereznik, some 125 miles from Archangel on September 3rd. It was here that Poole planned to set up his winter base. On the railway front, the allies had got as far as Obozerskaya some seventy-five miles down the line.

The day after Bereznik fell the Americans landed at Archangel; 4,477 soldiers of the 339th Infantry, the 310th Engineers, the 337th Field Hospital and the 337th Ambulance Company under the command of the Australian-born Colonel George E. Stewart. They had been training at Camp Custer, in Battle Creek, Michigan, to fight in France when they were shipped off to England and told that they would be going to North Russia. They landed at Liverpool on August 4th and marched through the city with the church bells ringing and people lining the streets to watch the Yanks pass by. They then took the train south to Camp Cowshot in Surrey where they drilled and marched and were issued with Russian rifles and arctic underwear, neither of which met with their approval.

They also got passes to go up to London: a much nicer prospect. As Corporal Frank Douma, later to become Superintendent of Schools at Ottuma, Iowa, wrote in his diary:

> August 12. This evening we went to London. Was in the finest saloon there, the bar-tenders were all girls. Women drink in the saloons the same as the men and also smoke a great deal . . . August 17. Got another pass for London . . . Visited the Tower of London, the Houses of Parliament, and St Paul's Cathedral which was very beautiful and awe-inspiring. Visited some more swell saloons and had plenty to drink. We ate supper at the Eagle Hut and went to the Strand Theatre in the evening. The men and women both smoke during the show and liquor is served between acts.

On August 26th they sailed from Newcastle in a convoy of four troopships escorted by busy little destroyers which chased round them shepherding them away from danger.

The crossing was smooth, and they were delighted by the strange sights of the northern sea, the whales and polar bears and the midnight sun. But they had the flu amongst them and by the time they got to Archangel five hundred men were sick. The rest marched down the gangway, the first American soldiers in Russia. They were supposed to parade through the town, but it was raining and the parade was cancelled. On September 7th one battalion was packed into boxcars and sent down the railway to help maintain the situation at Obozerskaya, some seventy-five miles south while another battalion was put on board filthy coal barges and sent up the Dvina to Bereznik where the Royal Scots and the Poles were pushing on towards Kotlas and where, it was hoped, they would join the Czechs.

The Americans lost their first man four days after arrival. He died of flu and exposure on a coal barge and with the bugler playing the Last Post he was buried in a tiny village by the river.

This use of the Americans by Poole was quite contrary to President Wilson's terms of reference which said that they could only be used to guard the stores and give "such aid as may be acceptable to the Russians in the organization of their self defense". Wilson had made it quite plain that the doughboys were not to "take part in organized intervention . . . from either Vladivostok or Murmansk and Archangel." Yet there they were being rushed into the front line.

The reason was simple. The Americans who, with the *Olympia*'s sailors and marines, numbered 4,800, now formed the bulk of the Allied forces. The British numbered only 2,420, many of whom were base personnel with most of the fighting troops being officially classified as unfit for active service. There were 900 French, most of whom were Colonial Infantry unsuited to fighting in northern latitudes, 350 Serbs worn out with fighting and scurvy, a handful of excellent Polish soldiers, and only the rudiments of the Slavo-British Legion. If the fronts were to be held against the Bolsheviks' reorganised and numerous forces the Americans had to go into battle whatever President Wilson said.

They were soon in the thick of the fighting. Sergeant Silver Parrish of B Company records in his diary that they fought their first battle on September 16th. Parrish was weak on grammar and spelling, but had a fine turn of phrase and his diary gives a vivid account of the role played by the American Infantry in the intervention in the North. His company had gone some twenty miles up river, south of Bereznik, by a combination of steamer and "hiking" and were making breakfast over bonfires when a Bolshevik gunboat steamed into sight, shelled them and landed some riflemen. "They saw us and opened up on us," wrote Parrish. "Almost every man was rattled until I went down over an open field holloring [sic] for our men to follow and I formed a skirmish line and with the assistance of a few Russian regulars and one platoon of Scots we drove them back on their boat and then our gunboat hove in sight and sunk the enemy boat." (This was probably the small British Monitor M252.)

On the 19th, Parrish was in Tulgas, a village on the Dvina which was to be the scene of bitter fighting, changing hands several times throughout the Allied occupation:

At two in the afternoon the enemy field pieces and gunboats opened up on us and gave us hell. We were in a graveyard at the time (a good place to die). At seven in the evening the captain sent me back to town to see if our machine guns and gunners were there. I got into town about eight p.m. and the enemy gunboats and field pieces were blowing hell out of things but I went from place to place until I got all the men and guns. I arrested a spy who was flashing signals from a loft to the gunboats and then I went on a long hunt for the company for they had moved up into the woods closer to the enemy. I had fourteen men and eight Lewis guns and we were in one hell of a rain of shrapnel and H.E. [High Explosive] for two hours and it was dark as pitch and raining and we were hungry as we had no food.

We found the company in a ravine huddled together to keep warm. But we should worry. We had Lewis guns now and all the enemy had was gunboats, pom-poms, machine guns, rifles and field pieces and trenches. But orders were to keep on our full packs and these we did keep on for about 52 hours. Sept. 21. 10 a.m. We formed a skirmish line. B Company on the right flank. C on the left and D in reserve. We went into battle with full packs and water knee deep. The enemy was entrenched and we were in the open. We advanced against their machine emplacements and trenches, me in charge of the right flank of our company where I took 2 machine-gun crews and about ten other men. We tried flanking movement which made the enemy fall back and when I placed my men and started back to inform the commanders of my success to my surprise I saw that our men were retreating and the enemy were going the other way. So I went back to get my men and then we found the company and dug ourselves in and at 5 p.m. the Russian artillery composed of two three-inch guns opened up and after an hour's barrage, A, B and C companies formed a skirmish line and took the town of Selsoe. We lost four dead and five wounded. These were all in my little team . . . Next morning I was called before the commander and informed that I was recommended for a commission for making a good thing out of a bad mix-up.

Frank Douma who was with D Company was also involved in the fracas of September 21st:

Started to hike at 9.00 a.m. Our whole battalion went at one time, our company being in the lead. I was the runner between Captain and Major all day. Was extremely hard work running through the heavy mud. We came upon the Bolos at Selsoe at 2.30 p.m. I was on the point with the Captain and they opened up on us with machine guns and pom-poms. We had to dig in right where we were. That night we moved back to a fence at the back of which we dug a system of trenches. We slept in the trenches all that night. It rained constantly and we were soaked to the skin by morning. A Bolo gun boat opened up on us early this morning. Our rations were very low and I divided up my last can of bully at 2.00 p.m. Our artillery came up and saved the day for us.

We were ordered to advance at 5.00 p.m. We chased the Bolos out of their trenches and captured a number of prisoners. The Bolos retreated and left considerable ammo and guns. We took three villages and established out posts. We have no rations and all we ate today was turnips and cleba [bread].

This was the pattern of fighting in the swamps and forests south of Archangel with small forces clashing in the woods, struggling through the mire to attack villages and with gunboats making forays along the Dvina and its tributaries. It was hard, bloody work with the fog of war made even more confusing by poor communications and the impossibility of knowing what was going on only a few hundred yards away where a battle could be completely screened by the forest and cut off by impassable swamps. In such fighting the Engineers became priceless. The men of the Royal Engineers and the US 310th Engineers were working well together to build the bridges and blockhouses and to provide the accommodation which was to be vital when winter clamped its iron fist on the battlefield. Jay H. Bonnell of the 310th Engineers later remembered going up the Dvina for about a hundred miles "then I was left off the boat with ten other soldiers two of them being a sergeant and corporal. Proceeded to the fighting line about twenty miles away. Built a bridge in thirty-six hours with the help of 18 Russian labourers." He spent two months at the front building bridges and repairing roads. It was hard graft, enlightened one day by being put in charge of a ration barge. "The boys had a good time, and forgot their hardships for the time for they broke into the rum and got drunk, all but Dan and I."

While this little war was being fought, virtually unknown to the outside world, Poole was running into trouble in Archangel. Food was short, and there was a thriving black market. The YMCA had stopped selling chocolate because it was being resold at exorbitant prices. Recruitment of local Russians into the Northern Government Army was so bad that conscription was introduced. Poole found himself denied the reinforcements he so badly needed and indeed two days before the Americans fired their first shots, the United States announced that no more American soldiers would be sent to Archangel or Murmansk. As there seemed to be no chance of building an effective Russian force to oppose the Bolsheviks, America insisted "that all military effort in northern Russia be given up except the guarding of the ports themselves and as much of the country round them as may develop threatening conditions . . ."

And then there was Poole himself. He had rubbed the Americans up the wrong way by taking too literally the agreement that the British should be in charge of operations and therefore insisting that British officers should command all aspects of the expedition. The Americans were particularly irked by what they saw as the British tactic of promoting officers and even NCOs to field rank to ensure that they were senior to the American officers. There may have been an element of truth in this charge, but there was also a great lack of good British officers to replace those succumbing to old wounds, the flu and the whisky bottle.

Poole's major problems, however, were with the government of Tchaikovsky. Relations between the two men grew increasingly difficult with Poole trying to run an army of occupation and Tchaikovsky trying to run a Russian government on Russian soil. It did not help that his was a socialist government bitterly opposed by the bourgeois of Archangel and by Tsarist officers such as Georgi Chaplin who looked on Tchaikovsky's ministers as hardly better than the Bolsheviks. It was obvious that matters could not continue as they were. Chaplin was the man who brought the crisis to a head. On the night of September 5th, he and a group of other former Tsarist officers kidnapped Tchaikovsky and five of his ministers and packed them off to Solovetski Island in the White Sea, an island with a history of British intervention. At that time there still remained evidence of English round shot fired at one of the towers of the island's great monastery during the Crimean War. In folklore the monastery is famous for its seagulls which left its monastery walls when the British warships opened fire, flew off to the British ships and made such a mess with their droppings that the English sailors ceased firing and withdrew.

The mess they made was nothing to the mess that Poole was now in. He took the news of the coup calmly, so calmly that it gave rise to suspicion that if he wasn't involved in it he was at least privy to it.

But when the Allied ambassadors got to hear of it they were enraged, especially the American Ambassador, David Francis, and as a result of his protest to Washington, President Wilson informed the British government that unless Poole changed his attitude towards the Russians the American force would be removed from his command. At the same time a general strike was called in Archangel and bands of armed peasants appeared on the streets demanding the return of Tchaikovsky and his ministers. Meanwhile the Allied diplomats had telegraphed Kem, the nearest port to Solovetski and ordered a British warship to pick up the castaways and return them to Archangel. On their return Tchaikovsky agreed to get rid of some of his more socialist colleagues and to moderate his policies. Poole then agreed to abolish Colonel Donop's post of Military Governor and allow Tchaikovsky to appoint a Russian Governor-General. In this way a modus vivendi was established. But it was too late for Poole. On October 14th he was recalled to England "for consultations" and never returned.

His place was taken by Major-General Edmund Ironside who had disembarked from HMS *Czaritsa* on October 6th to be Poole's Chief of Staff. A huge man, six feet and four inches tall and over nineteen stone in weight, he dwarfed everybody around him and was, of course, nicknamed "Tiny". At thirty-seven he was one of the youngest Major-Generals in the British Army. He was a natural linguist and when a young lieutenant worked undercover in German South-West Africa where he disguised himself as a Boer oxen-driver and joined a German punitive expedition against the native Hereros in the then German colony. The Germans thanked him for his good work with a medal. While he was in South Africa he met John Buchan who was working for Lord Milner, then High Commissioner for South Africa. Buchan was so impressed by Ironside's exploits that he made him the model for Richard Hannay, hero of *The Thirty-Nine Steps*.

Ironside lived up to his reputation in Russia. Unlike Poole he did not remain in Archangel but took himself to the battle, travelling fast on a horse-drawn sleigh and appearing suddenly out of the forest to frighten Allied commanders more than the Bolsheviks did. He was no respecter of persons and he seemed to dislike the Bolsheviks, the Jews, the French and the Germans in that order. Nor did the Americans meet with his approval.

One of his early actions in Archangel was a proclamation which said:

There seems to be among the troops a very indistinct idea of what we are fighting here in North Russia. This can be explained in a few words. We are up against Bolshevism, which means anarchy pure and simple. Any one of you can understand that no State can possibly exist when its own internal affairs such as labour, railways, relations with Foreign Powers, etc., are so disorganised as to make life impossible for everybody. Look at Russia at the present moment. The Power is in the hands of a few men, mostly Jews who have succeeded in bringing the country to such a state that order is non-existent, the posts and railways do not run properly, every man who wants something that somebody else has got just kills his opponent, only to be killed himself when the next man comes along. Human life is not safe, you can buy justice at so much for each object. Prices of necessities have risen so that nothing is procurable . . . In fact the man with the gun is "cock of the walk" provided that he does not meet another man who is a better shot. The result is that the country as a whole suffers and becomes liable to be the prey of any adventurers who happen along. Bolshevism is a disease which, like consumption, kills its victim and brings no good to anybody. Undoubtedly things will be changed after the war, but not by anarchy and wholesale murder. Bolshevism to start with was only commenced with the sanction of Germany to rid the latter of a dangerous enemy. Now Bolshevism has grown upon the uneducated masses to such an extent that Russia is disintegrated and helpless and therefore we have come to help her get rid of the disease that is eating her up. We are not here to conquer Russia, and none of us wants to stay here, but we want to help her and see her a great power, as at present she is lying helpless in the hands of the adventurers who are simply exploiting her for their own ends, and who, in order to attain their ends, kill off their opponents from the highest to the lowest including those who have the best brains in the country, and whose powers could be utilised to restore her prestige and place among the nations. When order is restored here we shall clear out, but only when we have attained our object, and that is, the restoration of Russia.

The *Jewish Chronicle* in London learnt of the proclamation after it had appeared in an Archangel newspaper. Following correspondence between the editor of the *Jewish Chronicle* and the Foreign Office, a Foreign Office memorandum agreed that Ironside's remarks about Jews were "unfortunate" and suggested that the War Office should tell Ironside to issue a new proclamation making it clear that nothing detrimental to the Jewish race was intended. Ironside was told to refer his proclamations to London in future. The *Jewish Chronicle*, meanwhile, was asked not to make any reference to the proclamation.

But although Ironside may have been publicly silenced, the pencilled drafts of his reports, made for him by Major Sturdy on the back of old maps reveal that he had not changed his attitudes. Referring to the bad state of moral [*sic*] of the troops under his command he blamed it in part on the "insidious Bolshevik propaganda . . . broadcast by the polyglot Jews and renegade journalists on the other side."

The Americans and the French also came in for fierce criticism. He accused the French of refusing to fight and of "general ill-discipline and slovenliness" while the American officers were "incompetent" and their men "worthless". The Americans, he maintained, "have never been good fighting troops".

However, his account of the Bolshevik offensive along the Dvina which lasted from October 4th to November 15th showed that his British troops were not beyond reproach. The offensive started when the British gunboats and barges withdrew down the river for fear of being frozen in. This meant that the soldiers were deprived of transport, communications and, most important, of their artillery which was mounted on the boats. When the British boats withdrew, the Bolshevik boats reappeared and on October 4th "opened a bombardment on our positions at a rate of about 1000 rounds a day".

He noted that a reinforcement of three officers and 200 other ranks of the Royal Scots arrived at the front on the night of the 12th/13th October after a week long journey from Archangel. The journey itself must have been terrible enough and they were thrown into the rearguard fighting the moment they arrived. "The continuous shelling," he wrote, "sorely tried the moral of the Royal Scots, who were all of low category [B2 and most of them previously wounded] and whose vitality was much reduced by their previous exertions and the extremely severe conditions under which they had been fighting."

On October 20th he reported that fresh troops were needed but more were being sent out . . . the position was very extended for the available troops . . . Brigadier-General Finlayson reported he was impressing labour to dig defences . . .

Finlayson also said that he could only hold his position as long as the gun (solitary 130 mm gun mounted on a barge) kept going. Later in the day Finlayson reported that an enemy 4.8 inch gun in Troitskoye had sunk the barge and the gun had been lost.

On October 23rd, Ironside recorded, an enemy attack was repulsed by Captain Boyd of the 339th US Infantry. It was a fight in which Silver Parrish was, as usual, heavily involved. In his spidery scrawl he recorded: "October 23rd. Enemy bombardment all day from the gunboats. We make no reply for we have nothing to reply with. At 6 p.m. the enemy attacked our open posts with a bayonet charge and we had two hours fast fierce fighting and we drove them back."

Four days later the Royal Scots with a platoon of Lithuanians and a detachment of Poles made an attack on Kulika on the right bank of the river. But the Red troops had got wind of the attack and were well prepared. They opened up with machine-gun and rifle fire and smashed the attack. Ironside noted:

The Lithuanians immediately bolted. The platoon officers of the Royal Scots became casualties and the enemy then delivered a counter attack.

The Royal Scots turned and fled, throwing away their arms and equipment in a state of absolute panic and demoralisation. The Poles on the left flank were the only troops who behaved well and did not succumb to panic. They covered the retirement and brought back all their wounded. Four Canadian artillerymen and four marine artillerymen who accompanied the Royal Scots in the attack behaved very gallantly and were the last to be withdrawn after making their presence very severely felt on the enemy.

The Canadians had been sent to Russia – to the far north as well as the far east of which more in Chapter 10 – with much reluctance after intense pressure by the British government. In Archangel there were sixteen of all ranks performing administrative duties, there were ninety-two instructors on the Murmansk front and 16 Brigade of the Canadian Field Artillery numbering 497 (all ranks) who took part in the fighting. They performed extremely well and met with nothing but praise from Ironside.

The Bolsheviks continued their attacks, with small but bloody encounters in the forests, and charges across open ground supported by fire from their gunboats. The mosquitoes had gone, the snow had started, cold was becoming the real enemy to both sides. On November 10th, Silver Parrish recorded that he had been on patrol every day since October 23rd. On November 11th, the day World War I ended, some 2,500 Bolsheviks attacked the Allied positions around Tulgas which were manned by about 400 men. The fighting continued for four days and, according to Parrish, "we licked the Bolo good and hard but lost 7 killed and 14 wounded and the Canadians lost quite a few and the Royal Scots lost 36 men and many wounded. The Bolo lost about 475 men."

The Bolshevik offensive came to an end on November 15th when, said Ironside, "the enemy was forced by the freezing of the river to withdraw all his ships back to Kotlas for the winter. He had lost very heavy casualties and many of his troops had been scattered and lost in the forest whilst the rest were in a state of utter demoralisation. Five of the chief enemy leaders had been killed and the enemy were finally convinced that these attempts to drive us down the river were hopeless."

On that same day, Parrish, now Platoon Sergeant, took part in a counter-attack, "and was ordered to burn a small village where the enemy could do effective sniping. Women opened fire on us and we had to advance without firing upon them. But we took 14 enemy prisoners and killed two. Then we burned the village and my heart ached to have the women fall down at my feet and grab my legs and kiss my hand and beg me not to do it. But orders are orders and I was in command of the fifteen men who went across that field. So I done my duty."

While Parrish did his duty there were others who did not. There had already been trouble among the Russian recruits many of whom sympathised with the Bolsheviks. On August 29th a section of the Slavo–British Legion, a unit raised from local Russians and officered by the British, had fired on its officers and deserted and on October 29th conscripts at the Alexander Nevski Barracks refused to go on parade. They gave four reasons: 1. Their Russian officers were still wearing their Tsarist badges of rank. 2. They would not fight for the English King. 3. They would not salute. 4. They wanted larger rations.

On December 3rd there was a more serious affair when the 1st Archangel Regiment mutinied. It was ended when British officers bombarded the mutineers' barracks with a Stokes Mortar, which had been developed for trench fighting on the Western Front, and forced them to surrender. Ironside, true to the custom of the Western Front where some 300 British soldiers faced the firing squad for desertion, cowardice and similar offences during the course of the war, had thirteen of the mutineers shot.

It was not only the Russians who were disaffected. Once the news of the Armistice spread among the troops there were few who wanted to continue fighting in this strange land in a war they did not understand. As far as they were concerned the war was over. It was time to go home. The French made it plain that they would soldier no more and the Americans, republican to a man, had no wish to restore the Tsarist regime. A number of them were of Russian and Polish families – one man actually met his mother in Archangel – who had fled from the cruelties and poverty of Tsarist rule. Many of them sympathised with the Bolsheviks. And, while few of the British troops were Bolshevik sympathisers, most of them now considered their war over. The only body of troops that showed any real enthusiasm for the fight were the Poles who, like the Czechs, were fighting to prove that they deserved their independence. And they hated all Russians anyway.

There were one or two exceptions among the malcontents. The Canadians who had been sent so reluctantly to provide a united Empire flavour to the intervention, uniformly fought well. There were also professional British soldiers, both officers and other ranks, who, despite having been at war for nearly five years suffering wounds and gassing and the traumas of trench warfare, still took pride in their ability to carry out their duties like true professionals.

There were also some extraordinary White Russians, men out of the pages of *War and Peace*, who fought for honour and for love of their country. One such man was the fighter pilot, Alexander Kazakov. He won his wings in February 1915 and the following month brought down his first German. The primitive machines of that time had not yet been armed with machine-guns and so Kazakov devised his own aerial weapon – a weighted grapnel suspended from a wire cable. Armed with this he took off to chase a two seater Albatross which was spotting for the German guns. He positioned himself above the Albatross and began to unreel the grapnel while the German observer fired at him with a rifle. But he only managed to get a few feet of wire unwound when the winch jammed. Unperturbed, Kazakov dived on the German and rammed it with his undercarriage, sending it crashing behind the Russian lines while he made a belly landing.

Although the intensity of the air fighting was nowhere near that of the Western Front Kazakov continued to be successful. He had a Maxim gun fitted to fire upwards from his Nieuport "Bebe". But to use this weapon he had to attack from below, positioning his plane rather than aiming the fixed gun. In 1917 he was given command of No. 1 Fighter Group of four squadrons flying French Morane Saulnier monoplanes and the excellent Nieuport 17. They were known as the "Death or Glory Boys" because of the skull and crossbones painted on their tails. By the time the Russians stopped fighting Kazakov had shot down 17 German planes.

He was a religious man who had an Ikon of St Nicholas screwed to the instrument panel of his plane and always tried to attend the funerals of the men he shot down. He was described as "possessing an austere and imperious countenance," but being "unassuming and almost naive".

When the Bolshevik Revolution took place he, like most pilots in the Imperial Air Service, was in a most invidious position. Many were murdered, others imprisoned and, when their mechanics tried to fly their planes on behalf of the new regime and crashed, were then pressed into Bolshevik service under threat of death.

Kazakov was one of the few who got away, largely due to the efforts of George Hill, who in his short-lived role as Trotsky's Inspector of Aviation, organised an escape route for the pilots. In his secret report when it was all over, Hill said: "I guaranteed 10,000 roubles to the pilot of each aeroplane landed with all accessories in the Czecho-Slovak lines: 2,500 roubles to each observer on condition that they went over in flights or squadrons." The reason for this condition was that when pilots escaped singly the other members of his squadron were brutalised by the Bolsheviks.

Kazakov eventually arrived at Archangel with thirty-seven pilots and ground crew from the Imperial Air Force along with a small RAF contingent and eight DH4 bombers. They commandeered some Sopwith 1½ Strutters and Nieuports 17 c-Is which they found, still in their crates just as they had been unloaded at Bakaritza many months before, and which had been missed by the Bolsheviks when they carried away the Allied stores from Archangel.

Kazakov and his men went into action almost immediately, flying from an advanced field on the Dvina Front. The enemy were known to have a Nieuport 28 fighter and a flight of Caudron G 111A 2 reconnaissance aircraft in the region, but they rarely put in an appearance and most of Kazakov's activities consisted of straffing positions and spotting for the guns on the British river boats.

When the Bolsheviks launched their October offensive on the Dvina his squadron was cut off. They dismantled their aircraft, loaded them on sleighs and set out for safety, fighting their way past patrols through ever thickening snow. Taking refuge at Siy Convent, they fought off attacks for a week before slipping away to the Allied lines under cover of darkness still dragging their aircraft behind them. Once safe they assembled the planes and were in the air almost immediately, machine-gunning the Red Guards who were attacking the Canadian gun pits.

Kazakov was made a Major in the British Army and awarded the DSO for this exploit.

Winter now clamped its bone-hard arctic fingers on the battlefield. There was little flying, the soldiers took turns between tending their machine-guns and stoking their stoves. On November 26th the temperature was recorded at 60 degrees below zero. There were patrols, alarms and excursions, but military activity was dictated not by General Ironside or Comrade Samuolo but by General Ice and Comrade Snow. Christmas came and Ironside spent it like some huge improbable Santa Claus swathed in furs in his pony sleigh visiting the troops in the front line.

Silver Parrish did quite well. He spent Christmas at Shusuga and had "pine-fed pheasant for dinner and some rum". Frank Douma's platoon who were in rest billets but still within patrol range of the enemy were each given a wild turkey. Then on Christmas Eve, "we had a programme at the Y [YMCA]. Captain Boyd played his mandoline for us. It is the best music I have heard for a long time. We each received a sock filled with candy, raisins, dates and cigarettes and an extra pair of socks, I wish I was at home. This is so different from last Christmas. Lieut. Mills presented us each with another bird."

On Christmas Day "the Russian children came all morning singing carols, expecting sweets from us. Lieut. Mills called us to his billets and gave us each a drink of rum, and another of cognac. We had dinner at the Y at 12.00 but this was a failure. The meat was rotten and it made a number of the boys sick."

Such are the realities of war.

Nicholas II, the last Tsar of Russia, was held prisoner by the Ural Soviet in Ekaterinburg in July 1917. He was executed with his family shortly after this picture was taken.

Lenin and his sister on their way to a meeting of the 5th All Russia Congress of Soviets held in Moscow's Bolshoi Theatre.

Vic Clow on board
"Z" Flight's special
train as it steamed
through the heartland
of Russia towards
Moscow.

"Z" Flight's RE8
bombers strapped to
their flatcars ready to
move off in support of
General Denikin's
advancing White
Army.

Dual control RE8
used to teach Russian
pilots to fly by the
RAF Training Mission
at Taganrog on the Sea
of Azov where
General Denikin had
his headquarters.

British sailors marching through the streets of Odessa, the Black Sea port, after disembarking from HMS *Ceres*. The hotel was renamed after the collapse of the Intervention.

Major-General Ironside inspects a newly raised and trained White Russian regiment at Murmansk. Despite their smartness and good British equipment, many of these troops proved unreliable and deserted to the Bolsheviks.

British "Whippet" light tanks on their way to join General Denikin's army from the port of Novorossiysk. British instructors, despite being forbidden to join in the fighting, took their tanks into action alongside the Cossack horsemen of the White Army.

Major-General Maynard takes the salute as a contingent of American troops marches past the Union Jack at Murmansk in a parade to impress disaffected locals with the Allies' strength.

ussian peasants bargain with Allied troops on board a barge on the Dvina River. These shallow
:aught barges were used to transport men and supplies to the front, south of Archangel.

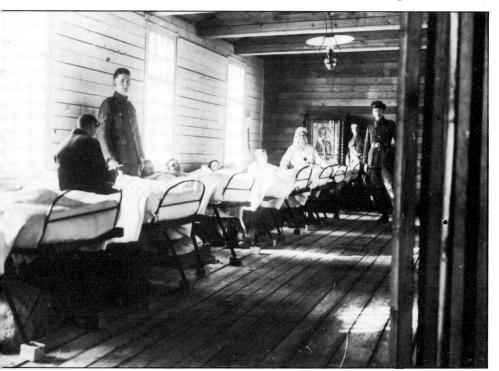

hospital for Russian troops run by British nurses and Royal Army Medical Corps personnel.
ote the ikon at the end of the ward.

Lev Trotsky as Commissar for War was the chief organiser and leader of the Red Army during the Intervention and Civil War.

Felix Dzerzhinsky created the Cheka, the Soviet political police, in 1917 and unleashed the Red Terror considered essential for the survival of the regime.

One of a handful of British Intelligence agents in Russia in 1918, Captain Sidney Reilly unsuccessfully attempted to organise a counter revolution.

Robert Bruce Lockhart led an official mission to the Bolsheviks in 1918 with the aim of keeping them in the war.

General Denikin's weary cavalry retreats across the Steppes. This photograph was taken from "Z" Flight's train, steaming to safety before the advancing Red Army.

The victorious Red Army, exhausted and riddled with typhus, marches into Irkutsk in March 1920. Their arrival in the Siberian railway town followed the defeat and execution of the White leader, Admiral Kolchak.

CHAPTER 10

Cattle Truck to Omsk
Siberia, August–December 1918

Private Reardon of the 25th (Garrison) Battalion Middlesex Regiment had been sitting out the war in Hong Kong. He and his comrades, not fit enough to fight in France even when Britain was so desperate for men to put into the trenches that skilled craftsmen were being conscripted from the aircraft works and the tank factories, had been looking forward to the end of the war, rapid demobilisation and the joys of civilian life when they were ordered to Siberia.

Not being a battalion which breathed fire and brimstone and itched to get into action, this was hardly a move which met with their whole-hearted approval. They left Hong Kong and the many delights it had to offer foreign soldiers and sailed on the *Ping Suey* on July 27th, 1918 for Vladivostok, a place they did not know but suspected quite rightly would be uncomfortable, cold and dangerous.

Nevertheless, it started well enough with a Japanese destroyer courteously steaming out to escort them into Vladivostok on August 3rd, the day after Poole had landed at Archangel. They then marched through the streets with a guard of honour supplied by HMS *Suffolk* and a Czech Legion band playing rousing military music, to their quarters in the Old Siberian Barracks.

As the first Allied infantrymen to reach Siberia it was considered essential that, fit or not, they would have to show the flag and so it was arranged that half of them along with forty-three machine-gunners should go up to the front on the Ussuri river where the Czechs and their White Russian allies were holding the Reds while other Czech units tried to fight their way through Irkutsk from the west. It was agreed, however, that the Middlesex would only act as second line troops. So when they moved up to the Ussuri on August 10th it was to take over positions from a Cossack unit which was going to advance. But there is no safe place on any battlefield and Reardon recorded in his diary three days later: "First enemy shellfire." Thereafter his diary reads:

August 15: started trench digging amidst marshes. Pestered with mosquitos. Working all night under terrible difficulties.

August 18: Heavy shell fire from enemy guns and armoured trains.

August 20: Digging bunkholes to make cover from shells.

August 21: Retired at noon four hours after Czech and French troops. Very heavy shell fire.

August 22: First Division of Japanese troops arrive.

August 24: Ordered to advance with Japanese at 2 a.m. Czechs and French as line of support. Japs make a brilliant victory.

The newly arrived Japanese, well-trained, well-armed and spoiling for action, completely defeated the rag-tag Red Army and a few days later the Czechs forced their way through Irkutsk without any help from the Allies who had come to "rescue" them. The Czechs now held the Trans-Siberian from west of the Urals all the way to Vladivostok, some four thousand miles away. Their westernmost outposts were established at Kazan and Samara where they captured the train carrying Russia's gold and platinum reserves. These successes momentarily raised British hopes that the Allied forces moving down the Dvina River from Archangel, and the Czechs established at Kazan, could join up at Kotlas and lay the foundation of a new Eastern Front – even though it was hundreds of miles away from the nearest Germans.

This was just wishful thinking. The plan was doomed from the start. The Japanese had no intention of moving further west than Irkutsk. The Americans were under strict orders to do nothing except help the Czechs leave Russia and guard the military stores. And the Czechs, while ready to defend themselves, had no desire whatsoever to stay in Russia.

They suffered their first defeat on September 5th when Trotsky took to the field with his reorganised Red Army and drove them out of Kazan. From that moment the dreamers of a new Eastern Front woke up to reality. There would be no Eastern Front. In fact there was no longer any need for one. The Germans had shot their bolt.

Nevertheless Colonel Ward loaded his "Die-Hards" on to the Trans-Siberian and set off for Omsk, 3,500 miles west of Vladivostok. It took them a month and there they stayed, as Reardon wrote, for "six months of a terrible Siberian winter" which they saw through with the help of winter clothing supplied by the Canadians. They saw no more action, although, when their band visited a forward position, their playing so enraged the Bolsheviks that they started a bombardment.

146

By now some 70,000 Japanese troops were based in the Pacific provinces of Russia and China, commanded by General Otani who claimed the title of Supreme Allied Commander in Siberia. The Japanese played a cynical game of self-interest. As far as they were concerned they were there to stay, and they were not over particular about their methods. One of their chief allies was Semenov, the vicious and unpleasant Ataman who had originally been given arms and money by the British in the mistaken belief that he would bring order to the anarchic situation in Eastern Siberia. The British had dropped him when it became obvious that far from bringing order, he was an old-fashioned warlord while his Mongol and Cossack horsemen were dedicated believers in the ancient military habits of rape and pillage. This did not stop the Japanese, however. They supplied Semenov with weapons, money, artillerymen and "advisors". He, grateful to his benefactors, carried out operations for them which they had no wish to acknowledge. It is one of the quirks of history that although the British rapidly disowned him and the Americans actually had a bloody encounter with him, it is the Allies who the Russians blame for the reign of terror which he spread across Siberia and into Manchuria where he settled in 1921. The Bolsheviks caught up with him eventually. The Red Army arrested him in Manchuria in 1945 and he was executed the following year.

The first contingent of the American expeditionary force arrived at Vladivostok on September 2nd, just twenty-four hours after the Czechs they had come to rescue broke through at Irkutsk thus making the Americans' journey unnecessary. Eventually there were nearly 9,000 US troops in Siberia. Of these 5,000 came from the Eighth Division. Other contingents were the 27th and 31st Infantry Regiments posted from the Philippines along with a field hospital, an ambulance company and a telegraph company. They were commanded, albeit reluctantly, by Major-General William S. Graves who had been given his assignment in a conversation lasting about ten minutes with the US Secretary of War, Newton Baker, at Kansas City railway station. Baker gave him a copy of President Wilson's statement of July 17th and told him: "This contains the policy of the United States in Russia which you are to follow. Watch your step; you will be walking on eggs loaded with dynamite. God bless you and goodbye."

Small wonder then that Graves arrived in Siberia determined to do nothing outside his brief. But that was ambiguous in the extreme. He was supposed to protect the Czech forces, but they had shown that they needed no protection. He was also supposed to guard the military stores "which may subsequently be needed by

Russian forces . . ." What Wilson's aide-mémoire did not spell out was: which Russian forces? As Graves later grumbled: "I could not give a Russian a shirt without being subjected to the charge of trying to help the side to which the recipient of the shirt belonged."

President Wilson had also urged in his memo that, among others, "Red Cross representatives and agents of the Young Men's Christian Association" should be sent to help the people of Siberia. And so they were. Eventually the Red Cross had over 2,500 workers there, five hundred of them American. The YMCA sent teams and so did the Knights of Colombus. Their presence perhaps highlighted the unbridgeable aims and policies of the so-called Allies in Siberia. They represented President Wilson's muddled hope for good to come out of an evil situation.

The other nations had different reasons for being there. The British had sent their worn out Die-Hards in order to maintain their influence on the conduct of affairs: the French a Colonial battalion of 1,100 men for similar reasons; the Italians 1,700 men to prove that they were indeed members of the Alliance. In addition the British and the French had sent strong Military Missions to train the new White Russian Army.

The Canadians, who had given in to the pressure from London, sent 4,186 men, many of them illegally for they had been conscripted under the Military Service Act which stipulated that they could only be used for the defence of Canada. Unlike their comrades in Archangel they saw no fighting and were used in a logistic role for the Middlesex and, later, the Hampshire battalions. Rumanian, Serbian and Polish contingents were there for the same reason as the Czechs: their fierce determination to prove their right to run their own nations. And the Japanese were there in pursuit of their expansionist ambitions which were to reach their zenith after Pearl Harbor twenty-three years later.

The fragmentation and jealousies of this "alliance" were matched only by the rivalries, intrigues and treachery among the various groups of Russians who made up the White forces fighting the Bolsheviks.

At one stage nearly a score of different bodies claimed to be the real government of Siberia with each one hoping to come to power once the Bolsheviks had been defeated. Minor warlords flourished and small groups of men with guns and food claimed the right to rule huge areas of territory. It must be remembered that at this time, apart from the towns and the land bordering the railways which flowed like great civilising rivers through Siberia, the far side of the Urals was still untamed country whose hinterland belonged to tribes run by Shamans (witch-doctors). It was like the American West before the US 7th Cavalry put down the tribes.

The most influential of the early opponents to Communist rule were the Socialist Revolutionaries – many of whom had been exiled under Tsarist rule to Siberia along with the Communists. When it was all over surviving Socialist Revolutionaries claimed that it was they who started the fight against the Bolsheviks in Siberia rather than the Czech Legion. But this is a claim which is hard to sustain. It may be that the SRs were plotting against the Bolsheviks but it was the Czechs' determination to fight their way to Vladivostok which precipitated the Civil War in Siberia and brought about the Allied intervention there.

It is, however, indisputable that the SRs co-operated with the Czechs in fighting the Bolsheviks along what became known as the Volga Front from Kazan to Samara. The SRs, led by former members of the Constituent Assembly who had fled from Petrograd, set up a government in Samara which they claimed was the real government of Russia and put together an army of some 10,000 men to fight alongside the Czech Legion. At the same time a conservative group set up a five-man provisional government in Omsk on the other side of the Urals. This junta, which claimed sovereignty over Siberia but not the rest of Russia, set about destroying every vestige of Communism. Former Tsarist officers and kulaks – the rich peasants – flocked to its standard, although there was no love lost between them. However, under the pressure of events – the Czechs were driven out of Samara by the Bolsheviks on October 8th – they came together to form the All-Russian Provisional government in Omsk on November 5th.

It lasted just twelve days. On the night of November 17th in a coup reminiscent of Chaplin's action against Tchaikovsky and his ministers at Archangel, a group of White officers kidnapped four socialist members of the Omsk government. Their reason was the same as Chaplin's: they wanted to replace what they regarded as a weak, government overly influenced by its left-wing members with a strong military regime. But where this ploy failed in Archangel, it succeeded in Omsk.

The following day the government was dissolved and all power, civil and military, was placed in the hands of a "Supreme Ruler", Admiral Alexander Kolchak, War Minister in the Omsk government.

Kolchak, a Crimean Tartar by birth, was an imposing man. According to an over-fulsome report from the *Times* correspondent in Siberia: "His swarthy, smooth-shaven, aquiline features, his black hair and black piercing eyes, and a long head like a Norman, make up a portrait that recalls the British quarter-deck rather than his native Cossack steppe." He was a noted Arctic explorer and oceanographer, played a leading part in the defence of Port Arthur in 1905 and was a successful commander of the Black Sea Fleet in operations against the German–Turkish fleet 1916–1917. He became an expert on mines which were used with devastating effect by both sides in the Russia–Japanese war and in April 1917 he went to America to advise the US Navy on their use. He was thus out of danger when the Imperial Navy mutinied and turned on their officers.

When the Bolsheviks seized power from the Provisional government in Petrograd he was actually in Tokyo on his way back to Russia. He immediately made the quixotic gesture of calling on the British Ambassador and offering his services to the British. He asked to serve in the Army rather than the Royal Navy on the basis that the Navy would be embarrassed by having to accommodate an officer of his high rank. His offer was accepted. He was to be posted to Mesopotamia, but before he could take up his new duties it was suggested that he could serve his country better by returning to Siberia to help form a new Russian Army to oppose the Bolsheviks.

And so it was that eventually he came to Omsk. He was a brave, intelligent, but serious and autocratic man imbued with the discipline of the old Imperial Navy, who came to regard himself as the legitimate successor to the Tsar. He was also active and honest and created a good impression on the British officers of the military mission who were beginning to despair of finding a senior officer who was not either incompetent or corrupt. General Knox was especially impressed. What he wanted was a strong man in charge at Omsk capable of imposing the conditions in which the new Russian Army could be raised and trained. Kolchak was Knox's man and he welcomed the Admiral's assumption of power as Supreme Ruler. Later, General Maurice Janin, Head of the French Military Mission, accused Knox of organising Kolchak's coup for perfidious British reasons. But, as we shall see, Janin probably had good reason for trying to cloud the Kolchak story.

Knox, later asked by a cunning editor to review part of Janin's memoirs, wrote that the coup was "carried out by the Siberian government without the previous knowledge and without in any sense the connivance of Great Britain".

Colonel Ward, now established with his battalion in Omsk with orders to keep the peace in the town, was another of Kolchak's admirers. He recorded in his book *With the Die-Hards in Siberia* how, when he heard of the kidnappings he turned out his soldiers and set up machine-gun posts to cover the streets in case there was trouble around his barracks. As it happened the barracks were next door to the building where the Council of Ministers met to decide on its own dissolution. As he wrote with his tongue firmly in his cheek: "That these arrangements gave the Ministers greater confidence to proceed with their policy I have no doubt. That was one of the inevitable consequences of the preparations for our own defence . . . it did steady the situation."

One man opposed to Admiral Kolchak was General Graves, the American commander, who was totally against the restoration of a Tsarist style regime in Siberia. Despite Knox's urgings to co-operate he drew Wilson's aide-mémoire round him like armour plate and refused to step outside its confines.

Edith Faulstitch records what he had to say about his dilemma in her book *The Siberian Sojourn*: "I have often thought that it was unfortunate I did not know more of the conditions in Siberia than I did when I was pitch-forked into the mêlée at Vladivostok. At other times I have thought that ignorance was not only bliss in such a situation but was advisable."

Ten days after Kolchak seized power reinforcements arrived for the British. The 1/9th Hampshires, originally a Cyclists Battalion of the Territorial Army, arrived at Vladivostok on board SS *Dunera* from India. Unlike the Middlesex, they were all graded A1. They comprised thirty-two officers and 945 other ranks and were commanded by Colonel Robert Johnson, a peace-time civil servant. Among his NCOs was Corporal Arthur Waide who recalls that he had joined the Territorials when he was only sixteen because "I was a keen cyclist." With his elder brother Walter he was called up for coast patrol duty at the beginning of the war but in 1915 as the Western Front ate up men the Hampshires were sent to India to replace regular troops who had been transferred to France. During three years enjoying the garrison life of India, they had taken part in a minor campaign in Waziristan and were beginning to look forward to the end of the war. Corporal Waide was on leave in Simla sitting in the theatre waiting for the curtain to go up when a sergeant-major walked on to the stage and announced: "Will any member of the Hampshires report to me in the foyer." That was the start of an odyssey which took Waide and his comrades from their cantonment at Ambala in the East Punjab to Bombay, Colombo, Singapore, Hong Kong, Vladivostok and Omsk. Waide was relieved they went by sea; someone in the barracks had suggested that they were going to march over the Himalayas to Siberia. They were at sea when they learnt of the Armistice. "Some of the bright boys said we won't be going on after this. But we did."

On August 16th, Colonel Johnson had written a rather despondent letter to his mother telling her that he hoped to be away from Ambala "for a fortnight or so after hill pheasants out Chakrata way. A reviver in preparation for this wearisome camp and manoeuvre training which comes round with the cold weather – but I must take care not to overdo myself this time. It has been one of the worst hot weathers on record, always 10 degrees at least above the normal for this time of year . . . Not a drop of rain yet – already 6 weeks overdue . . ."

Later in the letter he writes of his hatred of war and his longing to get home to his wife and family: "Oh Lord how I wish this terrible orgy was over . . . And how I wish I could afford to go into Parliament after this war and help in the abolition of all soldiers!"

"Even when demobilisation does come," he complained, "there will be ships for Yankees, Australians, Canadians, Irishmen, Welshmen, Scotchmen, Chinese, Japanese, Indians, Hottentots . . . but none for Englishmen and least of all if they are Territorials!" He was soon to find himself on a ship heading for a much colder climate and a new war.

On December 5th Johnson was writing to his father: "Here we are in Vladivostok waiting to complete clothing and equipment which is expected to arrive from Canada this week after which we start on our long journey to Omsk."

He told his father of the extreme confusion in Russia – "this seething pot of murder and madness" – the divided counsels of the Allies. "You can well imagine the reluctance of all the Allies to take on fresh commitments now the war is over – especially with troops enlisted for the war only." But, he insisted, "whether they like it or not they will find that the task of restoring settled government to Russia is unavoidable."

About the magnitude of the task and how long it will take opinions differ, but the British view (which is also that of non-Bolshevik Russians) is that it is an easy business if tackled firmly and with resolution and that a very few good troops acting resolutely will soon restore order . . . The idea is to form new Russian armies trained and at the beginning officered by English and French and hand over when they are able to stand on their own. So far in Siberia all the work has been done by the

Czecho-Slovaks – magnificent fellows. But they naturally want
to get home now to build up their new little state in Bohemia and
the question is, who is to take their place? At present the only
people who can do so are the 9th Hants and a few old garrison Bn
[Battalion] men who are already up the line – but even the 9th
Hants is hardly a sufficient substitute for the Canadians neither
for several thousands of Czechos.

It was with this attitude that Johnson took his men off on the
month-long railway journey to Omsk. They travelled at a comfortable 15 miles an hour in cattle trucks which had been roofed in,
equipped with a stove and boards to sleep on. Corporal Waide was
one of the advance party. Now fully equipped with Canadian
sheepskin coats they set off from Vladivostok on December 5th and
steamed for Harbin, Chita and Irkutsk. Waide spent much of his
time on the footplate armed with a revolver to make sure the driver
and fireman behaved themselves. By Christmas day they were a
few hundred miles short of Omsk. The temperature in their truck
was −40°F and they celebrated Christmas with an extra tot of rum
as they travelled.

Following on with the main party ten days later Johnson spent his
Christmas in Chita. A religious man, he was gratified to be able to
arrange a Christmas communion in a Greek Orthodox church
before collecting his 250 men together and holding a Christmas
service in a hall near the station. He read the lesson, the men sang
Christmas hymns and the Greek Orthodox priest blessed them all.
Then they set off on a march round Chita to show the flag, wrote
Johnson, "bugles blowing (until frozen up) and drums beating, the
big drummer very smart in his Indian tiger skin."

Johnson marched his men off to the house of Ataman Semenov
who, the Colonel observed: "rules Chita and district with a rod of
iron."

He is, said Johnson in a letter to his mother,

an interesting personality and one of the great difficulties in the
situation out here. He is strongly anti-Bolshevik . . . but he has a
personal disagreement with Admiral Kolchak, the head of the
Siberian Government at Omsk and consequently will not recognise the Govt . . . As he controls the railway in these parts this is
very awkward, he takes his toll of supplies going up to Kolchak
and the front, intercepts telegrams and as Kolchak has now
declared him a traitor to Russia, the situation is very strained.
Three days before our arrival he was bombed but escaped with

but slight injuries and now lies injured in bed. I drew my detachment up before his door and walked in to enquire how he did. I had rather to guess whether this was in accordance with policy but he was satisfied that it was so; although in disgrace for not coming into line he has no quarrel with the British and shares the general anti-Bolshevik view which recognises our disinterestedness and welcomes us as deliverers. Coming just after the attack on him which he declares (quite without ground) to have been instigated by the Kolchak party this formal visit from the British Commander of Omsk was an immense joy to him and he was obviously hugely gratified.

The good colonel obviously had no idea on what dangerous ground he was treading. Semenov's depredations had already horrified the British and American governments and if Johnson had known of his host's catalogue of crimes he would undoubtedly not have been so civil.

But he was in unstoppable form . . . "Having been introduced to his bedchamber, however, I then proceeded through my interpreter to deliver a lecture to him which I knew was in accordance with policy." It was indeed a very pompous lecture on the need to pull together to fight the Bolshevik. "It was intolerable that the restoration of settled government in Russia should be held up owing to a personal quarrel between two great men like Semenov and Kolchak."

Imagine the scene; the bloodthirsty warlord lying in bed nursing his wounds from an assassination attempt and being lectured on his behaviour by a former president of the Oxford Union – a civil servant turned soldier who had just come from celebrating Christmas communion.

"He was obviously impressed," wrote Johnson, "and said the relations between British and Russian were excellent and that he had no idea of disturbing them. I replied that in that case the relations between all good Russians must be equally good. We parted with toasts of champagne and a speech from his chief of staff to my bewildered men."

Johnson rejoined his men for Christmas dinner "principally consisting of pheasants which I had bought for them in Harbin." The party was joined by Semenov's staff officers who "got rather drunk on our rum". The Hampshires then trooped off to the bath house before rejoining the train which steamed out of Chita to a "royal round of cheers" from Semenov's men.

An extraordinary episode. But then everything was extraordinary in Siberia during the Christmas of 1918. Johnson's encounter with Semenov merely reflected the confusion that prevailed, and the persistent lack of a coherent Allied policy.

CHAPTER 11

The Lockhart Plots
Moscow and Petrograd, August–December 1918

August 1918 was a traumatic month for Lenin and his followers. The Germans, breaking the Brest-Litovsk Treaty, seized the Crimea, the Don region and the Ukraine and moved into the Baltic states. The Allies landed at Archangel and Vladivostok. The Czechs established themselves along the Trans-Siberian. General Denikin and his White Army was on the move in the south and had captured Ekaterinodar (Krasnodar). Other White forces were gathering in the north and east while the opposition parties, defeated in Moscow and at Yaroslavl, remained a threat.

The Bolshevik perspective of the world from Moscow where Lenin had established his government in the Kremlin was a precarious and insular one: surrounded by enemies bent on the destruction of their new order. It is a perspective which in essence remains the same today and so does the Soviet reaction to it: brutal repression.

Suspicion quite rightly settled on the British, French and to a lesser extent, the American representatives in Moscow and Petrograd. Captain Cromie had his cabling facilities removed, and was not allowed to travel. Britons living in the two cities were detained, interrogated and after being released were effectively put under house arrest. Hounded by the Cheka and hemmed in by Soviet Foreign Ministry restrictions, the official presence in Russia became a shambles. In Moscow Lockhart's offices were raided. There was now no official communication between the Allied missions and the Russian government.

George Hill's agents told him that the Bolsheviks were divided over what to do with the Allied officers. Some wanted to arrest them all pending their expulsion from Russia while the others wanted "public executions as reprisals for the supposed shooting of some Soviet Commissars at Kem . . ."

He was not surprised therefore when there was a round-up of Allied officers on August 5th. Tipped-off, he left his rooms and escaped to Reilly's flat.

According to Hill, Reilly "knew nothing about the events in the town, but immediately got ready to leave his flat, packed up a few remaining things he had, destroyed his papers and a report he was writing, in my presence, and with me, after sending a warning to the American consulate, left his flat for our secret quarters."

In one of the biggest raids, on August 15th, the British Consul-General, Oliver Wardrop, burnt every document he could find in the fireplace of his bedroom just before the Chekists burst in. There was so much smoke that they had to wear wet cloths over their faces and in the end abandoned the raid. Wardrop crushed the burnt remains and contacted the Foreign Office – as Consul-General he was still allowed to cable – saying there was "not now in the building a single scrap of paper of a strictly confidential kind," and there was no longer any point in sending or receiving such cables.

Nevertheless, despite the Chekists' close attentions and the threat to their lives, Lockhart, Hill and Reilly were determined to attempt the overthrow of the Bolshevik government. Lockhart remained in the open, still acting as head of the British mission but Reilly, according to Hill's secret report, "got a job in a technical department while I received papers as a film actor and had an interest in a curio and fancy goods store".

Hill was preoccupied with setting up his courier service for supplying information "to the commanders of the allied troops operating from North to South". He also set up groups to –

> find out the best roads, know of all the traps, take stock of the disposition of the Soviet troops, guns, food stores, dumps and morale of the army, and send these reports verbally to the Allied advance detachments and scouts, also carry out, if desired, reconnaissance work required by these advance units. If necessary they were to occupy themselves with gentle sabotage. They should also know all those who were pro or anti-ally, reliable and unreliable, for our use during subsequent occupation of villages by us.

They were formed of men "who had suffered and lost everything they possessed owing to the Bolsheviks". Nine of them were to lose their lives as well, caught and executed by Chekists in the Vologda district.

Meanwhile, Lockhart and Reilly were pursuing another course. Their attention focused on the Lettish soldiers who had lost their country to the Germans but remained a cohesive, well-disciplined and well-trained force. With nothing to lose they threw in their lot with the Bolsheviks during the Revolution and became the military corner-stone on which Lenin's government rested. They were given special facilities, good food and pay. According to Hill "they guarded the Kremlin, gold stock and the munitions. At the head of the Extraordinary Commissions, the prisons, the banks and the railroads were Letts. The nucleus of strength on the fronts consisted of Letts and wherever fighting was to be done they were sent. Russian troops could only be relied upon to act if backed up and coerced by the Letts."

If they could be seduced away from their alliance with the Bolsheviks then Lenin and his comrades would find themselves in very serious trouble. There was hope that this could be accomplished. The civilian Letts who had fled from the Germans were growing restive under Communism and their discontent was beginning to affect the Lettish soldiers, increasingly dismayed by the role of executioner which had been thrust upon them and by the possibility that they would be called upon to fight against a full-scale Allied invasion.

At least, that was the belief that prevailed in the British and French missions in Moscow. A meeting was set up between Lockhart, Reilly and the French Consul-General, M. Grenard, and Colonel Berzin, commander of the artillery battalion of the Lettish Rifles. It is still unclear whether the initiative for this meeting came from Berzin or the Allied representatives but what we do know is that Reilly reported to Hill after the meeting that the Letts could probably be won over to the Allied side as a number of them now believed it would be in their interest.

It is worth quoting Hill's report at some length here because he set out precisely what the Allies hoped to gain from the Letts and how the plot was to be organised:

> Certain sums of money for propaganda and work were promised [to Berzin] and it was arranged that, if on the departure of the Diplomatic Corps all the money had not been handed over, drafts would be left with Lt. Reilly to enable us to carry out the scheme.
>
> The scheme which the Allied Diplomatic representatives worked for was: a definite relief on our Northern and Czecho-slovak fronts which was to be brought about by certain Lettish units turning over to our side and thereby weakening the main force against our troops.
>
> The Allies, the Czechoslovak and White Guard troops were straining their utmost to join up with each other and to form a united front. The staged Yaroslavl affair had worn itself into a disastrous failure; the confidence of the White Guard organis-

ation was shaken in the Allies and it was impossible to rely on any mob of theirs for support of the Allied troops . . .

The only sound scheme left was to back the Letts. This had been conceded as sound by most people who knew the conditions in Russia, but a few have had doubts as to the rights of staging a revolution internally in Moscow and Petrograd.

The proposed turning of the Lettish troops to our cause on the fronts could not be achieved without seriously affecting the Moscow and Petrograd centres. The simultaneous change on the fronts and at Moscow and Petrograd would have destroyed the Soviet Government, and automatically the White Guards would have come into power and the ammunition, arms and supplies would have been at the disposal of this new force.

Destruction gangs organised by us for a time would have prevented any possible attempt at interference from the Germans until the Allied forces had linked up, and a national White Guard Army formed.

Supplies from the North, corn from the East and produce from the Volga, with a White Guard force, and there would have been no fear of any trouble from the people. This was the possibility of success. In the event of failure and our being found in any plot, Lt. Reilly and myself should have simply been private individuals and responsible to no one. As we hourly expected the departure of the Allied representatives, the whole brunt would have been borne by us.

It will be seen from this account of Lockhart's dealings with Berzin that the British representative who, only a few weeks before, had been urging the government to co-operate with the Bolsheviks, was now attempting to bring them down. It must be assumed that he would not have entered into such a plot without the explicit orders of the government working through "C" at MI6.

However, Lockhart was not involved in the detailed planning. That was left to Reilly. Hill, too, played no part in the planning but Reilly reported to him after every meeting so that if anything happened to Reilly, Hill would be able to take over.

Reilly initially met Colonel Berzin in the Tramble Café in the Tverskoy Boulevard (now Gorky Street) to thrash out the details. Later their venue was a flat belonging to a member of the Committee of Letts formed from friends of Berzin. They proposed to use the civilian Lettish refugees to spread propaganda and they estimated that the plot would be ready in five or six weeks. Hill says that telegrams were sent to General Poole in Archangel, telling him what they were doing but we have not been able to trace any record of these messages.

By the third week in August Reilly had the bit between his teeth. He told Hill that Berzin wanted to assassinate Trotsky and Lenin rather than arrest them because their marvellous oratorical powers would so act on the psychology of the men sent to pick them up that it was not advisable to risk arresting them; moreover, their assassination would create panic among the Bolsheviks and therefore there would be no resistance to the coup. Reilly said that he had been very firm in dissuading Berzin from such a course and that he had impressed upon the Lett that the policy should be "not to make martyrs of the leaders but to hold them up to ridicule before the world".

Reilly's plan was to arrest the Bolshevik leaders on August 28th at a meeting of the Soviet Central Executive Committee in the Bolshoi Theatre, where the Lettish Riflemen would be on guard. He would then strip them of their trousers and underpants and march them through Moscow to the jeers of the populace.

By this time the British had taken over from the French as the financers of the counter-revolution. Lockhart distributed large sums of money to people who promised their help when the time came. Patriarch Tikhon, head of the Russian Church, was one of the recipients. Reilly and Hill called on him with two large suitcases stuffed with money. In exchange for five million roubles, then worth about £143,000, Tikhon promised that solemn divine services would be held in Moscow churches to mark Russia's release from the Bolshevik yoke.

With so much money in circulation and with so many people now involved in the plot it was inevitable that the Bolsheviks would hear about it through their highly developed system of informers. However the question is not whether they knew about it but whether they set the whole thing up in order to trap the Allies.

According to the Soviet version of the affair they knew every move that Lockhart made because Berzin was an agent provocateur loyal to Bolshevism. The counter plot, they add, was set up by Moise Uritsky, head of the Cheka in Petrograd.

This version claims that Uritsky planted a youth called Smidchen on Captain Cromie who used him to carry messages to Lockhart in Moscow. Smidchen was a mysterious figure and it was not until 1966 that a Russian newspaper published an account of his exploits. This Soviet version said that he was really Yan Buikis, a Lett working for the Cheka, and that the man he was reporting to was Colonel Berzin. Smidchen was with Berzin on August 15th when he met Lockhart at the British diplomat's flat in Khlebny Lane.

In Lockhart's discreet version of the affair the Letts said they were not prepared to fight for the Bolsheviks against the Allies and they wanted safe conduct passes to reach the British forces in Archangel. He gave them the passes and put them in touch with Reilly. The Soviet version confirms that Lockhart produced the passes but claims that he also offered them some six million rubles to bribe the Lettish soldiers. Altogether, say the Russians, the British actually handed over one million, two hundred thousand roubles which the colonel passed on to his superiors in the Cheka.

Lockhart was able to acquire all the roubles he needed in Moscow by doing deals with rich Russians who wanted to get out of the country. Lockhart relieved them of their useless currency and gave them promissory notes to be repaid by the British government. That particular chicken came home to roost a few years later when the notes were presented with the threat of a long court action if they were not honoured. The case was hushed up; presumably the holders of the notes were paid off, because the British government feared what revelations might be made in court.

Just how much the Cheka did know remains unclear but they certainly knew enough to postpone the Central Executive Committee meeting for a week. At the same time the Bolshevik government signed a trade agreement with Germany which seemed to make it even more important to the Allies that the Bolsheviks should be overthrown. The agreement gave the Germans what they had long coveted: oil from Baku, the use of the Black Sea Fleet and a large indemnity. In return German troops would be used to help the Red Guards deal with the Allied intervention in the north, and Berlin would withhold its support of the Don Cossacks who had declared their independence.

Reilly left Moscow for Petrograd on August 28th to meet the Lettish organisation there and to confer with Cromie and Boyce, the MI6 station chief. Berzin had gone ahead of Reilly to set up the meeting. Soviet documents record that Berzin told the Cheka what he was doing, and the papers state specifically that Berzin's courage and resourcefulness played a major part in frustrating the "Lockhart Plot".

This version is supported by the fact that the Cheka raided two of Reilly's hideouts in Petrograd while he was still in the city. How he escaped arrest remains a mystery, but one story has him going to the Cheka headquarters in Gorokhovaya where friends told him to forget every alias except one – that he was a Chekist Commissar called Rilinsky.

But all this plotting and counter-plotting came to an abrupt and bloody end on August 30th. Uritsky, head of the Petrograd Cheka, was shot dead by Leonid Kanegisser, a twenty-two-year-old Jewish student, and that night Lenin was seriously wounded by three shots fired at point blank range. The would-be assassin was one Fanny Kaplan, a pretty twenty-eight-year-old Jewish revolutionary who had been sentenced to death twelve years previously for attempting to blow up the Tsarist Governor of Kiev. She had been spared execution by the Tsar's judges but sent to Siberia for life, a sentence from which she was released by the Revolution.

Ironically, Uritsky was one of the few men in the Cheka leadership who was against executions; he insisted that they generated hatred and fear and were counter-productive. As he was also a member of the Central Committee his views carried weight. However, he had the misfortune to uncover a plot among some artillery officers. His discovery led to the execution of twenty-one of the officers and he signed their death warrants. He has since been described as a merciless butcher and two weeks before his death a cable to the Foreign Office in London from the Consulate General had referred to him as a "venomous Jew" who was threatening to murder British diplomats.

Unluckily for him, one of the men whose death warrant he had signed was a friend of Kanegisser's who belonged to a small group connected with the Right SRs. The young student took his revenge, both personal and political, shortly after eleven in the morning when Uritsky walked into the former Tsarist Ministry of Foreign Affairs.

He escaped on a bicycle but was tracked down and caught in the English Club used by British diplomats – a coincidence which was to lend support to the Bolshevik accusations that the British were behind the assassination. Poor Kanegisser. When Felix Dzerzhinsky, head of the secret police, was told of the murder at Cheka headquarters in Moscow he summoned an armoured train and headed for Petrograd. Kanegisser was tortured and then interrogated by Dzerzhinsky himself. He insisted that he had acted alone. But the Cheka boss was certain that the British were responsible. Then, that night he received a telegram telling him of the attempt on Lenin's life. Given that he knew of Reilly's plot, the killing of Uritsky and the wounding of Lenin must have seemed to this dedicated, cold-hearted man the signal for the start of the counter-revolution.

He decided to strike back. The next morning he ordered gunboats to take up station in the Neva opposite the British Embassy and then he sent his hardest men into the building. As the Chekists battered on the heavy wooden doors with their pistol butts and rifles, Boyce started to destroy his top-secret documents, especially the codebook and incoming cables while Cromie stood guard with his service revolver in his hand at the top of the wide sweeping staircase which had seen so many grand diplomatic occasions. Imagine the scene; a warm Saturday afternoon, the sun sparkling on the Neva, the gunboats with their cannon trained on the Embassy, a group of 20 shouting men breaking the doors off their hinges and facing them, an archetypal British hero figure, handsome and courageous, defying the mob once again while the all-important documents are destroyed.

Cromie's life almost seemed destined for this moment. As we have seen, he had frightened off gangs of looters with his pistol while he was scuttling his submarines four months previously. But the men who broke into the Embassy were not so easily frightened; they were picked trigger-men of the Cheka who in the normal course of events had little regard for human life and on this day were enraged by the murder of Uritsky and the wounding of Lenin.

Cromie shouted at them to get out, to leave British territory at once. The Chekists took no notice but advanced up the staircase yelling, "Hands up, hands up." Cromie then opened fire into the crowd and men fell dead and dying. But some of the Russians must have got behind him on the first floor for he was shot in the back as he was going down the stairs. Mrs Natalie Bucknall, one of the embassy clerks, later made a sworn statement of what happened.

She was, she stated, in the Embassy's passport office talking to a clerk when she heard shots and "terrible screams". As she went into the hall she saw several Red Guards running down the stairs behind Captain Cromie, who fell on the bottom step. There was a great deal of wild shooting and upstairs there were shouts of, "Come out of the room, come out of the room or we will use our machine guns on you." After kicking the mortally wounded Cromie a couple of times the Red Guards returned upstairs and Mrs Bucknall and another woman went into the hall and spoke to Cromie. His eyelids moved and he spoke, but so faintly they could not hear what he said. Red Guards then reappeared and pointed their guns at the women and shouted: "Get upstairs or we'll shoot you."

In the Chancery there were several diplomats standing with their hands in the air. One of them was Boyce who must have been experiencing some qualms about his choice of profession. A senior Chekist told them that the Embassy had been seized in the name of the law and the Soviet government. When Mrs Bucknall told him that Cromie was probably dying downstairs he replied, "He can lie there. We have no time to look after him."

"The room was full of soldiers and sailors who were most brutal in their behaviour," said Mrs Bucknall. "Orders were given that the Embassy was to be searched from top to bottom, and the hall porter was led into the room with a revolver held to his neck. His guard threatened to shoot him if he did not obey him and open every door. We were taken downstairs four by four, and at the bottom I saw Captain Cromie's body lying under the hall window. He was already dead."

The Britons were taken to the Cheka prison at Gorokhovaya. The women were put into a small room packed with thirty-five people. Mrs Bucknall was interrogated by a Chekist who asked her if she knew anything about Cromie's political views, and what political party her husband belonged to. She replied that no member of the Embassy belonged to a political party, English or Russian. She was told that five English people, one of whom was Boyce, were on the list for execution and a decision was shortly to be taken about them. "The man whom I saw was very rude and said that all the English would be killed because the Murmansk expedition was advancing."

The Soviet version is, naturally enough, somewhat different. Dzerzhinsky, it runs, had indisputable proof of criminal activities being carried out by British diplomats and decided to search the Embassy for evidence pointing to British complicity in Uritsky's death. He selected six Chekists, including his secretary Bronislav Brotnovsky who was later to hold responsible positions in Soviet Military Intelligence and the Comintern. The team was led by Joseph Standolin, a veteran Bolshevik who had lived overseas for many years and spoke fluent English. They entered through the front door to find smoke and ashes from burning papers floating through the building as the diplomats set about "hastily destroying evidence of their crime". As they started to walk up the stairs there was a shot. Standolin shouted in English: "Stop that shooting immediately." But he was hit by a bullet and fell bleeding on to the white carpet of the staircase. Behind him other men, one of them Brotnovsky, were badly wounded. Then, according to the Soviet version, the Chekists returned Cromie's fire and killed the "head of the British Intelligence Network in Russia because he had lost his self-control".

The fact that they had broken all the laws of diplomatic behaviour was not lost on the Bolsheviks. Their version of the events insists that they would never have searched the Embassy in normal circumstances but that they could not remain inactive "when the Embassy is converted into quarters of conspiracy for plotters and murderers when officials in our territory weave . . . a net of bloody intrigue and monstrous crime."

Dzerzhinsky's men made a thorough job of searching the Embassy while the diplomats were held at Cheka headquarters. On September 2nd the Danish Minister in Petrograd sent a telegram to his government saying: "The archives were sacked and everything was destroyed. Captain Cromie's corpse was treated in a horrible manner. Cross of St George was taken from the body and subsequently worn by one of the murderers. English clergymen were refused permission to repeat prayers over body."

On September 4th, the Dutch Minister W. J. Oudendijk who had been looking after Britain's interests in Petrograd since the departure of Francis Lindley, returned from Moscow where he had been negotiating the exchange of British and Russian officials being held as near-hostages by either country. He was outraged to find Cromie's mutilated corpse still lying in the English church.

No funeral had been organised because some of the diplomats – Britons among them – were frightened of provoking the hostility of the mob. Oudendijk would have none of this and he insisted that Cromie be given what was virtually a state funeral with all the neutral diplomats following the cortège as it wound its way through the city. There was no hostility. Even the undisciplined Bolshevik sailors on the rusting destroyers moored in the Neva came to attention as the procession passed slowly over the Nikolai Bridge.

Cromie's death in defence of the Embassy did more than any other single act to convince the British that the Bolsheviks were indeed barbarians. There was uproar in the press. When Winston Churchill heard of Cromie's death he wrote a note for the War Cabinet. In it he argued:

I earnestly hope that the Government, in spite of its many pre-occupations, will pursue the perpetrators of this crime with tireless perseverance. Reprisals upon various Bolshevik non-entities who happen to be in our hands are of no real use, though they should be by no means excluded. The only policy which is likely to be effective, either for the past or the future, is to mark down the personalities of the Bolshevik Government as the objects upon whom justice will be executed, however long it takes . . .

The government did take action against the "Bolshevik non-entities" in British hands. Maxim Litvinov, Lockhart's counterpart in London, and his staff were taken to Brixton Prison as hostages and twenty-five Russians selected by Litvinov for repatriation as a goodwill gesture by the British had their passages cancelled.

On September 4th Foreign Minister Arthur Balfour took up Churchill's theme and sent a telegram to the Russian Foreign Minister, Georgi Chicherin, demanding the immediate punishment of everybody connected with "this abominable outrage". Balfour left no doubt about the British Government's fury. His telegram went on in threatening tone:

> Should the Russian Soviet Government fail to give complete satisfaction or should any further acts of violence be committed against a British subject His Majesty's Government will hold the members of the Soviet Government individually responsible and will make every endeavour to secure that they shall be treated as outlaws by the Governments of all civilised nations and that no place of refuge shall be left to them.

None of this, of course, helped the situation of Reilly or Lockhart, both of whom could feel the hot breath of the Cheka on the backs of their necks. According to an official Chekist version of events Reilly had arranged to meet Cromie for lunch at the Balkov Café on that fateful Saturday. He waited there for ninety minutes in a back room and when Cromie did not show up decided to walk along to the Embassy. When he got there it was all over. There were three bodies lying on the ground. Two were the Chekists Shenkamann and Yanson. The third was Cromie.

The Chekist account has it that a Red Army soldier recognised Reilly but as he knew the British agent only as Comrade Rilinsky of the Cheka he said: "Ah Comrade! See how badly it has turned out. The dog fired back. That's him over there."

Reilly had already been in touch with his friend and chief contact, the rich lawyer Alexander Grammatikov who had told him nervously, "The idiots. They acted too soon. They were supposed to co-ordinate the job. Uritsky has been killed. You must get away."

Despite the hue and cry mounted for him, he did just that. Reilly spent the night at the home of an SR contact, then, using his Cheka pass, bluffed his way by train to Moscow.

In Hill's official version Reilly had gone to his own flat in Petrograd where he met Boyce and spelt out the Lettish plan. Boyce was dubious, saying he thought the affair was too risky but agreed it was worth trying. He considered it was important for Reilly to meet Cromie, as Cromie had had a great deal to do with the Letts. According to Hill,

> he left Reilly at his flat to go to the British Embassy with the intention of returning by three o'clock with Cromie. Reilly waited in his flat until after six o'clock but no one turned up. He afterwards heard of Captain Cromie's death, but in no way connected it with the Letts affair. On Monday Reilly booked a sleeper for Moscow. He used the same passes that he had done on his journey North and arrived in Moscow . . . and only then got the first news of the crash.

In Moscow Reilly found everything in chaos. The British mission had been closed down. George Hill had gone to ground. Moscow's newspapers carried lurid stories about the "Lockhart Plot". Lockhart, they said, was the organiser, Reilly did the dirty work. Reilly's picture and description appeared on hoardings and a price of 100,000 roubles was put on his head.

The Cheka picked up six – some say eight – Russian women of various ages, shapes and sizes all of whom claimed to be married to Reilly. What happened to them is not known. It was another of his mistresses, Dagmara, the ballet dancer niece of Grammatikov, who saved Reilly. She put Reilly in touch with Hill and gave him a cache of two million roubles which she had been hiding. Dagmara was later arrested and shot, not because of her work for Reilly but because the Cheka established that she knew an accomplice of Fanny Kaplan. And that was enough to condemn her.

There was now no reason for Reilly to stay in Russia. His great plot had collapsed. He was hunted. His contacts and friends were being slaughtered. Reilly slept where he could and one night he lay low in a brothel. He later told the story of how a prostitute spent the night in his room, moaning in the last stages of syphilis. Eventually Hill gave him his own false papers and a train ticket to Petrograd. He arrived there on September 11th after sharing a compartment with German diplomats and pretending he was one of their number. He later wrote: "My aim just then was to get out of Russia as soon as possible. The Mission I had been entrusted with had ended in complete failure." He bribed his way on board a Dutch ship and by the first week in November he was back in London, lunching at the Savoy.

Lockhart was in even more trouble than Reilly. He was the official representative of the British government in Moscow and could not go underground. The night after Lenin was shot he was arrested by Pavel Malkov who before the Revolution had been a sailor in the Baltic Fleet but was now Commandant of the Kremlin and one of the Cheka's most dedicated executioners. Captain Hicks was picked up at the same time.

Another man in trouble was Commandant de Vertement, head of the French secret service in Moscow – codenamed Henri – whose flat was raided and stripped. The searchers found explosives but de Vertement managed to escape. "Henri" was convinced he had been betrayed by René Marchand, Moscow correspondent for *Figaro* who, on August 22nd, had attended a conference in the American consulate at which Reilly, de Vertement and Xenophon Kalamatiano, the American agent, were present. It has been suggested that as a result of what he heard, Marchand exposed the whole plot to the Cheka. But when Hill and de Vertement met in the safety of Finland and dissected what had happened they decided that while Marchand had probably betrayed de Vertement and one of Reilly's girls whose name was mentioned at the conference, he was unlikely to have given the whole game away.

Marchand was certainly indiscreet – when he was himself arrested he left on his table a most incriminating letter to President Poincaré of France. This letter gave a full description of the meeting of the secret servicemen in the American consulate and was seized upon with glee by the Bolsheviks. Like so many other aspects of this twisted tale the truth will probably never be known. What we do know is that when Marchand returned to France he joined the French Communist Party.

Malkov took Lockhart into a room at Cheka's headquarters in the Lubyanka – formerly the offices of a life insurance company – where he was confronted by a man he knew and had good reason to fear, Jacob Peters, Dzerzhinsky's deputy, a murderer who should have hanged for the shooting of three London policemen in the robbery which led up to the notorious siege of Sidney Street, in 1911. Peters, son of a Latvian farm-labourer, had moved to Riga when he was eighteen and joined the illegal Latvian Social Democrats Labourers Party. He agitated among the sailors of the Baltic Fleet against the war with Japan and in the repression that followed the 1905 uprising was arrested, beaten up and had his fingernails torn out. Eventually released in 1909, Peters fled to England and joined the swarming immigrant community in London's East End where he learned to speak English with a Cockney accent and became a member of several of the groups that plotted anarchy and world revolution in the mean houses of London's slums.

While their immediate schemes were directed against Tsarist Russia rather than Britain the anarchists nevertheless considered themselves justified in carrying out "expropriations" – in plain language, robberies – in London to finance their revolutionary activities. It was in just such an "expropriation" on December 16th, 1910 at a Houndsditch jewellers that a gang of Lettish revolutionaries was surprised by a group of unarmed policemen. The Letts opened fire. Three of the policemen were killed and two were crippled for life while one of the gang was mortally wounded by a bullet fired by one of his comrades.

It was Jacob Peters who killed the policemen, pumping bullets into them even when they were wounded. He was caught some time later after two of the gang had died in the Sidney Street siege during which Churchill, then Home Secretary, had turned out the Scots Guards. But when Peters stood trial he was found innocent due to an inept prosecution and a lax judge who allowed Peters to get away, literally, with murder. He stayed in London after he was set free and married an English girl, May Freeman, but left her behind in 1917 when he returned to Latvia to preach Bolshevism to the Lettish troops. His progress was rapid. Appointed to the Cheka, he dealt with all opposition without mercy.

When Lockhart first arrived in Moscow Peters had tried to cultivate his friendship. In April 1918, after Trotsky had decided to smash the Anarchists – who had been minor but useful allies of Lenin – Peters telephoned Lockhart and invited him to "come for a ride" in a Cheka car. He and Colonel Robins of the American Red Cross were taken to an area which had once been one of the most stylish in Moscow but had been taken over by the Anarchist "Black Guards". It had just been stormed by Cheka units and Lettish riflemen – once again in the thick of the action – and forty Anarchists had been killed and 500 taken prisoner. Lockhart gave a famous account of what he saw that day:

The sight was indescribable. Broken bottles littered the floors, the magnificent ceilings were perforated with bullet holes. Wine stains and human excrement blotched the Aubusson carpets. Priceless pictures had been slashed to strips. The dead still lay where they had fallen. They included officers in guards uniform, students – young boys of twenty – and men who belonged obviously to the criminal class and whom the revolution had released from prison. In the luxurious drawing-room of the House Gracheva, the Anarchists had been surprised in the middle of an orgy. The long table which had supported the feast had been overturned and broken plates, glasses, champagne bottles, made unsavoury islands in a pool of blood and spilt wine. On the floor lay a young woman face downwards. Peters turned her over. Her hair was dishevelled. She had been shot through the neck and the blood had congealed in a sinister purple clump. She could not have been more then twenty. Peters shrugged his shoulders. "Prostitutka," he said. "Perhaps it is for the best."

Now Lockhart was Peters' prisoner. The latter tried to question him, to implicate him in the attempt on Lenin's life. But Lockhart claimed diplomatic immunity and refused to answer any questions. He and Hicks were put in a cell and the next morning he had a visitor:

She was dressed in black. Her hair was black, and her eyes set in a fixed stare, had great black rings under them. Her face was colourless. Her features, strongly Jewish, were unattractive. She might have been any age between 20 and 35. We guessed it was Kaplan. Doubtless the Bolsheviks hoped that she would give us some sign of recognition. Her composure was unnatural. She went to the window and leaning her chin upon her hand looked out into the daylight. And here she remained, motionless, speechless, apparently resigned to her fate. Until presently the sentries came and took her away. She was shot before she knew whether her attempt to alter history had failed or succeeded.

It later emerged that Fanny Kaplan's attempt to kill Lenin was part of a Socialist Revolutionary attempt to destroy the leadership of the Bolshevik Party, but she gave nothing away at her interrogation in the Lubyanka. It was Malkov who was given the task of killing her. He later wrote that he took her, bound hand and foot, to a wood on the outskirts of Moscow, and shot her with his revolver at point blank range. Petrol was poured on her body and a match thrown. Her remains were buried in an unmarked grave.

Peters released Lockhart, probably at Chicherin's insistence. He was turned loose into a frightening world: the Cheka had been rounding up and killing "counter-revolutionaries" ever since the SR revolts of July. Now, with the assassination of Uritsky and the wounding of Lenin all restraint disappeared. The "Red Terror" was launched.

Within hours of Fanny Kaplan's bullets hitting Lenin the Central Executive Committee rushed out a statement signed by Sverdlov, the man who organised the Tsar's murder, declaring that: "Each drop of Lenin's blood must be paid for by the bourgeoisie and the Whites in hundreds of deaths. The interests of the Revolution demand it. The bourgeoisie have no pity, nor have we now."

So Dzerzhinsky went about his grim work, pitiless, remorseless, determined to cleanse Russia of the enemies of Bolshevism. Even before Lenin had been shot he had made his intentions clear. He told a press conference: "We exist on a basis of organised terror . . . We counter the enemies of the Soviet Government with terror and extirpate the criminals on the spot . . . The Cheka is obliged to defend the revolution and crush the enemy, even if its sword sometimes chances to strike the heads of the innocent."

He was supported by Lenin who attacked "narrow minded intelligentsia in the party who sob and fuss" over mistakes made by Dzerzhinsky and his collegium. That collegium included some bestial men and women who not only saw it as their duty to kill but positively enjoyed the torture and the bloodshed. Some 500 people were shot in Petrograd after Uritsky's murder, and over 300 prisoners were done to death in Moscow whereas it is doubtful if more than a handful were involved in the plots. They were shot "for Lenin". Such was the logic of the Red Terror. Peters himself was conducting interrogations on a production line basis at the Lubyanka, signing death warrants by the score and complaining he was sick and tired of sentencing people to be shot. But he never slackened.

The Moscow papers were howling for Lockhart's blood. A letter to the *Bulletin of the Cheka* complained:

The Cheka has still not got away from Petty-Bourgeois ideology, the cursed inheritance of the pre-revolutionary past. Tell us, why didn't you subject Lockhart to the most refined tortures, in order to get information and addresses, of which such a bird must have had very many? Tell us why you permitted him to leave the building of the Cheka "in great confusion" instead of subjecting him to tortures, the very description of which would have filled counter-revolutionaries with cold terror? . . . Enough of being soft; give up this unworthy play on diplomacy. A dangerous scoundrel has been caught. Get out of him what you can and send him to the other world.

Lockhart decided to brazen it out and called on the Russian Foreign Ministry to complain that the stories about him were all lies. Then on September 4th he went back to the Lubyanka to protest over the arrest of Moura Budberg, the latest exhibit in his large collection of mistresses; but she was something more than that. Highly intelligent and charming, she later lived with Maxim Gorky for twelve years and then came to the West and had a tempestuous affair with H. G. Wells. She was also probably a Soviet agent – Guy Burgess, the British diplomat who defected to Russia in 1951, was one of her friends – and it is quite likely that she had been "planted" on Lockhart. She was certainly quickly released by the Cheka and this was not due to Lockhart's protests, for when he arrived at the Lubyanka he was taken to see Peters who promptly re-arrested him.

"You have saved me some trouble," said Peters, "my men have been looking for you for the last hour. I have a warrant for your arrest." This time Lockhart was detained for a month, being interrogated at night by Peters who would urge him to tell the whole truth of the "Lockhart Plot" in his own interests. But the jailer must have realised he would get nowhere for he would suddenly change the conversation and chat about England.

After a time Lockhart was moved to a suite of rooms in the Kremlin where Moura would bring him newspapers – most of them demanding his execution – food and books. On September 19th he noted in his diary, "Lenin better and allowed to work again – a miraculous escape." It was a miracle for Lockhart as well as Lenin for there is little doubt that if Lenin had died, Lockhart would have been shot.

On October 1st he was taken to his flat and told to pack. His exchange for Litvinov had been agreed. The following day he was put on the train for Finland.

Among the party of some thirty British officials on the train was George Hill, who in his book told a somewhat romantic story of how he and his girl helpers escaped from the Cheka: "I could hear not only my own heart pounding but strangely the beat of Evelyn's as well. 'I am glad you let me do this work,' she whispered to me. 'It has been a wonderful experience. We have done good and no matter what happens now it has been worthwhile. Remember that, and don't have any regrets.'"

His secret report, however, was somewhat more prosaic: "Owing to the visible shortage of funds in the near future, and as our expenses were going up daily we felt that the work could not be carried on, and that I was in no way suspected, it would be best to come to life and try to get out of Russia as an official."

However he met resistance in the form of Consul General Wardrop who, found that it was impossible for me to be included in his official staff, as he said he did not dare risk having my name on paper, and thereby endanger the whole of his party. This was after I had explained to him that to the best of my knowledge I was in no way under suspicion, that none of my acts could be traced back to me. Captain Hicks, however, took up the matter, and it was thanks to him after a consultation with his American colleagues, that I was put on Mr. Lockhart's list as an official member (Lockhart was in the Lubyanka). I took off my disguise on the Friday afternoon (Sept 6) and appeared again under my own name and papers.

Hill continued to go about his business, getting Reilly off to Petrograd, sending a woman agent "H 1" off to Sweden "as I considered it no longer safe for her to remain behind" and dismantling his Moscow courier network.

He also noted that Kalamatiano, chief of the American Secret Service, was arrested:

All his documents were found. Lt. Reilly's last flat was raided and his agent "C" arrested at the Kremlin.

From September 3rd all British officers with the exception of one or two panic-stricken consuls, were either imprisoned or besieged in the American Consulate so that it was impossible to get any advice or to confer with anyone. I followed general principles.

I instructed the destruction gangs at Saratov to commence operations. About four trains of material were derailed a week. Preparations were made for the destruction of fuel and oil supplies here, and a section was sent to work on the Voronezh line.

He later learnt that twelve of his couriers had been shot "as had one or two of my independent agents".

Great credit [he wrote] is due to this body of men and to those shot, who could all have saved their lives by giving away the HQ address in Moscow.

This address was never given away, and every man shot showed the spirit of the 1914 Russian officers. I employed them collectively on one or two jobs in Moscow. As two of them came from the Baltic provinces, they were sent there, and finally the remainder were paid two months money and sent to the East, where I hope to pick them up again and resume work.

Hill, grudgingly allowed to join the official party, got as far as Finland where he was ordered to turn round and go back. The purpose of this mission has never been revealed but, probably, it was to continue blowing up bridges and railway tracks. He eventually reached London on the morning of Armistice Day, November 11th, 1918.

Given a DSC for his exploits, he was transferred from Military Intelligence to MI6. In December he and Reilly, who had been awarded (but secretly) the MC, went back to South Russia posing as British businessmen with the task of assessing General Denikin's situation. They were brought back to London after three weeks, long enough for Denikin to award Hill the Order of St George of Tsar Nicholas II. He was sent on one last mission and was in Odessa just before it fell to the Bolsheviks.

Hill was not finished with Russia. In an episode of supreme irony he was sent back to Moscow in 1941 when Britain and Russia were once again allied against German aggression. By then a brigadier, red-faced, bow-legged and bald, "Pop" Hill, the man who hated Bolshevism, was given the task of liaising with the NKVD, successor of the Cheka. While he was there he laid the groundwork for the reopening of the MI6 Moscow station, the first since 1918.

Lockhart arrived in London three weeks earlier than Hill, on October 19th, 1918. He had a long talk with Arthur Balfour and submitted a report for the War Cabinet. It was long and closely argued, pointing out that there were only two alternatives; either to come to an agreement with the Bolsheviks or to overthrow them by a massive application of force. He favoured the latter but the government chose neither and Lockhart disappeared to Scotland on a vice-consul's half pay. His only consolation was an audience with the King who displayed a great understanding of the Russian situation. Later he was to enjoy a distinguished diplomatic career but was to play no further part in Russian affairs although he knew more about it at close hand than any other British official.

Both he and Reilly were sentenced to death in their absence by the Bolsheviks in one of the first of their show trials. The two men drank to their conviction in champagne at the Savoy. One of their colleagues was not so lucky. Xenophon Kalamatiano, the American agent, had to stand trial in Moscow. He was sentenced to death and taken off to the Lubyanka to await execution. Offspring of a marriage between a Greek trader and the daughter of a Russian family with close connections to the Tsar's family, he had been brought up in the United States after his father had died and his mother had remarried. When the Revolution broke out he was selling agricultural machinery in Russia as a representative of the Case Company. The United States government asked him if he would provide information and he accepted in what Secretary of State Robert Lansing later described as a "soft recruitment".

There was nothing soft about his treatment by the Bolsheviks. He was twice taken out of his cell, given a last cigarette, blindfolded and heard the orders given: "Ready . . . Aim . . . Fire." There followed only the clicks of firing pins falling on empty chambers and he was led back to his cell for further interrogation. It is thought that he was saved from death by the direct intervention of Lenin who had no wish to antagonise the United States when the Americans, reluctant participants, were trying to disentangle themselves from the intervention.

Kalamatiano was then virtually forgotten in the Lubyanka where, however, he continued to gather information by tapping into the prisoner's grapevine and observing the prison's routine and his jailer's methods. He was released in 1921 and returned to America where he wrote a long report for the State Department. He then retired into academic life. There is a certain irony in that having survived the firing squad, he died of blood poisoning following a shooting accident.

Reilly was to be shown no mercy by the Bolsheviks. Lured back to Russia in 1924 through his old friend Boris Savinkov in a carefully manipulated plot, Reilly was shot soon after he crossed the Finnish frontier.

Jacob Peters met the end he so richly deserved. In the late spring of 1919 he took Uritsky's place as head of the Petrograd Cheka, then he went to Kiev and on to Turkestan and everywhere he went he justified his nickname of "Executioner". After 1922 he dropped out of sight but it is now known that he concentrated on building up the foreign section of OGPU as the Cheka became known in 1924.*
He may thus be regarded as one of the founders of the modern overseas arm of the KGB. He was last identified setting up a terrorist network in Berlin with the object of assassinating Russian émigrés. Then came the great purges and Peters, like so many thousands of his colleagues, was arrested on Stalin's orders and sent to that "other world" to which he had consigned so many men and women just under two decades earlier.

* The organisation went through a variety of name changes. It became the OGPU in 1924 but had become the NKVD by the time Hill returned to Moscow.

There is a curious footnote to the Peters story. On a number of occasions he asked his English wife to join him in Moscow. But she was reluctant and when she eventually arrived in Moscow with their daughter Mary, she found he had divorced her and remarried. However, she stayed in Moscow and eventually her daughter went to work for the British Embassy. In 1948, Mary like so many others working for foreigners, was whisked away by the secret police and did not reappear until Stalin's Gulag was dismantled in 1956.

There have been many different versions of the "Lockhart Plot". At one extreme there are the full-blooded Russian accusations that the British, French and Americans had conspired to kill Lenin and Trotsky – although Trotsky's name was deleted during the Stalin era – and to have organised the "White Guards risings in Yaroslavl, Rybinsk, Murom and other towns, the mutiny of the Czechoslovak corps in the Povolzhe and in Siberia, and the mutiny of the Left SRs in Moscow and Samara." And at the other there is the sanitised Bruce Lockhart version which claims that all he did was to meet Colonel Berzin and Smidchen and give them a note asking British troops in the front line near Archangel to allow a messenger safe passage to British headquarters.

Hill's secret report contradicts both versions. It shows that Lockhart quite deliberately put Colonel Berzin in touch with Reilly in order to bring about a mutiny among the Lettish troops and the arrest of the Bolshevik leaders. Lockhart may well have divorced himself from the details but he knew what Reilly was about. The report also explicitly states that Hill had organised saboteurs to wreck bridges and railway lines to prevent Bolshevik troops and material getting to the fighting areas. But nowhere is there a hint of British complicity in the murder of Uritsky or the attempted murder of Lenin. It is possible that Reilly may have had knowledge of such a plot through his links with the SRs, but, in view of his movements and actions during the hours covering the shootings, it seems unlikely that he was in any way involved. Moreover, if – as the Bolsheviks claimed – they knew everything about his plans they most certainly would not have allowed Uritsky and Lenin to be shot.

As for Berzin, it seems probable that he – and Smidchen – were indeed working for Dzerzhinsky although Reilly told Hill he thought Berzin was innocent of betraying them. But, as Reilly demonstrated when he was lured back to Russia, he was so blinded by his hatred of Bolshevism he was an easy mark for anybody professing a similar hatred. And this is a trait which, alas, has persisted until very recently in the ranks of the British Security Services.

The immediate, practical result of this imbroglio was the breaking of all official contacts between Russia and the West and the destruction of the British French and American spy networks in Moscow. From now on the Allies had no "assets" in Moscow and communications between the Bolshevik government and the Allies were maintained only by radio.

For the Bolsheviks there were two major benefits. The opponents, within the party, of the Chekists' use of terror were silenced: Dzerzhinsky and Peters were able to kill whoever they wanted without interference. And the hysteria calculatedly whipped up over the affair aroused the nationalism which is never far beneath any Russian's skin and convinced people who were not in favour of Bolshevism that they should now fight against the "foreign threat". The combination of nationalism and fear of the Cheka's executions effectively consolidated Bolshevik power as nothing else could have done.

At the same time the killing of Captain Cromie and the excesses of the Red Terror disgusted many people in the West who were sympathetic to the Bolsheviks and confirmed others in their belief that the Bolsheviks were indeed barbarians, capable of any cruelty. They agreed with Churchill when he told his constituents at Dundee: "Civilisation is being completely extinguished over gigantic areas, while Bolsheviks hop and caper like troops of ferocious baboons amid the ruins of cities and the corpses of their victims." And he, despite welcoming them into the fight against Hitler in the Second World War, never did change his opinion of the Bolsheviks.

CHAPTER 12

"Too Much of a Warlord"
London, November 1918–March 1919

The eleventh of November, 1918, was Armistice Day, the day the war ended, the war which had poisoned the fields of France and Belgium with millions of tons of high explosive and manured those same fields with the bodies of armies of men, the war which changed the world for ever. London, Paris and New York went noisily mad with that excitement that only comes with the bursting of pent-up emotion; bemused men, dazed by the silence which had fallen over the Western Front, wandered like curious tourists across the battlefield in which they had been deadly professionals a few hours before. The first incredulous thought in all their minds was: "I have survived." The second was: "I shall be going home." War correspondent Philip Gibbs wrote: "The fires of hell have been put out."

But not in Russia. As we have seen, the men of the Yorkshire Regiment celebrated Armistice Day – and their own deliverance from shipwreck – in the Orkneys. But they still had to go on to Murmansk to fight the Bolsheviks. Surely, now that the war was over, the Allies would withdraw from Russia? After all they had only intervened in order to save the stocks of war material from the Germans and to re-establish the Eastern Front.

Yes, but, things were different now. The British felt they could not turn their backs on those gallant Russians who had joined their cause in Russia when the Bolsheviks so treacherously made peace with the Germans and who would be doomed if the British withdrew their support. Neither could Britain forsake those states around the periphery of Russia who, after years of oppression, had seized the opportunity offered by the collapse of the Tsarist Empire to declare their independence. If Britain withdrew its support from them they would be gobbled up by the new Bolshevik Empire. And so a whole new set of reasons emerged for the intervention to be maintained.

This metamorphosis was completed in March 1919 when Field-Marshal Sir Henry Wilson, Chief of the Imperial General Staff, wrote in a War Office report: "The enemy of 12 months ago has for the time being ceased to exist and has been replaced by a more tangible but even more insidious foe in the shape of Bolshevism . . ."

Sir Henry, later to be murdered by the IRA, did not get much support from the Allies. However much they might have agreed with his reasoning, none of them had any intention of sinking further into the Russian quagmire with its appalling political and military dangers. The Americans, who had been so reluctant to become involved at all, had already announced that no more men would be sent to north Russia and they remained in Siberia only to make sure the Czechs got away safely and to keep an eye on the Japanese. The French, who had lost a considerable amount of money in loans to the Tsarist government would have been happy to see the Bolsheviks overthrown if only for sound financial reasons, but their army had been trembling on the edge of mutiny for two years and they recognised there was little they could do. The Japanese, unbloodied by the war, were going about their own business. They had never had any intention of setting up a new Eastern Front – in any case a logistic impossibility – and they were not particularly concerned with getting rid of the Bolsheviks as long as they were given a free hand in setting up their trading colonies on the Pacific seaboard. And the Canadians, finally, had given notice of quitting.

There was certainly no support for a new war among the soldiers and sailors of the Allied forces. They had fought the bloodiest war in the history of the world and all they wanted was a return to Civvy Street and a decent job in a "fit country for heroes to live in". Even that most patient and loyal of men, the British Tommy, was beginning to kick at the slowness and unfairness of the demobilisation procedure, and the prospect of further service abroad in a war which he did not understand against people of his own class who had overthrown a despotic tyranny. A favourite music hall song of the period was called "What are we waiting for now?" and it was sung with great gusto by the troops waiting for their release. So great was the discontent that from the beginning of 1919 the British forces became unreliable. There were demonstrations and mutinies in the Army and the Navy.

In January 10,000 men refused orders to return to France at Folkestone. Another 4,000 demonstrated in support at Dover. Senior officers were forced to meet the soldiers' representatives and actually negotiate a settlement. Then no less than 20,000 soldiers refused to obey orders at the transit camp outside Calais and discipline was not restored until two divisions had been recalled from Germany and the mutineers surrounded by machine-guns and fixed bayonets. Even the Guards were not immune. One report refers to an incident when "five battalions of Guardsmen marched from Shoreham to present a list of grievances to the Mayor of Brighton". There were demonstrations in Whitehall and on one occasion the disaffected soldiers besieged cabinet ministers in No. 10 Downing Street. Only the protests of senior officers prevented the Prime Minister, Lloyd George, from receiving a deputation.

The situation was no better in the Royal Navy. On January 13th, 1919, sailors on board HMS *Kilbride* at Milford Haven raised the Red Flag to the masthead and declared: "Half the Navy are on strike and the other half soon will be."

The unrest in the forces was matched in civilian life. Major industrial conflicts put off by the outbreak of war in 1914 erupted as the trade unions, strengthened by the social and political changes brought about by the war, presented far-reaching demands for reform. In August 1918, even before the war had ended, London's Metropolitan Police had gone on strike and throughout 1919 there was an average of 100,000 men on strike every day. The miners and railwaymen had presented demands which threatened to lead to damaging disputes. At the same time the Labour Party had emerged from the war stronger than ever before and Communism was gaining ground, especially in Scotland.

The legend of Red Clydeside was born in the last week of January 1919 when, the war contracts ending and the spectre of mass unemployment looming, the workers struck for a reduction in the working week. There was violence at a mass meeting on January 31st and the next day troops were moved into the city and tanks were parked in the cattle market. The government could only spare two battalions because the strike coincided with the mutiny at Calais. But they were sufficient. The leaders of the strike were tried on charges of incitement to riot. Manny Shinwell, later to become Minister of Defence and a centenarian member of the House of Lords, was sent to prison for five months; Willie Gallacher, later leader of the British Communist Party, received a sentence of three months.

It was natural in this turbulent, revolutionary atmosphere that there should be growing opposition to the intervention in Russia. There had been little objection while it could be presented as necessary for winning the war against Germany but now the cry went up: "Hands off Russia." There was also, even at this early stage, a conscious effort by the Bolsheviks to include Britain in their dream of world revolution. Close links had been forged between

British socialists and Russian émigrés at the turn of the century. Maisky, Litvinov and their colleagues had preached the revolutionary gospel in London. While Britain intervened by means of soldiers in Russia, the Bolsheviks intervened by way of propaganda and agitators in Britain. The prospect of revolution in Britain was frighteningly real in 1919, so real that the War Office sent a confidential questionnaire to the commanding officers of all units to find out if the troops would "remain loyal in the case of a revolution in England".

Among the questions asked were: will the troops in the various areas respond to orders for assistance to preserve the public peace? Will they assist in strike breaking? Will they parade for draft overseas, especially to Russia? Is there any growth of trade unionism? Have any soldiers' councils been formed? Is any agitation from internal or external sources affecting them? The existence of the questionnaire and the details of the questions were revealed in the *Daily Herald*, the irony of which is that the paper was given £75,000 by the Bolshevik government in 1920.

It was in this maelstrom of political and social change and military unrest that the British government had to decide what to do about Russia. On January 3rd, 1919, the *Daily Express* carried a story saying that there were signs that the government was about to launch a "gigantic campaign" against Russia and the newspaper made its position quite plain:

> We are sorry for the Russians, but they must fight it out among themselves. Great Britain is already the policeman of half the world. It will not and cannot be the policeman of all Europe. We want to return to industry and to restore the ravages of war. We want to see our sons home again. In fact, we want peace. The frozen plains of Eastern Europe are not worth the bones of a single British grenadier.

The *Daily Express* had by now come under the control of Max Aitken, newly created Lord Beaverbrook, and at that time was supporting Lloyd George, who had been re-elected Prime Minister on December 14th, 1918. But Beaverbrook was opposed to the intervention and displayed a sympathy for the Bolsheviks which surfaced again in World War II. Nevertheless, it is possible that Beaverbrook, in this instance, was reflecting Lloyd George's own views.

On the other side of the argument there were people in favour of crushing Bolshevism. Sir Henry Wilson had no doubts about what ought to be done. In his War Office paper he detailed the Allied dispositions in Russia and continued:

> At the beginning of 1919, we thus have the possibility of united action from the east and south-east against Bolshevism, while Allied occupation of the Northern ports, of the Black Sea ports and Bessarabia, together with their control of the Baltic closes most of the channels by which the flood of infection can reach Western Europe.
>
> If the Poles can establish and maintain their independence, it only remains to close the gap between this southern frontier and the north of Russia to complete the "Cordon Sanitaire" which will set a limit to Bolshevik expansion, and, by confining it to its own devastated districts, bring about its ultimate collapse.

Then there was Sir George Buchanan, the former Ambassador to Russia, and a friend of the Tsar. He had at first advised the government to follow a policy of conciliation towards the Bolsheviks but when Lenin destroyed the Constituent Assembly and then had the Tsar murdered, Sir George became a fervent advocate of military intervention. At one meeting in Edinburgh in March 1919 he argued that had such crimes as those of which the Bolsheviks had been guilty been committed under the Empire a storm of indignation would have swept through our country; but no, even when innocent children like the little Grand Duchesses had been murdered in cold blood, hardly a voice was raised in condemnation of the crime, while in certain quarters one found a latent sympathy with their murderers.

Lenin, he claimed, aimed at world domination and openly avowed his intention of creating a new Europe in which Bolshevism was to reign supreme . . . To prevent the spread of Bolshevist poison it had been proposed to draw a sanitary cordon round Russia, and to isolate her completely. He personally believed that such a policy would in the end cost us more, and be less effective than were we to strike boldly at the heart of the disease and eradicate the cancer that was sapping Russia's vital energies . . . One could never, as had been suggested, hope to save Russia by economic relief alone. Military assistance and economic relief must go hand in hand if we were to help the Russians to free themselves from Bolshevist tyranny. The task was not as gigantic as was generally supposed for the capture of Moscow and Petrograd would suffice to sound the death knell of Bolshevism . . .

It will be seen from the argument of both Wilson and Buchanan that the reason for intervention had now advanced from saving the stores and re-establishing the Eastern Front, through "we must not desert our allies" to "we must prevent the poison of Bolshevism spreading".

Which brings us to Winston Churchill. He has often been accused of being the architect of intervention, but as his biographer, Martin Gilbert, has quite correctly pointed out, for the first nine months of the intervention Churchill had nothing to do with it. He was Minister of Munitions and until November 1918 was fully occupied with keeping the shells flowing to the Western Front. It was not until 10th January 1919 when he was appointed Minister of War in Lloyd George's newly elected government that he became officially involved with events in Russia.

What is true, is that from that moment on he worked ceaselessly to bring about the destruction of Bolshevism. On the day he was appointed he suggested that Germany should be told that the Allies would have no objection if "she were prepared to organise her Eastern front against the ingress of Bolshevism". Later he proposed that the Bulgarians might "be given a chance to relieve their past misdeeds" by sending troops to fight alongside Denikin.

He went to Paris to try to convince the Allies that they had to adopt a "coherent policy" on Russia and his idea of a coherent policy was a combined effort to support the anti-Bolshevik forces in Russia. But he got nowhere with "Tiger" Clemenceau or Woodrow Wilson.

In London, Lloyd George told Sir George Riddell: "Winston is in Paris. He wants to conduct a war against the Bolsheviks. That would cause a revolution. Our people would not permit it." The Prime Minister had a much better perspective of what the people would or would not permit at that time and Churchill was suspect as a promoter of disastrous military enterprises. The albatross of the British defeat in the Dardanelles was still hanging around his throat, and Lloyd George wanted no Russian albatross to add to his problems. The debate dragged on in the Cabinet until March 4th, 1919. On that day it was decided that all British troops should be evacuated from North Russia by the end of June.

In effect the intervention had been written off. But Churchill was by no means finished. In the House of Commons later that month he spoke of the Bolsheviks who "destroy wherever they exist," but at the same time, "by rolling forward into fertile areas, like the vampire which sucks the blood from his victims, they gain the means of prolonging their own blameful existence."

Later the *Daily Express* warned: "Even with the undertaking given by the government to do the sensible thing, we must watch Mr. Churchill carefully. There is too much of the warlord about him."

However, the first problem in early 1919 was how to get the troops out of Russia without a military disaster. The Allied soldiers were uniformly discontented, many of them were mutinous and open to Bolshevik propaganda while the newly organised Red Army, outnumbering the Allied forces, was showing every sign of belligerency. It was to be no easy matter and, as we shall see, gave rise to further accusations that Churchill was determined to go to war with Soviet Russia.

CHAPTER 13

King George's Secret Orders
Murmansk–Archangel, January–March 1919

While these high-level decisions were being taken in London and Paris early in 1919 the soldiers in North Russia were concerned with more mundane questions: how to stay alive in the grip of a winter so bitter that few of them had ever imagined being so cold and, at the same time, fight off the increasingly bold attacks of the Bolsheviks. In Ironside's Notes on Operations covering this period he wrote: "As the fighting progressed it became more and more evident that the fighting was one of accommodation. If your accommodation was destroyed even to the extent of breaking your windows, you had to evacuate your position."

He was furious with the militant teetotallers in Britain who were waging a campaign against the supply of a rum ration to the troops: "I wish I could have had some of the placid prohibitionists on sentry-go for an hour in 72 degrees of frost and they would have changed their opinions as to whether it should be issued or not."

The Shackleton cold weather gear worked extremely well, except for the hated boots, but frostbite was commonplace. It seized hold in the time it took a soldier to take off his padded mittens to light his pipe. General Maynard suffered from it when pinning medals on three of his men. His fingers became so numb he did not notice he had driven the pin of a medal deep into his own finger. Men who were caught outside without shelter lost fingers and toes and those who fell asleep in the open rarely woke up. Journeys were planned in short stages from blockhouse to blockhouse and the winter's fighting depended on these wooden forts. They were built in groups of three with each one covered by the machine-guns of the others. They were each armed with an automatic weapon and seven men with rifles and were surrounded by barbed wire. Larger blockhouses holding two Vickers guns and their crews gave support to each group of three. They were quick to build. Moss rammed between the logs kept out the arctic wind and they were kept warm by big stoves on which the men slept, Russian-style.

Not all Maynard's men were so lucky. Some of the accommodation that was appropriated was unsuited to this sort of warfare, being heated by makeshift stoves that often caught fire and destroyed the buildings. One ship that brought over the prefabricated parts of Nissen huts turned up with only certain sections, the others only arriving a month later.

Among the men who suffered most were the fitters and mechanics of the Royal Air Force. The engines of their aircraft froze despite being heated day and night by means of flameless lamps and covers. Five gallons of hot water would be poured through the cooling system to take the chill off the metal, but often the drain cock froze solid after two gallons had passed through. Air intake pipes froze. Oil froze in the throttle joints. Every lubricant tried failed until, finally, the joints and fulcrums were cleaned and left dry. The bracing wires which held wings taut were liable to snap because the intense cold crystallised the metal wire. It was impossible for the men to handle metal with their bare hands because it would stick to their skin and tear it away. Bomb release gear froze during flights and in most cases the 20 lb bombs had to be carried in the observer's seat and dropped over the side by hand.

The cold also had an effect on guns and ammunition, considerably shortening the range of shells. The 18-pounder guns, for example, had to be ranged at 3,750 yards to obtain a range of 2,000 yards at temperatures of $-10°F$. The French 75 mm cannon which performed so brilliantly on the Western Front did not operate at all well in Arctic conditions. Rifle grenades often failed to explode in deep snow and the moving parts of machine-guns froze solid. Major T. Barratt of the Royal Army Ordnance Corps with his tongue firmly in his cheek made this report: "I am informed that a mixture of spirit (e.g. Vodka) has occasionally been used in the Russian machine-guns but that it frequently disappeared. The mixture is also of course extremely volatile."

In these circumstances the French and Italian skiers and the Canadians with experience of living in frozen forests were invaluable. Attempts were made to teach British troops to use skis and snowshoes but in Maynard's command results occasioned more despair than hope while Ironside commented with some bitterness: "We made plans to turn out hundreds of men on skis and snowshoes but none of the winter equipment arrived until after it was possible to use it . . . Had we been opposed to bodies of good skiers of even one quarter our numbers we must have been turned out of the country. Mobility when shown by either side met with instant success."

It was in these conditions that Ironside set out just before Christmas by pony sleigh to visit his scattered forces. At Seletskoe, where the left wing of the Railway Force had its headquarters, he sent a message ordering Sturdy there. When Sturdy arrived he found the British lieutenant-colonel in charge of the detachment "on the verge of the D.T.s" and with no arrangements made for an attack due to be made along the railway in a few days' time.

> I promptly got the detachment doctor to take the Lt. Col. sick, made out operations orders and mobilised all the women and children to take up sleigh loads of small arms ammunition and shells to the two wings of the detachment.
> The attack eventually failed, the USA troops on the right wing suffering about 30 casualties without advancing. The US head-quarters later complained that British GHQ always put the Americans in the most dangerous positions. The detachment MO (an American himself) reported that the wounds were all self-inflicted in hands and feet.

Ironside's judgement on this offensive was that "it failed utterly through the drunkenness of a chief column commander and the consequent disorganisation".

The Allied force was now uncomfortably exposed with extensive gaps between the strongpoints along the railway and the river. The White Russians and Americans at Shenkursk on the River Vaga were especially vulnerable. They were 180 miles from Archangel, stuck out in the middle of nowhere, surrounded by forest and frozen swamp. Ironside was later to admit that they "were too far advanced, but it was decided for political reasons to maintain them there during the winter".

On January 19th the Bolsheviks took advantage of this situation and launched a strong attack on Shenkursk, driving the defenders out and forcing them into a hurried retreat of some seventy miles. The Russian troops fighting alongside the Americans proved useless with one company refusing to obey orders to attack the advancing Bolsheviks. Frank Douma made terse notes in his diary:

> January 25 – Shenkursk fell today. The advance party came in this noon. They had 50 casualties. Troops are continually passing here in retreat. 8,000 Bolos attack 2,000 allies. The allies are leaving everything. January 26 – We have joined in the retreat. Set out at 1.00 p.m. and marched 7 versts [4½ miles] towards the Bolos. Acted as a rear guard as the others evacuated. We met the Bolos at 3.00 p.m. Several of the men are quite badly wounded. We stayed in skirmish until 9.00 p.m. and then marched back to

Shlgovari. Everyone had left the town. All the kit bags and personal belongings had been ransacked. All the souvenirs which I had collected had been taken away. All my personal belongings including a dress uniform, shoes, extra razor and 24 bars of soap. I shall miss the soap more than anything else. We started to hike in retreat at 10.00 p.m. We had lost everything except the clothes we had on. We had to hike in our stockings because the road was too slippery for Shackleton boots. The Cossacks burned the town after we left it. We hiked till 7.00 a.m. We arrived at Kitsa all in.

This was a serious setback for Ironside. The Allies' morale slumped and the Bolshevik advance threatened to outflank their positions on both the river and railway fronts.

Ironside appealed yet again to the War Office for reinforcements, an appeal to which it reacted by ordering Maynard to send two infantry battalions and a machine-gun company to Ironside's assistance. Maynard was not well pleased with this order as his force was rapidly shrinking. But there was nothing he could do about it except arrange the transfer of the men and their equipment in good order from his advanced base at Soroka to Onega, 150 miles to the east where Ironside's officers would take over the arrangements.

It was no easy task. The White Sea was frozen, there was no road from Soroka to Onega, little overnight shelter and there was no fodder on the route for reindeer, the best form of transport. Maynard was able to put 300 infantrymen and half the machine-gun company on an icebreaker making its last run to Archangel from Murmansk until the spring. The rest of the men, numbering some 2,000, were first taken down to Soroka by train. Dog teams were harnessed to ambulance sledges. Every available horse was requisitioned to carry supplies and the men set out across the bitter landscape, a white world where frozen trees burst with cracks like rifle shots. They marched in parties of up to 300 on fixed stages and the whole movement was carefully controlled. The men arrived at Onega with only a few cases of frostbite. But it was no picnic and it was especially unfortunate that the only infantrymen Maynard had to send Ironside were those same men of the Yorkshire Regiment who had suffered such hardships on the voyage to Murmansk and had then been employed in the back-breaking and soul-destroying work of labouring on their arrival there.

They were rushed directly to the front, but they refused to fight and Ironside, far from having a reinforcement of fresh soldiers, had a full-scale mutiny by surly, worn out men on his hands. He later rationalised their behaviour by arguing that their ill-discipline arose chiefly "from their long inaction at Murmansk and the sudden change from peace to war conditions". Whatever the reason he acted with his customary brisk decisiveness and put the ringleaders on trial. Two sergeants who "had spent the war in the Pay Corps" were sentenced to death by firing squad. But Ironside never had the sentence carried out because, as he explained in his book, *Archangel 1918–1919*, "King George had issued secret orders stipulating that no death sentences were to be inflicted upon British personnel after the Armistice. The sentences were therefore commuted to life imprisonment."*

The Yorkshires were not the only Allied troops who wanted to "soldier no more". Sergeant Silver Parrish and his platoon had been in the thick of the fighting ever since they landed at Archangel. He received a scalp wound in January and his diary shows that he was involved in close quarter fighting throughout January and February. On March 4th he drew up a resolution to "request why we are fighting the Bolos and why we haven't any big guns and why the English run us and why we haven't enough to eat and why our men can't get proper medical attention and some mail".

Everyone in the platoon signed, but "someone squealed" and Parrish was brought up before the Colonel who read the articles of war to him and pointed out where his offence was punishable by death.

However, fourteen days later, Parrish was awarded a British decoration for gallantry, the Military Medal. Ironside's citation read: "This NCO has shown exceptional initiative and good judgement in action and as a patrol leader his courage and personality have been valuable in keeping up the spirits of the company. His sense of responsibility and ability at sizing up situations have been of immense value to the company."

Parrish led a somewhat schizophrenic life from then on, taking pride in being a good and brave soldier but at the same time recording in his diary his sympathy for the people he was fighting against . . .

the way these kids and women dress would make you laugh if you saw it on the stage. But to see it here only prompts sympathy (in the heart of a real man) and loathing for a clique of blood-sucking, power-loving, capitalistic, lying, thieving, murdering, tsarist army officials who keep their people in this ignorance and

* There is no reference to these orders in the Royal Archives at Windsor Castle.

poverty . . . after being up here fighting these people I will be ashamed to look a union man in the face . . . The majority of the people here are in sympathy with the Bolo and I don't blame them, in fact I am 9/10 Bolo myself and they all call me the Bolo Leader and my platoon the Bolo platoon . . .

Clearly, not the sort of attitudes which allow a commanding officer to sleep easy.

Worse was to follow for Ironside. On March 16th the Bolsheviks opened an offensive against the railway front, attacking through the deep snow on sleighs. Ironside was harshly critical of the performance at Bolshoi Ozerke of the French Foreign Legion and 21st Colonial Battalion who "did not put up much resistance". When he went to find out what was happening, "I found myself obliged to relieve the French command at Obozerskaya as they were not equal to the occasion and took personal command until the arrival of Brigadier-General Turner from England ten days later."

The enemy's success, he said, was entirely due to the state of the French troops who were thoroughly disaffected and the weakness of the French command which had never really taken hold of the men. Ironside was in no doubt that if the Bolsheviks had pressed on with their attacks they "could have tumbled in our whole line" with very serious consequences for the forces covering Archangel.

Sturdy, who had displeased one of his superiors by being too free with his criticism of the conduct of operations, had been sent to the Onega front as a punishment but found himself enjoying his freedom from desk work:

I have been absolutely cut off from everywhere. Archangel seems as far away as England . . . I live like a savage, just roll up in a blanket on the floor at night at any old village I happen to be at, sometimes with a peasant and his wife in the same room, together with my Russian orderly, always with countless bugs. Generally travelling by sleigh from village to village and wading about in a couple of feet of snow. But I wouldn't have missed these months in the country for anything. I have got to know more about the Russians in that time than one could in years of town life. I have kept wonderfully fit and you would never guess I wasn't graded A1 . . .

Sturdy took part in the fighting at Bolshoi Ozerke and was awarded the 3rd Class Order of St Anne by the Russians – "they are handing them out by the dozen . . ." But he had to give up the country life when Ironside demanded his recall to headquarters where he helped draft the general's despatches and reports.

By this time a new problem had emerged for Ironside; an active Bolshevik underground operating in Archangel itself. It was small, numbering only about twenty militants, but effective. Its head was twenty-four-year-old Makar Boyov, who had lived briefly in the United States and spoke English.

Using this background and posing as a businessman willing to work with the Allies he struck up acquaintance with some American officers. Soviet accounts say that in January 1919 he wanted to mount a terror campaign against the British, murdering officers, and planting bombs in military installations. But other members of the underground insisted that they should confine their activities to propaganda, probably because it was safer.

Boyov's chief helper was his girlfriend Anna Matison, who worked as a waitress in the British Officers' Mess. An orphan, she was brought up in Latvia where she had learned English. Between them they distributed leaflets aimed at local workers, urging them to leave Archangel and join the Red Army in the forest. They also produced pamphlets written in English aimed at causing disaffection among the troops. One of them was headed "Why don't you return home?" and read:

> To the American and British soldiers. Comrades. The war is over, why are you not returning home? . . . Don't you want to mingle with your loved ones again? Do you really desire to bleed and die in order that capitalism may continue? . . .
>
> Form Soldiers Councils in each regiment and demand of your governments, demand of your officers to be sent home. Refuse to shoot our fellow workers in Russia. Refuse to crush our Workers Revolution.
>
> The Group of English speaking Communists.

These leaflets were stuck on doors and fences and tossed over factory walls. Some were distributed in churches. Soldiers would sometimes find them under their pillows. Others were slipped into packets of cigarettes.

Boyov and Matison also ran off reports in English of Red Army successes on other fronts. They acquired news for these reports through the Communist wireless operator of a hydrographic ship, the *Taimir*, which, curiously, was still carrying out research in the Barents Sea. Their efforts culminated in producing an underground newspaper, *The Call*. Matison's job was to put this in the officers' toilets. But, eventually, Boyov fell into a trap set for him by British counter-intelligence. Lured to a house where he believed he would meet a British contact, he fought it out for ten minutes before shooting himself.

Despite the attacks on his positions, the disaffection of considerable elements in his forces, and the campaign of subversion mounted in Archangel, Ironside was able, due largely to his own vigorous action, to contain the Bolshevik offensive and it petered out in the middle of April with the loss of some 2,000 Red soldiers.

While Ironside was enduring this torrid episode Maynard pushed along the Murmansk railway line. Already established at Soroka, he planned to drive the Bolsheviks down the line to Segezha thus securing his positions and opening up some 3,000 square miles of territory in which the White Russians could prospect for recruits. He launched the offensive on February 15th although with only 600 men it hardly deserved the description of offensive. The composition of the force would have caused Ironside misgivings for it contained only 50 British regulars in machine-gun and mortar teams. The rest were Canadians, French, Russians, Karelians and Serbs. But Maynard thought better of his Allies than did Ironside and he sent them about their business with his usual optimism. He needed to be optimistic because his men, split into four columns, were immediately attacked not by the enemy but by appalling weather. The temperature dropped to minus forty degrees fahrenheit and a knife-like wind drove snow squalls at the men as they struggled through the soft snow on skis and snowshoes. Two of the columns failed to reach their objectives but another, using sledges, covered 100 miles in sixteen hours and attacked Segezha under the cover of machine-gun and trench mortar fire.

Segezha fell with half its garrison killed. White Russian machine-gunners broke the railway line and ambushed a train bringing up Bolshevik reinforcements from the south. They perpetrated a dreadful slaughter and the train, with one set of wheels derailed and the engine riddled with bullets, steamed slowly away with its carriages dripping blood.

However, the Bolsheviks returned to the fight the following day, pushing forward infantry supported by cannon fire from an armoured train but the attack broke down against accurate fire from positions prepared overnight by Maynard's men.

Imagine the scene: a train slung round with armour, dimly seen among the snow squalls, belching shells which explode with a flash and a roar as men plod through the deep snow, their rifles held high, only to be mown down by the chattering machine-guns. Then when it is over and the survivors drag their wounded back to the train and it makes off into the grey distance, the snow falls again to cover the already frozen dead and soon the battlefield is white and silent as if nothing had ever happened there.

It was a neat little victory for Maynard. But he, like Ironside, was having trouble with his troops. The Karelians, who lived along the Finnish border, wanted to set up their own state and the twists and turns of politics had made the Red Finns untrustworthy. They had protected Murmansk against the White Finns and the Germans but now their enemy had been transmogrified into the Bolsheviks whose ideals and ambitions they supported. Not only could they not be trusted, care had to be taken that they did not decamp to mount an attack on the White Finns in their homeland.

The invaluable French ski troops who had performed well in the capture of Segezha had also become disaffected, asserting that they had not been sent out to Russia to fight. Maynard was forced to withdraw the whole company of 200 men from the front line. He pointed out in his memoirs that these were not the only Allied troops to go wrong, but refusing "to wash soiled linen before even a limited public, and still less to furnish it with a detailed laundry list . . . I will therefore confine myself to the general statement that, before the undertaking reached its close, there were units of nearly every nationality upon which I could not rely with absolute confidence."

Maynard who was far from being one of the unfeeling officers whose behaviour precipitates mutiny, sought to explain but not excuse his men's behaviour in a despatch to the War Office:

Owing to the extreme shortage of civilian labour, I have been compelled to employ a great proportion of them [the troops] on permanent working and building parties and on similar tasks of an uncongenial nature; their accommodation has not always been as suitable as I could have wished; the climate is severe, and trying even to the most healthy; leave to England is necessarily rare; local amusements are confined to such as we are able to provide; any movement of troops by rail is attended by great discomfort, owing to the shortage of suitable rolling stock. And, during the winter, transport by sea and road entails unusual hardships. Moreover my men have been surrounded for many months by an atmosphere of disorder, disaffection, and lawlessness, which cannot but affect adversely even the best-disciplined troops.

Maynard was undoubtedly correct in his diagnosis of the problem. But there was little he could do about it and we shall see just how seriously the disaffection grew and how close it came to causing a terrible tragedy.*

It was in these unpromising military circumstances that Ironside and Maynard were warned to prepare to evacuate North Russia by the end of the summer of 1919.

---

* He also had trouble with Bolshevik agitators in Murmansk. They were more violent than Boyov and his friends in Archangel and in January they murdered two British officers. His lengthening lines of communication also provided saboteurs with the opportunity to burn bridges and derail trains.

CHAPTER 14

"Shameful, Illegitimate Little War"
London–Archangel, April–June 1919

As seen from London the problem was twofold; how to prevent the
Bolsheviks turning the evacuation into a debacle and how to give
the British-supported North Russian government the time and
space it needed to establish itself. The War Office therefore proposed that the expeditionary force should undertake three tasks
before it was withdrawn. The first was to deliver sharp attacks on
both the Murmansk and Archangel sectors in order to dissuade the
Bolsheviks from interfering with the preparations for evacuation.
The second was to effect a proper union between the North Russian
forces and the right wing of Admiral Kolchak's Siberian Army.
Small parties had made contact between the two armies but what
was needed was the occupation of the river and rail junction at
Kotlas on the Dvina so that a unified front could be organized.
Finally the War Office proposed that a volunteer force of British
officers and NCOs should be formed to "organise, instruct and lead
Russian units".

This plan demanded large scale reinforcements. But the Army
had none to spare. Drained by demobilisation and the need to police
an increasingly restive Empire, it could scarcely find enough troops
to cope with the "Troubles" in Ireland. It was decided therefore to
appeal for volunteers. First of all the "reputable" press was enlisted
to stress the dangers and hardships being faced by our men in
Russia. *The Times* dutifully argued: "We shall, therefore, want
more men for Northern Russia, and regrettable though this need of
reinforcement is, we hope that it will be accepted without opposition." Other newspapers were less convinced, the *Daily Herald*
attacking "The gambler of Gallipoli, Winston Churchill," and his
"new war in Russia, to back reaction in the persons of Kolchak and
Denikin".

In Archangel Sturdy took a more relaxed view. He wrote to his
sister in some surprise because the newspapers were saying that
their situation was similar to that of the doomed British defenders
of Kut el-Amara on the Tigris who had been starved into submis-

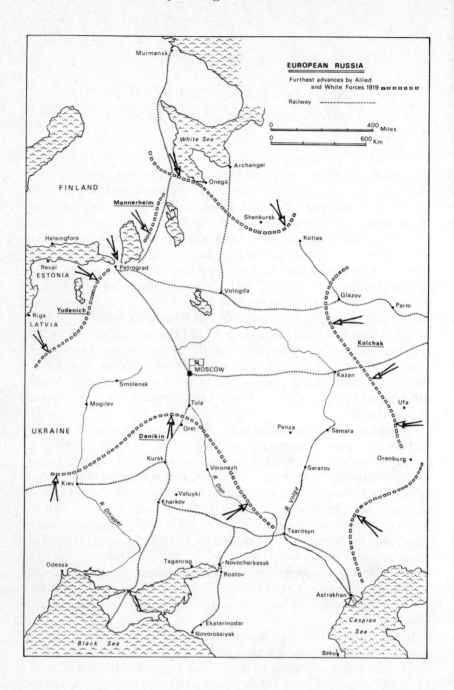

EUROPEAN RUSSIA

Furthest advances by Allied
and White Forces 1919 □□□□□□

Railway ·······

0   400 Miles

0   600 Km

Murmansk

White Sea

Archangel

Onega

FINLAND

Mannerheim

Shenkursk

Kotlas

Helsingfors

Reval

ESTONIA

Petrograd

Vologda

Glazov

Perm

Riga

LATVIA

Yudenich

Kolchak

Kazan

MOSCOW

Smolensk

Ufa

Mogilev

Tula

UKRAINE

Orel

Penza

Samara

Denikin

Kursk

Orenburg

Voronezh

Saratov

R. Don

R. Volga

Kiev

R. Dnieper

Valuyki

Kharkov

Tsaritsyn

Odessa

Taganrog

Novocherkassk

Rostov

Astrakhan

Caspian Sea

Ekaterinodar

Novorossiysk

Black Sea

Baku

196

sion by the Turks in 1916. To prove that this was not so he sent home a copy of the menu for a Mess night held on May 2nd:

Hors D'Oeuvres

– – –

Crème Gibier

– – –

Saumon
Sauce Hollandaise

– – –

Cotelettes de Veau
Petits Pois
Pommes

– – –

Glace Panachée
Café

– – –

And, he added, "I haven't got the programme of music with me, but we also had an excellent trio."

It was not however "base wallahs" like Sturdy who were having a rough time, but the infantrymen who had endured the long hard winter on basic rations. It was to them that Churchill addressed an appeal: "You are not forgotten. Your safety and well-being, on the contrary, is one of the main anxieties of the War Office, and we are determined to do everything in our power to bring you safely home . . . Only a few more months of resolute and faithful service against this ferocious enemy and your task will have been discharged. Carry on like Britons fighting for dear life and dearer honour, and set an example in these difficult circumstances to the troops of every other country. Reinforcement and relief are on the way . . ."

The ground prepared, the recruiting posters went up and volunteers were invited to join the Russian Relief Force to enable the hard-pressed men of the North Russian Expeditionary Force to return safely home. There was a great deal of purple patriotic writing about the scenes in the recruiting offices with men only recently released from the Army after the dangers and rigours of the Great War queuing up to go to the rescue of their comardes in arms. The *Daily Mail* reported: "The fighting spirit of the old army is aflame. Yesterday hundreds of veterans of the Great War were crowding Great Scotland Yard, Whitehall, to join the North Russian Relief Force." Former Colonels joined up in the ranks and some men were turned away in tears because they were no longer fit

enough to fight. Major Allfrey of the Royal Fusiliers recorded the
scene at Park Royal depot on May 5th, 1919. "Recruits are still
pouring in dressed in civilian clothes with medal ribbons on their
waistcoats and red handkerchieves round their necks. They have all
seen previous service and look the most ideal material from which
to form a battalion. The officers too are excellent, several Colonels
and seconds-in-command having thrown up their appointments to
command companies."

There were indeed many men who volunteered for patriotic
reasons but there were also many others, officers among them, who
had found that post-war England was not a "fit country for
heroes". They were unemployed, with no prospect of getting jobs
and would rather rejoin the Army than suffer the hardships and
indignity of such bleak prospects in civilian life. And, as Allfrey was
quickly to find out, they included a number of hard cases and
misfits.

Eventually a force of eight thousand men was raised, both
volunteers and some regular units. It was divided into two brigades
commanded by two fiery young brigadiers, G. W. St George
Grogan, VC, CB, CMG, DSO, and L. W. de V. Sadleir-Jackson,
CB, CMG, DSO. Two battalions of the Royal Fusiliers, the 45th
and 46th, were to serve in Sadleir-Jackson's Brigade. They boarded
the SS *Porto* at Newcastle on May 27th and there was trouble
immediately, for when the men were refused permission to go
ashore "to buy cigarettes" about forty of them rushed the gangway.
They were talked back and Allfrey had some sympathy with them:
"How the War Office have the audacity to put 1,400 men alongside
an amusing town and order them not to go ashore I'm blowed if I
know."

They sailed the next day. According to Allfrey it was quite a
performance:

> Great send off. People cheering. Ships' sirens, and drunken
> deserters running along quay as ship drew away. Taken off in
> launch. One fell into sea and had to be rescued. Commanding
> officer created sensation by personally escorting three very drunk
> men of D Company to the Guard Room. Every now and then he
> gave them a great clout on the head. One hung over the side and
> said he would drop off if he was not let go. Grabbed and put in
> irons.

The voyage was enlivened by the Regimental Sergeant-Major
getting very drunk and trying to murder the Lewis Gun Company

Sergeant-Major. "Luckily," wrote Allfrey, "the attempt was not successful although he put a bullet into the pillow of the man he tried to do in." However, apart from running aground in the Dvina, Sadleir-Jackson's Brigade reached Archangel safely on June 6th.

Grogan's men had already reached Archangel, having sailed on the SS *Stephen* from Tilbury on May 13th. One of their first duties had been to celebrate the King's Birthday Parade with a service in the cathedral and a ceremonial march past. The next day the 2nd Hampshires, a regular battalion who formed part of Grogan's Brigade, were loaded onto barges and sent up to Bereznik wearing the insignia of the Relief Force on their arms: a white star on a black background.

The convoy was commanded by Lieutenant-Colonel John Sherwood Kelly, VC, DSO, CMG, a man with a brilliant record as a fighting soldier. The *Daily Express* later said of him:

> He fought in Matabeleland and Somaliland and was so anxious to go to the front in the recent war that he enlisted as a private under an assumed name. He was promoted on the field during the second battle of Ypres, went to Gallipoli in 1915 and returned in the battle of the Somme.
>
> He won the VC after the Cambrai battle in 1917 by his skill and gallantry in covering the passage of a canal by his battalion of Inniskilling Fusiliers. He led the first company of the battalion over the canal then, under heavy fire, reconnoitred the enemy's position, and when his left flank was held up, brought a Lewis gun into position to cover the advance through the wire.
>
> He wears five wound stripes and was seven times mentioned in despatches.

The barges arrived at Bereznik at noon on June 5th and by teatime the Hampshires, along with the 238th French Mortar Battery and half a company of the 8th Battalion of the Machine-Gun Corps, had been sent further up river to relieve the River Column in the line at Kurgomen and Tulgas. This much fought over village of Tulgas had been recaptured by the Americans on May 18th after being handed over to the Bolsheviks on April 25th by the 2nd Battalion of the 3rd North Russian Regiment which had mutinied and gone over to the Reds.

The doughboys of the 339th Infantry were delighted to see the Hampshires arrive. Silver Parrish's company had already gone up river to Archangel but had run aground where it stayed for three days, passing the time by playing baseball on the offending sand-bank. But Frank Douma's company had been in action right up until June 2nd when it captured a Bolshevik patrol of twenty-five men. Douma recorded that the Hampshires took over their positions at 9.30 on June 6th. Two days later they were back at Archangel camped in tents at Point Economy.

"There are millions of mosquitos around," wrote Douma. "We saw autos, street cars and trains today, the first time in nine months. We also saw civilised girls for the first time, regular dresses and silk stockings. It surely seemed good. I am going to try to date up some of them as soon as possible and try to get a little loving. We must surely be on our way home by now."

Indeed they were. On June 14th they boarded the *Menominee* and sailed first to Brest and then, on July 12th, arrived in Boston. The "Polar Bears", as they called themselves, had lost 244 dead in Russia and despite Ironside's view of their fighting ability had fought as well as any of the Allied contingents and better than most. Strangely, only the division's home town of Detroit gave them any sort of welcome. They received no campaign medals and to this day most Americans do not know that an American expeditionary force fought the Bolsheviks on Russian soil. President Nixon seemed unaware of this piece of history when, in 1972 while on a visit to Russia, he appeared on television and told the Russians: "Most important of all, we have never fought one another in war." And twelve years later President Reagan suffered an attack of the same historical blindness in his State of the Union message, when, referring to the United States and Russia, he made a similar comment: "Our sons and daughters have never fought each other in war."

It seemed that once the "Polar Bears" had returned home, America's role in the intervention was pushed into the national subconscious. But the men who took part in it, however unwillingly, never forgot. John Cudahy of the Wisconsin meat packing family who, as a lieutenant, had taken part in the capture of Tulgas gave the name of the village to his daughter. He was later President Roosevelt's Minister to Ireland and Ambassador to Poland and Belgium and published his account of *Archangel: America's War Against Russia* in 1924. It was, he said a "mad man's war" and a "shameful, illegitimate little war".

But that was all in the future. With both the Canadians and the Americans gone Archangel became an almost entirely British "stunt". The Hampshires settled into the positions vacated by the Polar Bears and were thankful that they had not arrived in winter.

There was almost no night, the river had thawed, gunboats had made their way upstream and the RAF could give virtually twenty four hour cover to the soldiers. But it was the infantry who, as usual, suffered. They were plagued by clouds of mosquitoes and tiny stinging black flies and the swamps, passable when they were frozen, were now death traps of black mud. Most units lost men drowned.

By June 12th it seemed that the gallant Sherwood Kelly had slipped easily back into his fighting groove. The Hampshires' War Diary for that day records: "The C.O. took out No. One Platoon of W Company and ran into a Bolo patrol in a neutral village. Two of the enemy were killed and one wounded. The C.O. killed one man in personal conflict."

Then again, on June 16th: "The C.O. took out 9 Platoon on an all day reconnaissance of the route to Troitskoye. Marched 35 miles in 17 hours." Sherwood Kelly received a letter from Grogan which read:

> The GOC wishes personally to thank you on the very gallant way you led the patrol on June 13, 1919 which resulted in you killing three of the enemy at great personal risk to yourself.
>
> The information obtained by you was very valuable and the result of your encounter cannot but increase the moral [*sic*] of our men.

Ironside badly needed aggressive soldiering to boost the men's morale for the locally recruited Russian soldiers were showing themselves to be ever more prone to mutiny and the murder of their officers.

On May 14th the 1st Company of the 8th North Russian Regiment on the Pinega front had refused to embark to go up river and killed two of their officers. Ironside telegraphed Churchill: "I regret to report I had to shoot 15 but the companies are back at duty . . ." In fact the 2nd Company had to be disarmed and were made into labour troops.

Even more serious was the news that reached London on June 17th, from Siberia. The Czech General Gajda, commanding Kolchak's Western army which was supposed to link with Ironside's men at Kotlas, had been stopped in his tracks by an inferior force of Bolsheviks. The news of this defeat added to the growing feeling in London that no good would come of the plan to push British troops further into the Russian morass. Lloyd George in particular was anxious that Ironside should not get himself so involved that it would need yet more troops to get him out of trouble.

On July 2nd Allfrey made an interesting entry in his diary:

The C.O. was over to see Ironside today . . . Ironside told the C.O. that he had received a telegram from England to suspend all hostilities out here at once. This telegram merely makes Ironside smile, as he has no more intention of ceasing hostilities than the man in the moon, nor is it possible to do so, for the British force out here is involved pretty deeply in the operation and there is nothing between the Bolsheviks and thousands of Russians but us, and they would all be murdered at once if we withdrew. It is not known why the telegram was sent, but it is pretty certain it is, as usual, just a weak government pandering to the Labour people.

The rumour is that the coal miners have threatened that unless the British force in Russia is home within forty days they will all come out on strike on the grounds that we are interfering with the rights and freedoms of the Russian people. In other words they too are Bolsheviks and wish to support the Bolshevik movement . . .

What the War Office files in fact reveal is that Ironside had telegraphed on June 19th to say that he had no intention "of allowing British forces to get into such a position that they would require relief or that they could not withdraw". Moreover he made it plain that he thought the Kotlas operation could not be carried out if "the enemy puts up a stubborn resistance".

Nevertheless, the following day he set the first part of his Kotlas plan moving. Apart from fresh troops he now also had some excellent equipment. His fleet on the Dvina had been reinforced by Monitors and coastal motor boats. He was supported from the air by DH9 bombers and the very latest in fighters, the Sopwith Snipe, successor to the famous Camel. It was while he was flying one of these new aircraft that Kazakov, Russian ace and proud wearer of the DSO, MC, and DFC, met his death. He had flown brilliantly in support of Ironside's forces and it is claimed that he shot down fifteen enemy planes. This is somewhat doubtful because very few Bolshevik planes ventured into the skies of North Russia, but he certainly snapped up those of his former colleagues who crossed his path in aircraft now bearing the Red Star, the insignia of the infant Bolshevik Air Force. He took off one day soon after he heard that the British were going to withdraw, news which deeply affected him, started a low level loop, stalled his engine and went straight into the ground. Even the icon of St Nicholas which he always carried on his instrument panel could not save him.

Kazakov's death had little effect on the outcome of the fighting because the British had complete control of the air, and using the close co-operation tactics developed by the Camel squadrons in the last months of the war on the Western Front, gave the ground and naval forces first class support. But the Russian ace had been an inspirational leader of men, the sort of officer so desperately needed by the White Russians to offset the behaviour of those counter-revolutionaries who thought only in terms of a return to the ancient regime. Aloof, stern, intensely religious, he was a sort of Solzhenitsyn of his time and his death, especially the manner of it, dealt a severe blow to the morale of the White cause.

Another weapon now made available to Ironside was poison gas. This may sound horrific today but it must be remembered that ever since the Germans first used a lethal form of gas on the Western Front on April 23rd, 1915, it had been accepted by both sides as part of their armoury of weapons. In his *History of the First World War* Liddell Hart wrote: "The chlorine gas originally used was undeniably cruel, but no worse than the frequent effect of shell or bayonet, and when it was succeeded by improved forms of gas both experience and tactics proved it the least inhumane of modern weapons." And the only qualm felt at the War Office about the use of gas against the Bolsheviks was that the deployment of a new type developed too late for use on the Western Front might give away its secrets to potential enemies.

Churchill, who was initially against its use solely for this reason, eventually agreed and when, on May 29th, 1919, a Labour MP queried its employment in Russia, he replied: "I do not understand why, if they use poison gas, they should object to having it used against them." There are in fact no records of the Bolsheviks ever using poison gas in this conflict although there were at least two reports of gas shells being captured from the Red Army, and the Russian Army had undeniably acquired experience of gas warfare on the Eastern Front.

The War Office sent a telegram to Ironside advising caution: "The invention is very secret, and of course, once used, the secret would be divulged. It is only intended that this weapon should be used if specially necessary." And with that proviso they sent out nineteen Gas Officers, equipped with the new gas in cylinders and the "Smoke Generator No. 1, Mark 1".

It would appear from Sturdy's pencilled draft of Ironside's

Report on Operations covering the period from the arrival of the Relief Force (May 27th, 1919) to the final date of evacuation (September 27th, 1919) that Ironside judged its use to be "specially necessary" immediately it arrived. However, the gas experts were to find that conditions in North Russia were very different to those in France for, Ironside reported: "It was found impossible to empty the gas by ordinary hand discharge owing to the lack of wind in the thick forest. For a month we waited for a north wind and this method of discharge had to be abandoned." Ironside then wired to the War Office for gas projectors but these too were found to be useless because they arrived in an unusable condition. As so often happens the soldiers in the field found their own solution. Major T. H. Davies of the Special Company, Royal Engineers, invented the first gas bombs for use from aircraft. These bombs were made by the Ordnance Services and by the naval workshops on board the repair ship HMS *Cyclops* and, according to Ironside's report, "Gas bombing proved highly successful and materially helped the Russian operation."

Ironside's new attempt to reach Kotlas on June 20th was to have political repercussions in London far exceeding its military importance.

According to Allfrey the plan was for the 3rd North Russian Rifles to mount a frontal attack on the villages of Topsa and Troitskoye while Sherwood Kelly took two companies of his Hampshires on a long trek through the forest to appear behind the Bolshevik positions. Allfrey, who had made his way to the front in a Ford car, stopping to give joy rides to villagers who had never seen a car before, arrived at Kelly's rear HQ to see a village burst into flames and Royal Naval Monitors chasing Bolshevik gunboats up the Dvina. He passed about 150 Bolshevik prisoners on their way to the prison cages: "They looked a rotten lot of people, very dirty and with the most villainous uncivilised faces, very like the orthodox cartoons."

He recorded however, that "the morning's fighting has not worked out too well". Indeed it had not. Sherwood Kelly had, uncharacteristically, failed to press home his attack and had actually withdrawn his men, leaving his Russian allies to do the fighting.

The Hampshire's War Diary contains a bare account of that morning's work:

Attacked 04.45. At 10.30 as no news was heard or seen of 3rd N.R. Rifles on our right who were attacking Topsa and the enemy who were fighting very well had nearly surrounded us, the C.O. decided to withdraw from the position we had reached round Troitskoye village. After having withdrawn about two miles news was heard that the 3rd NRR had taken their objectives and Topsa so we marched into Topsa via the woods to the South.

Sherwood Kelly's own report on the failure of his mission was full of self-justification and blame for others

> . . . there was great difficulty in getting through the marsh . . . supposed to have been rendered passable by the R.E. but in a great many places little work had been done . . . no telephone cable linking the positions . . . running out of ammunition . . . the chief reason for me having to withdraw was the fact that I had no information of the success or otherwise of the attack on Topsa . . .

The Hampshires spent the next few weeks fairly quietly on the River Front before being transferred to the Railway Front. There, a few days after their arrival Sherwood Kelly was ordered to carry out a raid on some Bolshevik blockhouses under cover of gas. He promptly wrote a high-handed letter to the GOC of the front, Brigadier-General Turner, protesting that the raid would serve no purpose, "if the proposed operation is left to my discretion I shall not carry it out. I am continuing to make all preparations in case you order me to carry out the raid." Although he later insisted that his operation orders were approved by Turner except "for the exposed task I had allotted to myself" the tone of his letter was not acceptable. It was read as part and parcel of his arrogant behaviour at Troitskoye.

But Sherwood Kelly had already taken the step that would end his military role in the intervention and catapult him into the far more dangerous game of politics. He wrote a private letter to a friend at home in which he bitterly criticised the North Russian operation. He was later to argue that he had written the letter knowing that it would be opened by the censor and that he would be brought before the C-in-C to answer for it. He had written it, he said, because he was sickened by the waste of money and men on a "useless, aimless and ill-managed campaign", and "determined by some means or other to get back to England".

The letter was duly opened by the censor and the wheels of military justice started to grind. Brigadier Turner was asked for a report on his behaviour in North Russia. Turner was forthright: "He is a hot-headed and quarrelsome man who has rows with practically everyone with whom he has come in contact." Turner added: "He has a fine smart well-drilled battalion and his men like him, but I do not consider he is suitable for command of a regular battalion under the present conditions."

Sherwood Kelly was duly relieved of his command and on August 22nd the Hampshires' diary records without comment: "Lt. Col. D. M. Macleod, DSO, MC, DCM, 4th South African Light Infantry joined the Battalion and took over Command."

His offence, as he well knew, warranted court-martial, but Ironside interceded with the C-in-C, General Sir Henry Rawlinson, who had come out to take overall charge of the evacuation of the British troops. But, while Rawlinson was prepared to send Sherwood Kelly home without court-martialling him because of his fine record he was not prepared to withhold Turner's adverse report.

Sherwood Kelly (who thought he had made a deal with Ironside to refrain from writing a letter to Rawlinson "telling all" in exchange for the withdrawal of the report and a recommendation that he should have six months leave and the command of a reserve battalion at home) was enraged. So he wrote another letter. This time it was to the *Daily Express*. "I ask you, Sir, to publish this letter so that people in England may know the truth about the situation in Archangel and may be able to take steps to right it."

The *Daily Express* lapped it up. On Saturday September 6th, 1919, its front page splash headlines read:

Archangel Scandal Exposed
Duplicity of Churchill Policy
in Russia
The Public Humbugged
Famous VC appeals to the Nation.

Sherwood Kelly's letter was a slashing attack both on British policies in North Russia and the way they were being carried out. He had volunteered with the Relief Force, he said, in the sincere belief that relief was urgently needed in order to make possible the withdrawal of low-category troops in the last stage of exhaustion due to fierce fighting among the rigours of an Arctic winter. But, he claimed,

I was reluctantly but inevitably drawn to the following conclusion: That the troops of the Relief Force which we were told had been sent out for purely defensive purposes, were being used for offensive purposes on a large scale and far into the interior, in furtherance of some ambitious plan of campaign the nature of which we were not allowed to know. My personal experience of those operations was that they were not even well conducted and they were not calculated to benefit in a military or any other sense a sound and practical British policy in Russia. They only entailed useless loss and suffering in troops that had already made great sacrifices in the Great War.

He went on to criticise the "much vaunted 'loyal Russian Army' composed largely of Bolshevik prisoners dressed in khaki" and the "puppet government set up by us in Archangel . . ."

The War Office replied with a statement refuting the letter as being "biased and entirely unfounded". General Sadleir-Jackson's move forward, it said, was of ten miles and was "purely a local affair." It was in accordance with sound principles of defence and was not a penetration "far into the interior". And, the War Office insisted, "There is not, nor ever has been the slightest intention of deviating a hairs-breadth from the settled policy of evacuation."

All this was, of course, meat and drink to the opponents of intervention who ignored the War Office denial. The *Daily Express*, armed with two more letters from Sherwood Kelly, mounted a great campaign against Churchill and his "Private War". Sherwood Kelly sent a message to the Trades Union Congress which loudly applauded him. And Sir Basil Thomson, Director of Intelligence at the Home Office, in one of his weekly reports on "Revolutionary Organisations in the United Kingdom" said that the letter had effects in Liverpool, Newcastle, Nottingham and Glasgow where the "outburst of resentment has been remarkable".

Inevitably Sherwood Kelly was court-martialled. He pleaded guilty on October 28th at the Middlesex Guildhall to charges of contravening King's Regulations by writing three letters to the Press. His only defence was a justification of his actions: "I plead with you to believe that the action I took was to protect my men's lives against needless sacrifice and to save the country from squandering wealth she could ill afford. I leave this matter in your hands, hoping you will remember my past services to my King and country."

The court did, in fact, treat him with great leniency, sentencing him only to a severe reprimand. Nevertheless his career in the Army was finished. He retired and although he tried to rejoin on several occasions he was always turned down. His life ended sadly in 1931 when he died at the age of fifty-one, a solitary man in a nursing home. He was buried with full military honours, the Army sending two buglers to sound the Last Post over his grave.

There were those who insisted that the whole affair stemmed from his loss of nerve at Troitskoye and all that followed was a snowballing attempt at justification. Lieutenant I. H. Bowen of the gunboat *Moth* operating on the Dvina wrote: "We had read one of his interviews ourselves and thought most of it awful rot; five years of fighting must have disturbed the gallant officer's mental faculties."

But even if everything he had to say was true did it make any difference? The answer is no. Certainly Ironside would have pressed on to Kotlas if the way had been open. Certainly Churchill would have continued to wage war against the Bolsheviks if he had been allowed to. But Lloyd George had made his position clear: "The mere idea of crushing Bolshevism by military force is pure madness." And perhaps what is more to the point, by the time Sherwood Kelly's original letter was published, the Archangel expedition was already packing its bags to come home.

CHAPTER 15

Mutiny and a Victoria Cross
Archangel, June–September 1919

By the summer of 1919 General Alexander Samoilo, the Tsarist officer turned Bolshevik, had a proper military organisation, the Sixth Army, under his command. As well as rifle regiments, field gun batteries, machine-gunners and a "mine-throwing" unit, Samoilo had observation balloons and a number of aircraft including a Nieuport flown by S. F. Smirnov who was, he said, known to the British as the "Red Devil". Samoilo also had a very effective fleet on the Dvina which regularly engaged the British gunboats and supported army operations with fire from their big guns.

The unusually low level of the River Dvina that year helped Samoilo, for while he could get supplies down river from Kotlas the British supply barges going up river from Archangel found getting past the sandbanks increasingly difficult. Troops who should have passed easily along the river to the front were forced to march, arriving at the front line worn out.

But Samoilo's most effective weapon was the mutinous state of the Russians enlisted in the Slavo-British Legion and the North Russian regiments. It was their disaffection which, more than anything else caused the British to abandon whatever hopes they might still have had of opening up the way to Kotlas. Ironside was forced to guard as much against his so-called allies as against his enemies. Ultimately he had to send to England for a tank unit to come out, not to fight the Bolsheviks – the tanks would have been useless in the forests and marshes – but to impress their presence on would-be mutineers in Archangel as the intimidating power of this new weapon had been quickly realised.

So anxious were the British to build up the Russian forces that almost anyone was acceptable and many of them either already had Bolshevik sympathies or were easily swayed by the agitators who infiltrated their ranks. There were also those who, knowing very well what their fate would be once the Allies had withdrawn, preferred to go over to the Bolsheviks rather than have their throats cut.

Ironside was also short of fighting officers and made up a number of noncommissioned officers and privates to commissioned rank to officer the new regiments.

One of the men that Ironside commissioned was a young Canadian private called Dyer who had been decorated for gallantry with the DCM and MM. Dyer was given what were described as "one thousand criminals" and told to turn them into a battalion of fighting soldiers. He did. His men worshipped him; they became the 1st Battalion, "Dyer's Battalion" of the Slavo-British Legion and when he died, probably of the flu, they carried a large photograph of him just as the old Tsarist regiments used to carry ikons when on the march. However, his influence did not last long after his death.

On July 7th the battalion, still known as Dyer's though now commanded by Colonel Wells, was in reserve positions in the area of Topsa – Troitskoye where Sherwood Kelly had come to grief. At 2 a.m., during the short period of twilight that passes for night in midsummer in those latitudes, the 3rd Company, along with the machine-gun company of the 4th North Russian Regiment, sprang a carefully organised plot. First they tried to wipe out their officers by shooting and bayoneting them. Four British and four Russian officers were killed and two British and two Russian officers were wounded, one of them escaping by swimming out to a gunboat despite having twenty-five bayonet wounds.

The mutiny was put down by gunfire from the river flotilla and by nearby British troops who captured some of the ringleaders. The rest, some 200 men, fled into the woods to join the Bolsheviks, who took advantage of the subsequent disorganisation to capture the village of Selmanga. The 46th Battalion of the Royal Fusiliers was drawn into the fighting and two companies of the 45th were hurried up to support them on the C-in-C's house-boat – which had a suitably shallow draught.

"A" Company, commanded by Allfrey, stayed behind. It had a different job to do; to keep the disarmed remnants of Dyer's battalion under guard and to arrange the execution of the ringleaders. Initially there were forty men condemned to death and they were put in charge of a platoon armed with Lewis guns and orders to open fire if there was any trouble. Allfrey met Colonel Wells: "He is very overdone, poor fellow, and is also a good deal gone in the nerves."

Those members of the battalion who did not mutiny were billeted in the Fusiliers' camp. "I have established machine-gun posts all round the camp they are to occupy when they arrive, and if there is the slightest trouble I shall pump lead into them harder than they have ever seen bullets fly before. The machine-gun nests are quite neatly arranged, and are concealed, each one being in a bell tent, which is quite a common sight round these parts and will not be suspected."

One of the privates in the battalion was a woman who had been a company commander in the women's battalion which had defended the Winter Palace. She had not taken part in the mutiny and was overcome with shame at the conduct of her comrades.

Allfrey also discovered an English-speaking Russian among the condemned men who said that he lived in Scotland where his wife was working in a coalmine. Allfrey decided that he was probably innocent of murder and after some argument secured his release from Colonel Wells.

July 12th and 13th were spent in trying the "condemned" men by British court martial. Much to Allfrey's disgust most of them got off. "I think it would save a lot of trouble if they would allow me to shoot the lot just as they are now, as I have several times applied to do. However, they won't allow me to do this." On the 14th one of the prisoners tried to escape and was killed by a sentry.

By now the arrangements for the executions were being completed. Twelve were to die, shot by their own machine-gunners. Five hundred newly mobilised Russians were to witness the executions, doubtless to discourage them from any thought of emulating the men they were to see die. "Judging from the people who have asked me lately when I am going to shoot Dyer's men," wrote Allfrey, "I think it would be an excellent thing to swell the Company funds by having a little stand put up."

The executions were carried out at eight o'clock in the evening of July 17th. To make sure there was no trouble, the Russian machine-gunners, one for each condemned man, were issued with only five rounds so that if they turned their guns on the British they could do little harm. In addition Allfrey had the whole area covered by Lewis guns and took his own men on to the parade ground with guns loaded and bayonets fixed.

Something like 1,200 men were paraded, forming three sides of a square. Twelve execution stakes completed the square and a machine-gun was set up in front of each one. The prisoners were marched out, tied to the stakes and blindfolded. The paraded soldiers were silent, but suddenly a large group of off-duty British soldiers arrived to see the show. "It seemed," said Allfrey, "in awfully bad taste."

It was an oppressively hot, still, evening. The men fidgeted under the attacks of the mosquitoes. The order to fire was given and the

machine-guns rattled off their five rounds. But only four of the
twelve were killed outright. Seven were left wounded, squirming
in pain at the stakes. One man, a sergeant, was not even scratched.
The machine-gunner must have deliberately aimed to miss. The
execution squad was then doubled off the parade and Allfrey and
officers from Dyer's Battalion "had to go with our revolvers and
polish the prisoners off".

Allfrey also recorded that when the sergeant, "who behaved like
a man although he is a murderer", realised that he had been missed,
"he took the bandage off his eyes and shouted out: 'Long live the
Bolsheviks'. I was glad when somebody fired at him and killed him,
for he was uncannily cool and collected."

Six more men were due to be executed but the following day
Ironside received a furious telegram from the War Office criticising
his action and the six men were reprieved.

Just four days after the executions on July 21st a far more serious
mutiny took place near Onega, the joining point of the Murmansk
and Archangel commands, when the 5th North Russian Regiment
seized their officers and went over to the Bolsheviks leaving the
whole of the Onega front in Bolshevik hands.

The mutiny was led by soldiers in the regiment's 2nd company,
and particularly by one of its NCOs, Viktor Shchetinin, then aged
twenty-four. On the fiftieth anniversary of what the Soviet Union
describes as the "liberation of the north" Shchetinin recalled that his
company, and others on the front line had long been infiltrated by
Bolsheviks and there had been earlier plans made to mutiny which
for different reasons had failed.

The commander of the regiment was a Colonel Danilov, but
Shchetinin said that the man in overall charge was a Colonel Laurie,
and military operations were planned by him and a small group of
British officers.

On July 18th, the Reds began a push and occupied two lines of
White trenches. The 2nd Company were brought up to defend a
key railway track in the line of advance and when they reached their
positions in and around a hamlet bestriding the track they were told
to dig in. The company commander left to visit the regimental
headquarters at Chekuyevo and Shchetinin and other Bolshevik
agitators went to work. They decided to mutiny that night. It went
smoothly. The handful of White Officers were arrested in their
beds, ammunition was loaded on to carriages, and the company
marched to Chekuyevo.

According to Shchetinin's version not a shot was fired. The bulk of the regiment was scattered around five villages, and the Bolshevik soldiers simply marched up to the houses where the officers were sleeping and arrested them. There was no opposition from ordinary White soldiers "because they knew our cause was right". It was not until the afternoon that the mutinous troops decided to take the regimental headquarters, and it was apparent that no news of the revolt had yet filtered through.

Shchetinin claims the credit for the arrest of Colonel Laurie. He recalled:

At the British offices the day was passing in its usual way. Everything was calm. There was no fuss or noise. Colonel Laurie was sitting in his well lit office, studying a wall map with white and blue flags on it. The white ones were for the Interventionists. The blue ones were for the Reds.

We rushed in and our arrival was definitely not expected. We pointed our rifles at the Colonel. He was so surprised he just sat there, as if he was nailed to the chair, and he refused to move. Our lads knew what to do and they went over and picked him up still in the chair and took him out to where we had lined up the rest of the British officers. It was all over. We had got the lot. We were now three rifle companies, a machine gun detachment, a machine gun training school company, a cavalry detachment, and supply and medical units. We had also captured ammunitions, food, and three boats. I was elected the new Commander of the regiment.

Shchetinin said that the regiment then linked up with the nearby 154th Red Army regiment. Soviet historians tend to argue that this mutiny was the beginning of the end for the intervention, but that was already long past. What it did spell out in unmistakable terms was that there was no chance that the Provisional government in Archangel could hold out against the Bolsheviks once the Allies had left – for while there were individuals who were prepared to give their lives in the anti-Bolshevik cause there was hardly a unit that was not riddled with subversion.

In practical terms the Onega mutiny was a severe embarrassment to the Allied Forces, cutting the land link between Maynard and Ironside and creating a two-way threat. If the Bolsheviks struck to the east they would threaten Ironside's men strung out along the railway while if they turned west they would threaten Soroka, a key point on Maynard's line of communications. Onega remained a threat until September 8th when the Bolsheviks, fearing an Allied attack, set fire to the town and marched away.

It was in these circumstances that Sir Henry Rawlinson ("Rawley the Fox" as he was known), was sent out to Archangel as C-in-C of Archangel and Murmansk to co-ordinate the withdrawal of both forces. His appointment was greeted with something like hysteria by the *Daily Express* which argued that "there will be a combined naval and military operation and the choice of one of the most experienced British generals to direct it suggests that it will be on a large scale. We are, in fact, in peril of drifting into a new war." And it added: "This will open the eyes of the British public to the grave consequences of Mr Churchill's gamble in North Russia . . ."

Whether Rawlinson's appointment was necessary is doubtful. Maynard and Ironside were quite capable of carrying out the evacuation. But neither of them publicly objected and when he arrived at Archangel on August 9th Ironside met him on the quayside.

Ironside had already set in motion a series of strong raids on the Bolsheviks designed to give them, in a later general's words, a "bloody nose", to persuade them not to interfere with the evacuation and to give the Provisional government's forces breathing space once the British had left.

The Royal Fusiliers were in the thick of it, urged on by the thrusting Sadleir-Jackson. One of the officers of the 45th Royal Fusiliers was Edward Sutro who later became famous as a British eccentric. He drove round London after World War II in a white Rolls Royce, took a coffee grinder and supply of beans with him wherever he went in the world, and, resplendent in an opera cloak, attended some 6,000 theatrical first nights. But out in the forests around Archangel he lived a different sort of life and was awarded the MC for gallantry. When he returned to England he took with him a little dog he called Dvina and swore it had saved his life. His mother, however, disliked the dog and when one day she discovered a puddle on the kitchen floor, she banished Dvina from the house, whereupon Sutro, protesting the puddle had come from a leaking refrigerator, stormed out of the house with his dog, and booked passage for them both to New Zealand where he stayed for sixteen years. When he returned to England he would never allow hunting over his land because, he said, he had found out what it was like to be hunted in Russia. Among Sutro's papers is the copy of a song sung by the 45th to the tune of a popular music-hall song:

Sadleir, Sadleir, Sadleir my boy,
Where are you taking us now?
You promised to take us home after the show
Ever since then its been all push and go.
All the Company
Keep on asking me,
Which day, what day?
I don't know what to say.
Sadleir, Sadleir, Sadleir my boy,
Where are you taking us now?

The answer to that question was into the swamps and forests and mosquitoes to kill as many Bolsheviks as possible.

On August 10th, the day after Rawlinson's arrival, the Royal Fusiliers and White Russian units attacked the Bolshevik-held village of Seltsoe. The plan was for the Russians to make a frontal attack while C Company of the Fusiliers attacked the flank and A and D companies went off on a long trek to attack the villages behind Seltsoe. It turned into a confused and bloody affair. The Fusiliers, making their way through the forest two days before the attack, found it impossible to get their heavy equipment through the marshes. Everything had to be manhandled, the mountain battery could not get forward and packs had to be left behind. When the actual attack on Seltsoe went in, it was broken up by Bolshevik machine-gun fire. D Company was then attacked by Red soldiers landing from boats which also opened up on them at two hundred yards range. Major De Mattos was mortally wounded and Major Sheppard was killed. Small groups of men fought individual battles among the pine trees. Allfrey's A Company carried the village of Pipovets with a bayonet charge, digging out Bolsheviks from chimneys and underneath mattresses.

They then withdrew through the forest, picking up stragglers from other units and with 400 Bolshevik prisoners carrying the wounded. Exhausted and hungry and almost out of ammunition, they were ambushed while crossing a single plank bridge across a small river. The men on the plank were knocked into the river by machine-gun fire while the captured Bolsheviks dropped the wounded and ran.

For a time there was that total confusion that can be found nowhere else except on a battlefield. Bullets thudded into the pine trees, men crashed through the undergrowth and the wounded screamed as they were carried away by the river. The situation was saved by Captain S. S. Harrison of the Irish Guards who was serving with the Machine Gun Corps. He kept his head, rapidly mounted his guns on the river bank and drove off the ambushers. He got a bar to his MC for "gallantry and good work".

For days afterwards the woods were full of lost men, both Bolsheviks and British, as they struggled to find their way to safety, occasionally meeting and clashing before resuming their hunt for their own positions. British planes flew low over the forest, firing coloured lights to lead stragglers in the right direction while buglers constantly sounded "the rally" at the edge of the forest to guide the lost men home. Eventually most of them, including the Fusiliers' tough Australian commander, Colonel Davis, reached safety. But four officers had been killed in the operation along with one Company Sergeant-Major and twenty other ranks. One of the dead officers was Lord Settrington who, if he had lived, would have become the Duke of Richmond and Gordon.

Despite the casualties and the confusion, the operation was judged by the British to be a success: the Bolsheviks had lost many more men and had been so disorganised by the Fusiliers' attack on their rear that they made off through the forest, abandoning Seltsoe which was now occupied by the White Russians.

The 45th were involved in another desperate affair a fortnight later at Emtsa on the railway. The village changed hands several times during furious fighting before finally being held by the Fusiliers. It was there on August 29th that Sergeant Samuel Pearse died winning the Victoria Cross. It was the only VC awarded to a soldier throughout the intervention although, as we shall see, three naval officers were also to win the medal. Pearse had been born in Wales, but grew up in Australia. He joined the Australian Army as soon as he was old enough in 1915 and became a machine-gunner on the Western Front where he won the Military Medal. He volunteered for the Relief Force, transferred to the British Army on July 18th, 1919, and sailed to join the Fusiliers. He was in action almost immediately and at Emtsa, according to his citation: "During the operation against the enemy battery position north of Emtsa . . . Sergeant Pearse cut his way through the enemy barbed wire under very heavy machine-gun and rifle fire, and cleared a way for the troops to enter the battery position. Seeing that a blockhouse was harassing our advance and causing us casualties, he charged the blockhouse single-handed, killing the occupants with bombs. This gallant non-commissioned officer met his death minutes later, and it was due to him that the position was carried with so few casualties. His magnificent bravery and utter disregard for personal danger won him the admiration of all troops."

The fierceness of the fighting for Emtsa was recorded by Samoilo. Two British battalions, he wrote, "were thrown into the attack on our right flank and came at us out of the forest. They reached our artillery positions and took them after six hours of fighting. They went on to try to capture Armoured Train No. 20. but although the crew was killed, it was started and went to the aid of the 1st Light-Artillery battery and took it to safety. The Interventionists set Emtsa on fire and destroyed the water tower. By midnight they had overrun all our frontline positions but 500 of our men plus ten machine-guns and four minethrowers managed to break out. The 155th regiment managed to hold on to the railway station for nearly two days. But no reinforcements could get through. The British attacked again and again and set the station on fire. Our men were exhausted and surrendered."

There were of course other regiments involved in the actions around Archangel. The Royal Scots who had endured the worst of the winter fighting had gone home in June to be demobilised but their place had been taken by a number of famous regiments. There were Royal Warwicks attached to the Ox and Bucks Light Infantry in Grogan's Brigade. There were men of the Wiltshires serving with the Hampshires who had returned to the front line and acquitted themselves well under their new CO. The Highland Light Infantry were there and so were the Durham Light Infantry and the Liverpools. The two Yorkshire battalions had been rehabilitated and had won a number of awards for gallantry. All the supporting arms were represented and the Royal Marines served as both soldiers and sailors on board the river gunboats. And, as the British Army had learned the lesson of the machine-gun the hard way on the Western Front, the Machine Gun Corps was everywhere. The Tank Corps detachment had arrived with its three Mark V heavy tanks and three Medium B "Whippets" and its official mascot "Nell", a messenger dog, wounded in action in France.

Grogan's Brigade, holding the Pinega River front to the east of the Dvina, followed the same policy as Sadleir-Jackson's, delivering a series of sharp blows against the Bolsheviks like a boxer jabbing to sap his opponent's strength. Aircraft were used extensively in these operations, developing a system of co-operation with the ground forces which, alas, had to be learned all over again by the British in World War II. Poison gas was used extensively and a list of precautions issued to the troops following up a gas attack from the air:

A. No man to enter the 'smoked area' until one and half hours after the last bomb is dropped.

B. Cellars and cavities will be avoided.

C. No water in these villages will be drunk.

D. Earth is contaminated where bombs drop. Skin contact will be avoided.

Closed houses will be specially watched as padded doors may keep out the gas. Cigarette smoking will give some relief if gas is inhaled.

One of these gas attacks was ordered for September 4th: "Pocha and Vekhtovo will be heavily gas bombed by our aeroplanes. Immediately afterwards these places will be raided and destroyed."

We have a rare opportunity in this instance to read reports from both sides of the same action. Grogan's HQ War Diary records: "Aeroplanes dropped 200 gas bombs on Pocha. One plane forced to land North of Priluk and was afterwards destroyed by us. Gas bombs only partly successful."

The Russian account was sent by teleprinter from Operations Chief Burenin and Military Commissar Popov of the 6th Army:

Northern Dvina district. Pinega position (2nd Brigade). On Sept 4th the enemy shelled positions of the 481st Rifle Regiment in region of Ust-Poga (Pocha) village with six-inch weapons. Enemy aircraft were used as spotters to correct shelling. One of the aircraft caught fire and came down near village of Prilutskaya. During Sept 4 enemy aircraft dropped up to 100 bombs in our positions of which most were suffocating gas. One person killed. One wounded. Several persons poisoned by the gas. Two horses killed. One wounded . . .

One of the reasons for the lack of effectiveness of the gas was simply that the Bolsheviks had been issued with gas masks.

The pilots were busy young men. Flying a variety of planes and often exchanging them, they flew missions almost every day. The Log Book of 2nd Lt L. W. Mason shows him "Bombing gunboats on Dvina . . . Raid on Bolo airport. Nieuport in flames . . . Bombing Bolo fleet . . . Sent gunboat up in flames . . . Troitskoye, strafing trenches." Another pilot, Major Carr, landed on a Bolshevik aerodrome and taxied round shooting it up before taking off again. One of the pilots flying from Bereznik airfield was the World War I Ace Captain Ira "Taffy" Jones who had shot down forty Germans over the Western Front.

But these were only the last flickers of a dying battle. The Allies pulled back into Archangel with the Royal Fusiliers providing the rearguard, a somewhat risky business, the Dvina being so low that their transport barges often stuck on sandbanks. The Bolsheviks, who had suffered heavy casualties in these final actions, took their revenge by sniping at the stranded boats and killed several men. Some boats were destroyed by mines floated down the river. HMS *Glow Worm*, one of the gunboats, was blown up in this fashion and the captain killed. HMS *Sword Dance*, a minesweeper, was also destroyed.

It was decided that two of the newly arrived tanks, one Heavy and one Whippet, would be given to the Russians to form the North Russian Tank Corps and a tank school was hastily set up to teach the new corps, commanded by Colonel Kenotkenich, how to use them. Two nights before the evacuation this brand new corps entertained their British tutors to dinner at the Club St Georges in the Petrogradski and heaped honours and decorations on them. The Forces newspaper, the *Archangel Gazette* printed its last edition. The troops did some last minute bargaining, called "Skolkering" after the Russian word *Skolka* meaning "how much?" Most of them wanted to take furs home. The YMCA closed its doors. The Slavo-British Boys Legion faced an uncertain future. And those citizens who knew very well what their future would be under the Bolsheviks applied to be taken to England.

Units which were no longer needed had been sent back during late August and early September. On September 9th GHQ North Russia closed down, on the 23rd all British troops withdrew to the city and then on the 27th under cover of a curfew a convoy of some forty-five ships sailed from Archangel. A rearguard of C Company of the 45th Royal Fusiliers and a Lewis Gun Company covered the evacuation while seaplanes patrolled overhead and coastal motor boats sealed off the river. HMS *Fox*, steam up and guns trained on the city, stood by to deal with any interference. Rawlinson and Ironside boarded the transport *Tsaritza*. The wind blew half a gale, howling through the deserted, silent city. The Fusiliers were taken on the ocean-going tug *War-Karma* and carried down river to board the *Kildonan Castle*. There being no room on any of the ships for one of the coastal motor boats which had done such a good job on the Dvina, she was pumped full of tracer bullets until she was destroyed.

That night Sadleir-Jackson's staff on board the *Kildonan Castle* got very tight in the smoke room and debagged certain of their colleagues who they considered bumptious. It was a peculiarly British way of mourning a failed enterprise.

When General Ironside arrived at Liverpool on October 6th, a reporter asked him if he would care to say anything about the expedition. He replied that he thought too much had been said about it already, but added that he thought the expedition had done its work and that the Russian loyalist forces would now be able to stand by themselves.

But, inevitably, once the British had sailed away, the North Russian Army succumbed swiftly to the Bolsheviks, although there were certainly great deeds of individual bravery by those left to fight. Major J. N. L. Bryan who had commanded the tank Corps detachment, told in the *Tank Corps Journal* how he had received a cable from Colonel Kenotkenich who had gone into action with his two tanks shortly after the evacuation. It read: "Proud keep traditions, English Tank Corps. Took in glorious fight five fortified points and Plesetskaya Station."

But it could not last. And Colonel Kenotkenich's Heavy Mark V now stands in Archangel as a Soviet memorial to their victory over the "forces of capitalism and imperialism".

CHAPTER 16

The Last Battles
Murmansk, April–October 1919

Throughout the summer of 1919, Maynard, in Murmansk, although under orders to do nothing to risk casualties, had conducted a small but professional war in which, apart from a few minor setbacks, he had always come out on top. In April, Major Anderson, the officer commanding at Segezha, learning that the Bolsheviks were gathering at Urosozevo, some twenty miles down the railway line, to attack him, had launched a pre-emptive attack and routed them. They left fifty dead, and forty prisoners were taken to be sent back to the once-proud battleship *Chesma*, now converted into a prison ship. Anderson's men captured, among much else, two field guns with 7,000 shells and twenty-two freight cars along with much valuable railway repair equipment. Maynard later paid generous tribute to the French crew of an armoured train: the success, he said, was largely due to their gallantry. Allied losses were one dead and five wounded. In the subsequent operations to tidy the battlefield, newly trained Russian troops, under a first class officer, Captain Davidov, mopped up a series of Bolshevik positions in actions which encouraged the White Russians to push further south.

This placed Maynard in something of a quandary: although the occupation of the northern tip of Lake Onega now seemed an attainable and worthwhile objective, he was constrained by orders from London to a policy of non-offence and the Russians were not yet sufficiently trained in strength to undertake what in Murmansk terms was a major offensive.

Maynard, however, felt that it was worth asking the War Office for permission to mount an attack. He pointed out that the establishment of a new line running from Povenets in the east to Medvezhya Gora in the west would put him in a much stronger tactical position. He also felt he now had the troops to do the job: he had been reinforced by two special companies, one from the Middlesex Regiment and the other from the King's Royal Rifle Corps, and had also acquired two companies of American railway troops who proved to be invaluable. They were not only expert

221

railwaymen, they also had to be restrained from seeking out the fighting. Moreover he now had sufficient artillery.

Somewhat to his surprise he won approval from the War Office for the offensive and subsequently went at his preparations with an enthusiasm which drew groans from his already over-worked staff. He had a pair of 4.5 howitzers mounted on railway trucks, sent an ice-breaker and trawlers to fetch a field battery from ice-bound Pechenga and gathered together a flotilla of ancient boats to serve as a navy on Lake Onega. The flagship was a submarine-chaser armed with 37 mm guns and rechristened the *Jolly Roger*, and the whole fleet was hoisted on to flat cars ready to be taken south by rail.

The only department with which Maynard now had some difficulty was air support. His six RE8s were in such a dreadful condition that only three of them ever flew, and their pilots, unlike the aces who had been sent to other parts of Russia, were inexperienced youngsters.

Maynard split his 3,000 men into columns on three lines of advance: British, French, Italian, Serbian and Russian troops were all involved while the Americans rebuilt bridges, re-laid tracks and then guarded their work. The offensive lasted from May 1st until May 21st when Medvezhya Gora fell. It had been held up by the onset of the thaw which left the men struggling through marshes and rushing streams but ended in complete success.

The Onega fleet now came south down the line and the *Jolly Roger* was launched on June 4th. It proved to be an unlucky ship for her engines repeatedly broke down and on June 8th she burst into flames and exploded, killing five men. But for the moment she was invaluable and her fleet, including some boats which had been left in the now melting ice by the retreating Reds, numbered six motor boats and two steam launches.

Maynard who finished the offensive with just one of his RE8s flying – and that was more an act of faith by its pilot than airworthiness – also acquired a new air force, a flight of Short seaplanes and a flight of Fairey IIIC seaplanes, delivered to Murmansk by the seaplane carrier *Nairana* whose aircraft had frightened the Bolsheviks out of Archangel the previous August.

Arriving by rail from Murmansk on June 4th, the first plane took off from Medvezhya Gora two days later. They first showed their worth on June 8th when four armed Bolshevik steamers put in an appearance. They were bigger and more heavily armed than Maynard's flotilla which, nevertheless, sailed out to do battle. It could have ended in disaster but the seaplanes took off, surprised the Bolshevik ships and sent them scurrying for safety under a hail of bombs and machine-gun fire and with the motor boats nipping at their heels. Lieutenant-Commander J. H. Mather, serving as a major in the Royal Engineers, won the DSO in this action for taking his four boats out to attack the Bolshevik gunboats.

One of Maynard's strengths was that he had a number of officers who delighted in taking independent action with small bands of locally raised "partisans". One of them, Captain M. B. Burrows of the 5th Dragoon Guards, had won the MC during the May fighting for landing with a party of ten men on the Sunga Peninsula on Lake Onega. According to his citation, he "raised partisans, and by his energetic action against the Bolshevists covered the landing of a Russian battalion." Some weeks later, now a major, Burrows won the DSO for another mission behind the lines. "Taking 120 men across 15 miles of Lake Onega, this part being in the hands of the enemy, (he) landed them near Vate Navolok, 21 versts [14 miles] in rear of the enemy front line and captured the garrison of this place. He then took his party on to the railway west of Vate Navolok and by his skilful dispositions greatly assisted the column operating on the railway."

Another young officer who became something of a legend for his daring operations and would obviously have made a fine present-day officer of the élite Special Air Service regiment, was Lieutenant E. A. Small of the General List. He gathered together a group which became known as "Small's Partisans". They were described as being like "a huntsman and his hounds". Small's usual dress was a pair of oilskin trousers and a khaki cricket shirt.

One of his exploits was to bring back a traitor from sixty miles behind the Bolshevik lines. This man had betrayed an Allied agent who had been killed by having a sharpened stake thrust up him. The traitor was hanged.

His men were devoted to him and as one of his colleagues rather jealously wrote, "they saw to it that he always got his eggs for breakfast."

On another occasion, with thirty-seven of his men, Small captured a Bolshevik brigade commander, the brigade staff and fifty other prisoners, stole the breech block of a 3-inch gun and brought them all back to Maynard as a gift. His most daring and valuable raid behind the lines destroyed the vitally important bridge over the Suna River which carried all the Bolsheviks' supplies from Petrograd. The RAF had been trying to knock out this bridge for some time, but without success as it provided a small target and was well defended by high-angle machine-guns. One day Maynard, in exasperation, said: "I wish someone would burn down that wretched bridge." Small overheard him, gathered his partisans together and set out on July 18th. It took them five days, hiding during the day and hiking across rough country at night, always in danger of being betrayed or running into a Bolshevik patrol. But they arrived without being discovered, surprised the guard at the station, captured two machine-guns and then set fire to the bridge, completely destroying the northern end and making it impassable. Small was awarded the DSO for his endeavours.

During this fighting, the new Russian regiments were being trained with the utmost speed. Maynard needed them in the line because so many of his original force had gone home. The Canadians had gone; so all too quickly, had the American railway troops. And the admirable Serbs were thinking it was time they went back to their own country.

Moreover, the Russians had to be given experience in the field before the Allies finally withdrew.

Maynard was delighted, therefore, when the White Russian, General Skobeltsin, arrived from Archangel to take charge of the Russian troops. An attack was proposed on Siding 10 south of Medvezhya Gora in which the newly raised Russian regiments would be used in conjunction with the Olonetz Regiment formed of Russians and Karelians from the Finnish border which had already proved its worth in a number of engagements. The attack was to be supported by British artillery.

The Olonetz performed admirably but the new Russian formations fled once the Bolsheviks opened fire and the attack broke down. Maynard, for morale reasons, could not allow this defeat to remain unavenged. The Olonetz went back into action with the support of a company of Serbs and the unwilling Russians had a backbone of Serbs inserted into their ranks and were given a relatively easy task while the main attack was undertaken by British infantry and machine-gun detachments. The attack went in on June 13th. Accurate artillery fire demoralised the Bolsheviks and they fled, giving the British force a walkover without a single casualty.

The new Russians were, however, heavily counter-attacked on their push down the shore of Lake Onega to Fedotova and it is here that we pick up the trail of Captain Crawford, former "King of Restikent" whose diary had petered out. He had been put in charge of all the Russian machine-guns and led them forward. He beat off the Bolsheviks, advanced for another three miles and captured twenty-four prisoners and a machine-gun. He was awarded an MC, the citation saying: "His gallant leadership was of great service."

This success was followed by a well-organised combined operation against three Bolshevik ships at Tolvoya on the Shunga Peninsula where their guns were frustrating White Russian attempts to capture the port. Maynard had received reinforcements from England for his fleet: six 40-foot subchasers armed with 3-pounders and machine-guns and six 35-foot motor boats carrying machine-guns. These boats were under the command of Commander Curteis RN who had with him 14 officers and 120 ratings. They were much smaller than the Bolshevik's steamers which were based at the port of Petrozavodsk on the western shore of the lake. But they possessed the advantage of speed and manoeuvrability and they had the RAF's seaplanes which were unopposed in the air.

Four Fairey seaplanes opened the attack on the Red ships on August 3rd and their bombs panicked the Russian crews. Two of the ships headed south as fast as their engines would take them, while the third was run aground and abandoned by her crew. Then, while the seaplanes harried the Red ships, Curteis's subchasers surrounded them like wasps round bumble bees, stinging them with 3-pounder shells until they surrendered. The Allied boats then put a landing party ashore and, together with the White Russians, captured Tolvoya.

It was a highly satisfactory exercise; the booty included a 300-ton steamer and a small destroyer armed with two 3-inch guns and it put the whole of the northern part of the lake under Allied control.

Maynard, after conferences in Archangel with Ironside and General Eugene Miller (who had taken over as head of the North Russian government from Tchaikovsky and proved to be the first effective Russian leader in the north), returned to set up a final series of attacks before the Allies withdrew. As in the Archangel sector, the purpose was to hurt the Bolsheviks as much as possible and to give the White Russians time and space to ensure their survival. The attacks were to be made by some 9,000 troops of whom 6,000 were Russians organised in three columns. So little time was left before the Allies returned to Murmansk and boarded their ships for home that their soldiers were concentrated in the two central columns to make their return journey easier.

It is here that we must tell the story of the 6th Battalion of the Royal Marines Light Infantry. It has never been told before. The strictest censorship was imposed by the British War Office and Admiralty and the men involved were so threatened that one old man, possibly the last survivor of this unfortunate battalion, remains too frightened to tell his story.

The battalion had been raised, not to go to fight in North Russia, but for mainly ceremonial duties during the plebiscite being held in Schleswig-Holstein which would determine whether it would remain part of Germany or return to Denmark. For that reason the battalion included young men, mostly recruits, and men who during the war had been sent to sea after only a brief period of training. It also included men who had returned from the mental and physical hardships of imprisonment in German prisoner of war camps, and, incredibly, had not been given leave before being sent abroad again.

One company each had been provided by the Chatham, Portsmouth and Plymouth divisions of the Royal Marines along with a company of the Royal Marine Artillery. They had joined up at Bedenham, near Gosport, for training – but their training was in ceremonial drill rather than in warfare under difficult conditions. However, while they were preparing for what should have been a pleasant duty in a friendly country, the Admiralty was asked to provide a marine battalion to bolster the forces available to Rawlinson to cover the evacuation. The 6th seemed to fit the bill admirably, for it was not expected that it would have to do any fighting. So, under Lieutenant-Colonel A. de W. Kitcat, they were shipped to Russia, landing at Murmansk on August 8th. They entrained that same evening for Kem where they arrived on the 10th to find themselves far from being rear echelon soldiers. The men were on their way up to the front line to take part in Maynard's last push. And they were not very happy about it.

In the first place they had not been given the chance to volunteer for the Russian mission. The Royal Marines' Adjutant-General had simply "vouched" for them at the War Office. Secondly Kitcat had thought it wiser not to pay them the day before they left Bedenham so that he would not leave any drunks behind. And thirdly, with the war over, nobody wanted to risk his life on behalf of Russia. If it had been England they would have fought willingly, but Russia was a different matter.

The marines saw their first action on August 17th when C Company, supported by an armoured train, drove the Bolsheviks further down the railway line. Then on the night of 29th/30th C Company, under the command of Kitcat, attacked the village of Koikori. This was supposed to be a preliminary to the main thrust south and the Bolsheviks were expected to run away when the artillery opened up and the seaplanes started to drop their bombs. But the village was defended by the tough and experienced Red Finns and the marines were met with concentrated machine-gun fire from prepared positions. Kitcat was wounded in the foot, three men were killed, eighteen wounded and the marines fell back, eventually halting at Svyatnavolok, some ten miles away, at nine in the evening. They had had no food since midnight the day before and were exhausted. When they were relieved by the East Surreys, they left all their gear behind while they moved further back to Tivdiya, which involved a ten-mile row across Lake Limozero. It was an undistinguished action which foreshadowed the trouble to come.

On September 8th B Company returned to the attack on Koikori while D Company attacked Ussuna. The men of B Company had already made it clear to their officers that they should not try to win any medals. They ran into trouble immediately. When B Company's Russian guide disappeared it swiftly became evident that he was a Bolshevik agent for the marines were soon coming under heavy fire from their rear. Many of them were shot in the back. One of them was Private Davey who, when he was shot, simply said "I've copped it" and died. Private Pyle who was wounded and captured during this action said later that he had seen the guide in the Russian camp. Pyle was later awarded the DCM for his "gallantry and determination and loyalty" shown while he was a captive of the Bolsheviks for a year.

But there were few medals awarded to the marines that day. Major A. C. Barnby, the company commander, was wounded. So was Captain Noyes. Captain Watts, who should have taken over command, collapsed and the company fell back in disarray. Much the same thing happened to D Company and soon, instead of advancing, the British were retreating in some haste in the face of a counter-attack by Red Finns.

The flavour of the situation may be judged from the citations for the medals which were won that day. Lieutenant W. A. M. Lanson of the marines won the MC "when, although wounded he refused to leave the line thereby steadying his platoon". Captain W. Morris of the Machine Gun Corps was awarded the MC for handling "his guns most ably and, under heavy fire, successfully engaged the enemy while the infantry withdrew". Lieutenant W. G. Irvine-Fortesque of the Royal Engineers got a bar to his MC "for conspicuously good leadership in very trying circumstances. On the 8th when the attacking troops failed in their attempt and became disorganised, he took up his section with other reinforcements and successfully held the line."

These citations tell the story of brave men acting coolly in the face of disaster.

Lieutenant P. R. Smith-Hill now found himself in charge of B Company and, as he later reported,

> I reorganised the company and manned outposts on the Koikori –Svyatnavolok road. On my return from speaking to Major Strover (Machine Gun Corps) I found the company collected in the road. On asking why they had left their positions they informed me that a Major in the MGC had told them to leave their Lewis guns and "Get to hell out of it" as they were not needed and that he would find someone "who was some use to the position."
>
> I was told by the men that Major Strover had telephoned HQ informing them that he was sending the Marines out of it as he had no use for them and asking that they should be neither clothed or fed.
>
> The word had been passed to the men that those who did not wish to fight could march back. The men fell in and obeyed orders.

Koikori and Ussuna were never taken, but the rest of Maynard's attack, launched on September 14th, succeeded brilliantly. The Bolsheviks suffered heavy casualties, including a thousand men taken prisoner. Their largest ship on the Onega, a four-funnelled destroyer, was bombed and damaged by the seaplanes, and the whole front advanced some twenty miles so that Maynard was able to hand over to General Skobeltsin along the line of the River Nurmis. General Rawlinson had given orders that Maynard should not advance beyond the Nurmis in case his men would be too far forward to comply with the time-table for the evacuation.

By September 25th Skobeltsin and his new Russian Army had taken over and all the Allied forces were moving back to Murmansk. For them the war was over. It was also over for General Maynard, for after a year of unremitting war and staff work carried out in the most exacting conditions, his medical board finally proved to have been correct in its opinion of his health. Worn out by his physical exertions, he broke down and was forbidden to play any further part in the war which he had conducted so ably.

But for the 6th Battalion, Royal Marines, it was far from over. When they got back to Murmansk over one hundred of them were court-martialled. "A few days later," wrote Smith-Hill,

> the battalion was drawn up in a hollow square with the men who had been court-martialled facing the open side of the square. The

Commanding Officer read out the charge against them, cowardice, the finding of guilty, and the sentence – death. I was only a few yards away and saw that they merely looked bashful at the publicity, not shocked. The C.O. continued to read that the sentence had been commuted to seven years penal servitude with hard labour.

Captain Watts was also tried. He was charged with cowardice and "using words calculated to create alarm and despondency in that he did say 'the whole bloody company is lost' or words to that effect."

Poor Watts. Although it was pointed out that he had been wounded at Gallipoli and one of his arms permanently disabled, that he had a record of accidents and illness and on that fateful day had used up more than six field dressings bandaging the wounded, he was found guilty and cashiered.

He was given a suit of civilian clothes and sent home on a collier. He later joined the Black and Tans and worked in an undercover unit against the IRA, no job for a coward.

When the sentencing was over General Rawlinson addressed the officers of the battalion and told them that there were no bad men, only bad officers. After he had left, Kitcat said that as commanding officer he accepted the main responsibility. His career was in ruins. He was placed on half pay and then on the retired list. All the other officers, except for one captain and one lieutenant received "an expression of their Lordships' grave displeasure".

Smith-Hill survived this reprimand to become a Brigadier and be decorated with the CBE. He later reflected that "the Other Ranks suffered most and deserved it the least. They were transported two thousand miles by sea and 450 miles by rail; they fought a minor action lasting 2½ hours – and returned home. They achieved nothing. They were like disgruntled children in a strange land far from home."

The unfortunate 6th Battalion left Murmansk on October 8th on board the SS *St Elena* and arrived at Glasgow three days later where the companies dispersed to their parent divisions and the convicted men were taken to serve their sentences in the naval prison at Bodmin in Cornwall. Not a hint of the affair had so far reached the British public but rumours began to spread in government circles and the families of the convicted men had to be told that they had been imprisoned – although the families were given no details of the offences they had committed. Enough news seeped out for some Members of Parliament to start asking questions in the House. At first they were fobbed off but on December 22nd the

Conservative MP, Lieutenant-Commander Kenworthy, asked the
First Lord of the Admiralty if he was now in a position to announce
the decisions of the Admiralty on the cases of the Royal Marines in
Bodmin Prison "for offences alleged to have been committed in
Russia".

In a carefully phrased reply Mr Walter Long, First Lord of the
Admiralty, announced a remarkable measure of clemency for the
men, some of whom had been judged guilty of crimes deserving the
sentence of death.

He first praised the splendid and devoted service of the Royal
Marines throughout the Great War, then said:

> We have given these cases our most careful and anxious con-
> sideration, and have decided to deal with them in what we believe
> the House will regard as a spirit of clemency.
>
> About ninety men of the Royal Marines in North Russia were
> found guilty of insubordination and refusal to obey orders while
> engaged in active operations. They were serving with the Army
> in the field and were sentenced by military courts-martial.
>
> Subject in all cases to good conduct in prison, we have decided
> on the following reductions in the sentences:
>
> Of thirteen men sentenced to death commuted by the General
> Officer Commanding-in-Chief to five years' penal servitude –
> twelve to be released after one year; one to be released after two
> years.
>
> Twenty men sentenced to five years' penal servitude, to be
> released after six months.
>
> Fifty-one men sentenced to two years' imprisonment with
> hard labour, to be released after six months.
>
> Special consideration has been given to the cases of men under
> nineteen years of age at the time of the commission of the offence
> in question, in view of the Army instruction, that young soldiers
> were not, if possible, to be employed in front-line operations.
> Two of those who continued in a refusal of duty when others
> obeyed, will, in view of their youth, be released after serving six
> months. The remainder – six out of eight – have been released.
>
> The extent to which it could be urged that bad leadership on
> the part of the officers contributed to these incidents has been
> fully considered, and, where merited, disciplinary action is being
> taken.

Remarkably, no further questions were asked and no newspaper
attempted to discover what lay behind this act of clemency. The

affair was kept so secret that none of the generals involved, Ironside, Maynard and Rawlinson, mention it in their memoirs. It was of course quite shameful that the 6th Battalion should ever have been sent to Russia and even more shameful that its under-age soldiers and prison camp veterans should have been thrown into the fighting. The suspicion must be that Long's announcement was as much an admission of governmental responsibility as an act of clemency.

When the last troopship from Murmansk left on the evening of October 12th, another episode in British military history came to an end. The total casualties sustained by the British forces in both the Archangel and Murmansk sectors from the beginning of the campaign in the spring of 1918 to the final evacuation in October 1919 were 41 officers and 286 other ranks killed, 65 officers and 591 other ranks wounded. The total cost was calculated by the Army at £18,219,860.

The Russian government, for which the British soldiers fought and died, did not last long after the troopships had sailed away. Murmansk fell to the Red Army in March 1920 and thousands of its inhabitants were killed in the terrible revenge the Bolsheviks exacted from those who had worked for the Allies and the North Russian government. Their thirst for vengeance was insatiable and their arm was long. General Miller escaped from Archangel in an ice-breaker in February 1920, just before it fell to the Bolsheviks. He fled to Paris where he became leader of the White Officers' Emigré Organisation. In September 1937 he was kidnapped by Soviet agents and never seen again.

But that was in the future and when Maynard's troopships sailed from Murmansk, leaving the North Russian government to its fate, there was still a good chance that the Bolsheviks would be defeated by White Russian Armies fighting with Allied assistance on three other fronts. Admiral Kolchak, though hard pressed, still commanded large forces in Siberia, General Nikolai Yudenich's North Western Army, striking out of Estonia under the cover of the Royal Navy, was less than forty miles from Petrograd and, on the day after the last British soldier sailed away through the Kola inlet, General Denikin took Orel and prepared to march on Moscow.

CHAPTER 17

Defeat and Betrayal
Siberia, December 1918–February 1920

The situation of the anti-Bolshevik forces would have been better still had there been any determination among the Allies to crush the Red Army. When the Hampshires had arrived at Vladivostok in November 1918 they had increased the total of Allied troops in Siberia to nearly 180,000 well-armed men, a formidable fighting force in the Russian context at that time. It was a force which, properly used under a united command, could have defeated the Red Army in Siberia, joined up with Ironside in the north and Denikin in the south and enabled General Yudenich, the former Tsarist general now commanding the White Russians' North-Western Army, to make his thrust at Petrograd against weakened opposition.

What might have been achieved may be judged from the fact that Kolchak's badly trained, disorganised and largely unwilling soldiers advanced across the vast expanse of Siberia to within 500 miles of Moscow creating panic among the Bolsheviks. And they did this with virtually no help in the field from the Allies.

The Soviets have always presented the Allied intervention in Siberia as a united attempt by the capitalist powers to destroy their revolution, an attempt which was foiled by the gallant Red Army. In truth, apart from the initial flurry of action on the River Ussuri and the activities of gun teams landed by the Royal Navy, none of the allied forces in Siberia fired a shot designed to bring about the downfall of Bolshevism. The most the Allies did was to keep Kolchak supplied and to defend themselves against Bolshevik partisans and marauding bands of outlaws. The British sent two consignments of matériel, each sufficient to equip 100,000 men, and the Americans of the Railway Service Corps repaired the Trans-Siberian and kept the supplies rolling.

As we have seen, the American General Groves was sent to Siberia with only two objectives: to ensure the safe passage of the Czechs to Vladivostok and to protect the supply dumps. Groves, no lover of Kolchak, interpreted his orders to the letter. No American soldiers were employed on offensive operations against the Bolsheviks. And the Czechs, making local "don't shoot us and we won't shoot you" arrangements with the Red Army, were concerned only with getting home. Held up for months along the Trans-Siberian by lack of rolling stock and shipping, they had settled down in an elongated community stretching for thousands of miles, running their own commercial enterprises, including a bank and a newspaper.

The Japanese, while not averse to fighting the Bolsheviks, would only do so if their own expansionist plans to occupy the Maritime Provinces of Russia and Manchuria were threatened. They certainly had no intention of advancing further west than Irkutsk – a remarkable situation when their very presence in Siberia was brought about by the Allied hope that they would be rushed westwards to form a new front against the Germans.

Thus, with the Americans, Czechs and Japanese out of the game 151,000 men were effectively removed from the Allied Army. Moreover, once the Armistice with Germany had been signed, the Canadians, the Serbs, the Poles, the Rumanians and the Italians saw no reason to be in Siberia. What, on paper, was a powerful army was, in reality, a phantom.

The only Allied troops in Siberia committed to supporting the anti-Bolshevik forces were the two British infantry battalions and the Royal Navy's gun teams, the French Colonial battalion, and the military missions from France and Britain. Of these, the French battalion composed of "Tonkinese" from South-East Asia, bewildered little men in an alien climate, was useless; and the British infantrymen, mostly time-expired, were becoming increasingly restive at being kept in the Army while all the jobs were being snapped up at home by men already demobilised with far less service. They could see no point in being halfway round the world from their homes and doing nothing. It might have been different if they were in action, but they never once went up to the front line.

The only Britons who saw action after the Middlesex's baptism of shellfire soon after their arrival, were a few advisors attached to Kolchak's forces and the naval detachment of 29 men from the cruisers *Suffolk* and *Kent*. They mounted a 6-inch gun and four twelve pounders on an armoured train and did good work along the railway line between Omsk and Ufa until the end of November when the recoil cylinder froze on the 6-inch. However, when Kolchak captured Perm in December he also captured a number of boats, two of which were handed over to the naval detachment and, renamed *Kent* and *Suffolk*, were armed with the naval detachment's guns. Thus British seamen and Royal Marines found themselves fighting ship-to-ship battles on rivers in the heart of Siberia. This detachment was led by a Royal Marine officer called Tom Jameson who was awarded the DSO. He later became a Major-General and was made a CBE for his work in World War Two.

Surprisingly, it was the Americans who took most casualties despite their orders to avoid conflict with the Bolsheviks. In repairing and guarding the railway in small detachments they became targets not only for Red guerrillas operating behind the lines but for the various freelance groups of bandits and dissidents who wandered their bloody way across Siberia. In a number of brisk but small actions they lost 112 men.

When the Hampshires reached Omsk at the end of their long journey on the Trans-Siberian they moved into a girls' school. It was bitterly cold, just above freezing inside and 60 degrees of frost outside. There were no baths and just one smoky kitchen. But they considered themselves lucky for Omsk was crowded with refugees and soldiers, many of whom had no shelter. Colonel Robert Johnson of the Hampshires was horrified to find that the girls his battalion had dispossessed had nowhere to stay and were very badly off. He insisted that they should be given one wing of the building and he wrote to his wife: "If you were nearer I would ask you to get your friends to collect girls' underclothing and stockings and send them out to these poor creatures; their condition in this way is really deplorable."

Colonel Johnson was the very epitome of the late Victorian upper middle class, suspicious of the aristocracy, condescending towards but at the same time responsible for those worse off than himself. A fervent churchman, no doubt convinced that God was an Englishman, he certainly believed that the English soldier, especially the 9th Hants, was the best in the world, and he believed that his first duty was to look after the welfare of his men. He was also something of a prig and took great exception when Kolchak took a mistress and "displayed her in public".

Johnson was also afraid of the future: he had taken over command of the Hants as a Territorial Army Officer in 1911 and now, eight years later, had made no advancement, while his contemporaries had made brilliant careers in politics and wartime service on the battlefronts. His letters are full of envious surprise that "those rogues", Churchill, Lloyd George and F. E. Smith, were running the country. He, as much as his men, was fearful that all the best jobs would be gone by the time he got home. Eventually he was to become Sir Robert Johnson, Deputy Master and Comptroller of the

Royal Mint, a regular attender at the Hampshires' annual dinner where he always raised a shout of laughter by telling them that they were "a remarkable body of men".

But all that was many years and many thousands of miles away from the fearful city of Omsk where a meal for four in a restaurant cost £75 – a fabulous amount in those days – while there was such a shortage of bandages, medicine and ambulances that few of the men wounded at the front survived. The White Russian troops were so short of clothes that they stripped any prisoners they took and turned them loose naked to freeze to death.

One of Johnson's great problems was to keep his men occupied. The weather meant that training was cut to a minimum and the War Office refused to allow him to take his battalion into action – although he did send a small party on sledges to try to help at Orenburg which had just been lost to the Bolsheviks. He introduced ice-hockey – "it's all the rage" – dances were held each week, two for the men and one for the officers, and he even turned to amateur theatricals, getting his men to give a concert to Admiral Kolchak and his government.

Johnson wrote to his wife, Kathleen, that "it is a very great success in every way and has done a great deal to enhance the popularity of the British in Omsk . . . The most successful thing of all was a scene from the *Merry Wives of Windsor*, very decently acted indeed and the Elizabethan dresses all made out of simple material by the regimental tailor." Two of the women were played by young men of the regiment "quite as Shakespeare had planned it". Johnson planned to put on scenes from *The Merchant of Venice* at a subsequent concert – hardly a happy choice given the virulent anti-Semitism which flourished in the White Armies. The *Times* correspondent with the British Army in Siberia reported that they had also given an exhibition of Physical Training which "brought the house down" and that a three-round bantamweight exhibition of boxing which few of the Russians had ever seen before brought the ironic comment from the local newspaper, "a little too strong for our nerves".

The *Times* correspondent, Robert Wilton, was fiercely pro-intervention and pro-Kolchak and he used his despatches not for reporting the situation but for propaganda. After an interview with Kolchak, the "Supreme Ruler", Wilton reported that he had become more impressed with the indications of the "growing confidence and authority of [his] government. Also it had been borne in upon me that Admiral Kolchak was the centre of things and that people look to him alone. When a man who had ever played an unassuming role in affairs looms this large in the public mind we may assume that that man had come at the hour."

The most extreme criticism Wilton could manage was: "It seems a thousand pities that the most competent brains of Russia should not be available at Omsk."

However, it was only through such woefully inadequate and biased reportage that the world learnt anything of what was going on in Siberia.

Johnson gave the game away in a letter to his father dated January 28th, 1919: "When you read *The Times* Correspondent from Omsk you must read between the lines – we are of course in close touch – but think it inadvisable even to hint that Kolchak is insecure as that would give impetus to the policy of withdrawal which we are convinced would be fatal."

It is therefore to Johnson's own letters that we must turn for an insight into what was really happening in Siberia:

I am getting to regard the situation here as pretty hopeless . . . their army is useless . . . I never saw such an incapable lot . . . the army has no discipline. The regimental officers are useless. Kolchak is, I think, a determined man but he stands quite alone and may be murdered or upset at any moment and that would be the end. Indeed but for our own presence here he would already have gone, but what a hopeless situation if the head of the government here rests solely on 1,000 British bayonets.

Johnson got wind of a plot by discontented White officers to overthrow Kolchak. He –

promptly and ostentatiously prepared for a fight, letting it be known that I should not tolerate any disturbance of the peace or any armed attack on Kolchak and this squashed the whole thing. Kolchak has now gone off to visit his generals . . . all mutinous and with him have gone Captain Baring, my adjutant, and a guard of 9th Hants . . .

The men of the 9th Hants escort found a full general dead drunk in their railway carriage one afternoon and as he wouldn't or couldn't go away when they asked him, they had to lift him up and throw him into the snow. The next day he turned out on parade with his division to be inspected by Kolchak. He was still drunk.

In all sorts of ways the Russians are hopeless, unbusinesslike, unpunctual, corrupt, intriguing and without internal discipline of any sort, the latter the result of the Revolution. Then they are fearfully lazy and expect the Allies to do all the work for them while they sit tight and enjoy themselves – or try to make money.

I fancy that [the Bolsheviks] are better organised and have more enthusiasm . . . and I should be surprised if they didn't give these people here a good hiding . . . I am afraid the Russians are completely hopeless and that we are wasting time and energy and money in trying to help them.

Johnson's opinion of his ostensible Commander-in-Chief, General Janin of the French Army was hardly much higher:

He sits in his railway carriage here, a solitary though dignified figure . . . nominally C-in-C of the allies including the Czechs who refuse to fight under any circumstances, and ourselves. But he gives no orders and takes no responsibility, is thoroughly sick of the whole business and is pining to be back in France. Also there is the French jealousy of the British so he cannot even be taken into confidence especially as he is all for withdrawal . . . A ridiculous and pathetic figure, with his personal escort of 20 men – all the French troops he has except a battalion of Tonkinese who run on all possible occasions.

Janin in fact was C-in-C in name only. It was General Knox who exercised power on behalf of the Allies in Siberia.

By the early summer Johnson was having trouble with his beloved Hampshires, not that they would have run, and not with his original "terriers", but with conscripted men who had joined the battalion just before it left India. On March 30th he told his mother that they were not part of the family and also that, in the eighth year of his command, he was no longer a new broom. "The regiment has got used to me and I am not the power I was. Last week I had a very anxious time. Pilfering of government stores and I had to take strong action. As a result there was very nearly a mutiny incited by the draft men. It was touch and go for a short while but we succeeded in averting anything really serious – about a dozen poor fools who have been severely punished."

Then again, early in June he wrote: "We have had a rather nasty time – an attempt on the part of ten draft men to incite the rest to a kind of mutiny. It was an anxious moment but the discipline held and only a dozen men broke out of barracks and even they returned quietly in a very short time."

The fact of the matter was that the men were receiving long-delayed letters – they had to be fumigated because the trains were infested with typhus – telling them that family businesses were failing because their parents were getting too old to carry on and that employers who had held their jobs open for five years could no longer do so. It was a poor reward for patriotism and service and the men were justly angry at being kept in Siberia performing no useful function. "We played a lot of cards," said Arthur Waide.

Johnson, a devout Anglican, had another problem, a matter of religion: "My Chaplain, being a Canadian, has been recalled. They actually sent a Baptist to replace him: I am not, as you know, a narrow sectarian – least of all very 'high' – but I really could not stand that. And it would have made my co-operation with the Russian church impossible. So I have sent him back and asked for a C of E."

Imagine how that poor chaplain must have felt. He had travelled half way round the world to reach Vladivostok, then spent a month on a typhus-infected train constantly under danger of attack in order to care for the souls of the Hampshire regiment only to be put on the train again and sent back to Vladivostok – because the Hampshires' colonel did not like his brand of religion.

Johnson took on a new lease of life when he moved his men forward to Ekaterinburg "to have 8,000 Russians thrown at their heads to turn into a Russian brigade of 2 Regiments, each of 4 Battalions. The Brigade will be officered entirely by British officers and NCOs. The bulk of the officers will be training officers sent out to Knox; the NCOs from the Hants." The training officers were mainly regulars seeking advancement and adventure. One of them was Captain Brian Horrocks who had been severely wounded and captured in October 1914 and was only just resuming the military career which would flower so brilliantly in North Africa in World War II and lead to him becoming Lieutenant-General Sir Brian Horrocks.

"The Hampshire Russian Brigade," wrote Johnson, "will be dressed in British uniform, armed with British weapons and drilled in British style with British words of command . . . We hope to march into Moscow as conquerors. Hants and Russian Hants together."

At the end of April he was still writing optimistically. "It is difficult to be certain and foolish to prophesy but we all think here that Moscow may very well be taken by this army before the autumn and that Bolshevikism only wants one strong push to collapse altogether."

Siberia, December 1918–February 1920

A week later and his euphoria had disappeared:

Serious reverses have taken place in the South on the left of our
long line. Orenburg again, and a place between Samara and Ufa,
retaken by the Bolsheviks. A whole brigade of Ukrainian troops
deserted bodily to the Bolsheviks having murdered their officers
. . . And things are not too comfortable on the line to Vladivostok, constant risings, trains wrecked etc. The Americans doing
nothing at all and the Japanese and Semenov playing their own
dirty games. The latest is that Semenov has proclaimed himself
"Prince of Mongolia" no doubt at Japanese instigation. The
Americans are worse than useless being positively Bolshevik in
sympathy and the Canadians have left Vladivostok for home.
    Meanwhile it is an orgy of bloodshed and suffering every-
where – hideous cruelties on both sides.

He was working furiously to get the new brigade equipped and
trained. "It is up to us all to set an example to these poor helpless
Russians and show what just a handful of British can do."
    In the middle of May he wrote to his wife, "Tootsie": "Our first
750 Russkis coming in tomorrow and the next 1000 on the following day. The first thing we have to do is to wash them – they are
perfectly filthy and crawling with vermin – then entirely reclothe
from head to foot and burn their personal rags. Many of them are
Mongolian Mohammedans not speaking a word of Russian."
    While he pitied the recruits and was prepared to help them to the
best of his ability this very correct God-fearing man looked on the
middle-class people of Ekaterinburg with something approaching
hatred:

The bourgeoisie, are too cowardly to fight even though of course
they know that the triumph of the Bolsheviks would mean the
torture and murder of every man jack of them and every woman
jack too. Really, the bourgeoisie makes one almost a Bolshevik
oneself.
    Here is a rich town, full of quite rich people, the ordinary
population is short of everything including food because of the
fearful prices and the practical cessation of the railway for commercial purposes anyway, the army lacks everything, literally
everything an army needs – the hospital stinking with typhus
and crammed with wounded but with hardly anything at all – no
beds, shirts, mattresses, towels, bandages, swabs, surgical in-
struments, anaesthetics, medicines, literally without any of these

239

things – a frightful state of affairs. Yet not one woman of the bourgeoisie even goes near the hospital or dreams of sparing just an hour or even so much as meeting the train loads of wounded and offering them a cup of tea . . . the bourgeoisie goes nightly to the opera and then on to dance or what not until four or five even."

In almost every letter to his wife, Johnson urged her to contact his old friends now in powerful places, to plead the cause of himself and his men. In particular he asked her to "write to Jack Seely and tell him from me that I expect him to go and see his friend Winston [Churchill] and tell him not to forget us. This he should do not only as a friend who has professed gratitude to me – but as Lord Lieutenant of Hampshire . . ."

"Galloping Jack" Seely was a remarkable man. A Liberal MP from 1900 to 1922, he was Secretary of State for War from 1912 to 1914 but resigned following the Curragh incident. By 1918 he was commanding the Canadian Cavalry Brigade and it was he who led them on their epic charge into German machine-gun fire to retake the Moreuil Ridge, one of the key points in Ludendorff's attempts to crush the Allies in the spring of 1918. The Brigade lost 300 dead and wounded and 800 horses in less than half an hour but it saved the day and stopped the Germans. Seely was gassed later in the year and returned to politics to serve as Churchill's Under Secretary of State.

It appears that Mrs Johnson's approach to him worked. In the first week of June Johnson received a telegram from Seely telling him that the Ministry of Labour had applied for him to be released to take up a post at the Ministry, and that he "strongly advised" Johnson to accept. At first he was disinclined to do so; he was fed up with being a civil servant and working for politicians he despised and he did not want to leave his beloved Hampshires in the lurch. But it seems that the whole battalion wanted him to go home to plead their cause.

And so began an extraordinary journey of which, alas, we have only a fragmentary account. Instead of taking the train back to Vladivostok, Colonel Johnson set out for Archangel with twelve married men who were being demobilised on compassionate grounds. They left Ekaterinburg on June 4th, took a steamboat from Perm up the Kama, a tributary of the Volga, then transferred to rowboats to push north-west up a tributary of the Kama. Next they took to the forest to walk eighty miles to the headwaters of the Pechora river. There they picked up another rowboat before transferring to a river steamer for 460 miles and then, because the mouths of the Pechora were still blocked by ice where they ran out into the Barents Sea, they trekked for another 200 miles through the forest before hitting a river along which they rowed to the sea. There they were picked up by the Navy and taken round the coast to Archangel.

It was a hazardous journey. Writing from the Russian ice-breaker which was taking him to Lerwick on July 1st, he told his father "I only just got through in time. The Bolsheviks are already over part of my route and may soon be over the whole of it."

Johnson was luckier than he knew. It was while he was making his way through the northern wilderness that General Gajda, advancing towards Viatka and Kotlas to link up with the Archangel forces, was decisively beaten and the last chance of effecting a viable military link with Ironside was lost. Kolchak dismissed Gajda a few weeks later. He was one of the extraordinary galère of characters thrown up by the Revolution and Civil War. A pharmacist by training, he was conscripted into the Czech Army and was captured by the Russians in 1917. He became one of the leaders of the Czech uprising in Siberia and Kolchak promoted him to Lieutenant-General in command of the Northern Army. Furious at his dismissal by Kolchak, he tried but failed to seize power in Vladivostok in November 1919. He returned to Czechoslovakia in 1920 and was made Chief of the General Staff six years later but was dismissed and cashiered for taking part in an attempted coup by the fascists. He collaborated with the Germans during the war and was executed in 1945.

Gajda's attack on Viatka had been part of Kolchak's grand plan for linking with Ironside in the north and Denikin in the south for a general advance on Moscow. Kolchak, who had scored a great success in December by capturing Perm, launched his offensive in March with 130,000 men, 210 guns and 1,300 machine-guns organised into four armies. At first they did surprisingly well. They pushed south and north and in the centre they captured Kazan and pressed on until they were only some 450 miles east of Moscow. It was this advance which gave rise to Johnson's euphoric letter-writing in April. He was not the only one who at that time thought that Kolchak could be in Moscow by the autumn. Churchill was delighted by Kolchak's successes and put pressure on Lloyd George to recognise Kolchak's regime as the legitimate government of Russia. But there were grave doubts about Kolchak, not only among the British public but in the Cabinet. There was too much of the Tsar about him for British tastes and all Churchill could gain for him was recognition as "The Provisional Government of Siberia".

Not for the first time and certainly not for the last Churchill was fighting a lone campaign. Most of his Cabinet colleagues, all the parliamentary opposition and the majority of the public wanted to have done with intervention.

Churchill, however, fought his corner with skill, cunning and forceful language, so forceful in fact that he eventually prompted a written reply from Lloyd George which must rank as one of the most savage that any Prime Minister can ever have inflicted on one of his senior colleagues.

"I wonder," wrote Lloyd George, of Churchill's continuing desire for the Allies to drive Bolshevism from Russia, "whether it is any use my making one last effort to induce you to throw off this obsession which, if you will forgive me for saying so, is upsetting your balance . . . you won't find another responsible person in the whole land who will take your view, why waste your energy and your usefulness on this vain fretting which completely paralyses you for other work?"

Churchill's hopes were constantly being raised as one or another of the White commanders won splendid victories. But they flattered only to deceive and defeat followed victory with an inevitability and swiftness that constantly dashed Churchill's hopes and alienated him further and further from his colleagues.

So it was with Kolchak. His armies ran out of steam. Victory in April was followed by defeat in May. Stopped cold by the Red Army on the road to Nizhny Novgorod (now Gorky), Kolchak's forces were threatened with being outflanked when Orenburg fell. At the beginning of June he was forced to retreat over a hundred miles. Then, on June 17th came Gajda's defeat. In the first week of July the Red forces under General Tukhachevsky, the Bolshevik hero shot by Stalin in the 1937 purges, broke through the Urals and, taking the White Army by surprise, wiped out its 12th Division. The Siberian campaign was going disastrously wrong and on July 25th the War Cabinet decided the Hampshires and the Middlesex should be withdrawn as soon as possible. The naval detachment scuttled their gunboats, and, taking their guns with them, made their way back to Vladivostok.

Kolchak was now being driven back east of the Urals by the 3rd and 5th Red Armies. He lost Ekaterinburg and Chelyabinsk and retreated towards Omsk. However, he succeeded in stopping the Bolshevik advance in September and in a month pushed the Red Army back some hundred miles.

But it could not last. His army suffered from the same inherent weaknesses as all the other White armies; lack of organisation and

motivation. The selfishness that Johnson had noted among the
bourgeoisie of Ekaterinburg along with the appalling treatment of
the ordinary soldiers and the scheming and inefficiency of the
generals and the politicians gave the army no reason to fight. Why
should they go to battle for people who would leave them to die
without even offering them a cup of tea?

Kolchak left Omsk on November 14th hoping to set up a new
line of resistance at Irkutsk 1,500 miles to the east. It was a rout
more that an orderly retreat as the battle front disintegrated with
thousands of refugees – those same people who had spurned the
soldiers – all trying to escape the Red Terror which they were sure
would be visited on them.

Neither the Hampshires nor the Middlesex were involved. Both
had been pulled back to Vladivostok, and the Middlesex had sailed
for Canada and England on September 7th, with the Hampshires –
who had lost one man killed and three wounded in Siberia –
following them on November 1st. As their train steamed across
Canada, the Middlesex encountered the Prince of Wales in Alberta.
He had just been proclaimed Chief Morning Star by his "loyal
tribesmen the Stoney Indians" and the Middlesex were turned out
to be inspected by the Chief.

But not all the British had left. Some of the training officers –
whose idea of training invariably took them into the thick of the
fighting – remained. One of these was Brian Horrocks who was
caught up in the retreat. He was wounded for the second time – the
third time, in North Africa in 1943, would be almost fatal – and
captured by the 5th Red Army at Krasnoyarsk, 2,000 miles west of
Vladivostok. Typhus had tightened its grip on Russia and Horrocks
recorded in his book, *A Full Life*, that "there were reputed to be
30,000 cases in Krasnoyarsk alone. For long we had been living
with dead. Naked corpses stacked on the railway platforms, sleighs
packed with frozen bodies – these were common sights." Horrocks himself caught typhus but survived to come through his
second period of captivity with the dry humour and infinite
patience which were later to endear him to the men he led to victory
in World War II.

There was panic all along the line as the Red Army, itself in tatters
and riddled with disease, advanced – bringing the Cheka with it.
Refugees, gathered in their thousands at the railway stations, seized
trains reserved for the government and the Army and there were
trains running eastwards on both lines so that no supplies or
ammunition could reach those White soldiers who were still trying
to fight a rearguard action. No fuel could get through and once the

trees along the line had been used up the trains stopped running. By now the Siberian winter had set in and the refugees who survived the typhus froze to death so that there were whole trains motionless and silent in the middle of nowhere carrying only the dead on their abortive journey. The trains were also easy targets for Red guerrilla bands and Semenov's brigands as well as local villagers intent on rape and pillage.

Kolchak arrived in Irkutsk by train at the end of his long retreat on January 14th, 1920. His private carriage flew the flags of Great Britain, France, Japan, the United States and Czechoslovakia and a locked and guarded wagon contained the captured treasure of the Tsar, then worth some £100 million. Both he and the treasure were under the protection of the Czech 6th Regiment. But he found himself without friends. General Knox, who had supported him so ardently, had already left the city, retreating to Vladivostok with the British and French military missions, forced to accept the protection of the Japanese, the only viable military force in the area. Before Knox sailed from Vladivostok on December 26th, he had tried to impress on General Jan Syrovy, the former bank clerk who became commander of the Czech Legion, the importance of ensuring Kolchak's safety. He sailed away sure that the "Supreme Ruler" would be protected by the Czechs.

But the Czechs themselves were in a difficult position: the Poles who were supposed to form the rearguard had, except for one regiment, laid down their arms and surrendered to the Bolsheviks. And by now the last thing the Czechs wanted was to reopen hostilities with the Bolsheviks. They had almost reached Vladivostok after their long and painful odyssey and were determined to board the ships that would take them home to their new nation without losing another man. There was no reason for them to fight the Red Army and, although they held prisoner several high ranking Bolsheviks who could have been used as hostages in a deal with the Bolsheviks on Kolchak's behalf, they preferred not to get embroiled any further.

They did not interfere when armed members of the Political Centre – an alliance of Socialist Revolutionaries and Mensheviks – surrounded Kolchak's train and refused to allow anyone to go within fifty yards of it. At 9.30 on the morning of January 15th the "Supreme Ruler" was removed to Irkutsk prison.

The Czechs are often accused of surrendering Kolchak to the Bolsheviks. Perhaps they would have done, but the occasion did not in fact arise – for it was the Political Centre and not the Bolsheviks who were in control of the area surrounding the station.

It was not until the local Bolshevik Committee took over Irkutsk and the Political Centre disappeared (leaving Kolchak locked up in jail) that the Bolsheviks got their hands on him and the Tsar's treasure. The Red Army had still to arrive on the scene. On March 7th, 1920 the exhausted and typhus-racked 26th Division of the 5th Red Army, which had been mopping up White resistance and amalgamating local partisan groups into its ranks, finally entered Irkutsk.

By that time Kolchak, deserted by all his friends and allies – the men who had once called him the saviour of Russia – had been tried and executed by the Bolshevik Committee. He was taken out of his cell before daybreak on February 7th, 1920 and shot by the River Ushakovka. His body was then pushed through a hole in the ice to disappear for ever. He bore himself, said an eye-witness, "like an Englishman": in those days that was praise indeed.

Kolchak had certainly been dictatorial. A man of fairly limited intellect, he had nevertheless been honest and honourable. There was no need for him to have died. The Czechs could have bargained for his life using their high-ranking Bolshevik prisoners as hostages for his safety. General Knox, who sailed away from Vladivostok thinking he had ensured the Admiral's safety, could have made sure of it: the Americans could have taken him into their care. And the Japanese, the ruling military power in the area, could have protected him. But nobody moved to save the man on whom the Allies had rested their hopes and to whose armies they had sent millions of pounds worth of matériel.

Among Admiral Phillimore's papers there is a report from a British colonel which lays the blame on General Janin: "When the situation worsened, surely that was the time for Janin to come out of his retreat at Irkutsk and with all the authority vested in him by the allies to have compelled Syrovy to effect Kochak's security." The report added: "For Janin and Syrovy to stand aside and do nothing for fear of imperilling the evacuation, was criminal."

The Bolsheviks had no intention of interfering with the Allies' evacuation. As long as Kolchak's forces were destroyed and the threat from Siberia removed, they were happy to let the Allies move out in their own time. In any case their armies – which had chased Kolchak all the way across Siberia – were in no fit state to take on the Americans and Japanese.

The Americans, who had lost 192 men to bullets and disease, started to pull out on January 11th and the last doughboys left on board the *Great Northern* on April 1st. As they sailed away the

Japanese Army band on the dockside played: "Hard Times Come Again No More."

The Japanese stayed on, however, reacting to Bolshevik partisan attacks with great ferocity. When they caught Sergei Lazo, commander of the partisan forces in the Maritime Provinces, they handed him over to White soldiers serving under their command to be thrown, alive, into the furnace of a locomotive.

It took two and a half years before the Japanese were forced to evacuate Vladivostok and even then, despite the Red Army's destruction of Semenov's army and the remaining White forces in the Maritime Provinces and Mongolia, it was American political pressure which forced the Japanese to give up rather than the military pressure of the Bolsheviks. At the Washington Conference in July 1921, called by the United States to discuss the problems of the Pacific, the Americans made it plain to the Japanese that the United States would no longer tolerate their occupation of the Siberian seaboard. Here, then, were the portents of another, greater struggle when those hard times would come again.

CHAPTER 18

Spies, Torpedoes and Three Lame Tanks
The Baltic, November 1918–December 1919

Throughout the intervention the Royal Navy lived up to its reputation for daring and efficiency. Men and machines performed against the worst odds: the *Attentive* which opened the way to Archangel; the gunboats which fought the river battles on the Dvina; the hotchpotch flotillas which won command of the Caspian and Lake Onega; the naval guncrews in Siberia; and the sailors who carried out the slogging hard work of transporting and escorting men and matériel across a dozen seas to the Russian battlefields had behaved in the highest tradition of the Royal Navy. It was only in the Baltic, however, that the Navy operated as a fleet at war opposed by an enemy fleet of big ships armed with big guns.

The Baltic had been denied to the Royal Navy during the First World War with only the dashing Cromie being able to break through the German defences to reach Petrograd and then wreak havoc among German shipping in his submarine. Even after the war the Baltic was a perilous place, full of thousands of mines, and when Admiral Sir Edwyn Alexander-Sinclair was sent there with a small force of light cruisers and destroyers in November 1918, his first task was to sweep a safe corridor – "the Red Route" – through the minefields. Although the Navy was able to use German, Russian and Swedish maps of the minefields, so many mines had been sown and so many had broken free that it remained a highly hazardous exercise and the light cruiser *Cassandra* and several smaller boats were sunk during the clearing.

Alexander-Sinclair was succeeded in January 1919 by Rear-Admiral Sir Walter Cowan, who loved horses almost as much as he loved his ships. A short, sturdy man, he could be seen walking the quarterdeck of his flagship, the cruiser *Delhi* wearing riding boots and a red hunting waistcoat under his uniform jacket. His task was to protect the Baltic states of Finland, Estonia, Latvia and Lithuania which the Germans had wrested from Russia under the terms of the Brest-Litovsk Treaty and which the Bolsheviks were determined to bring back into the new Soviet Empire. In addition he was also supposed to make sure that the Germans, who had occupied these

247

new states, obeyed the terms of the Armistice while the Peace Treaty was being ratified in Paris.

Cowan was a fighting sailor of great personal courage but rarely had a British seadog found himself in a situation of such political complexity. He found the Finns, those same White Finns against whom Maynard had gone to war, bargaining for support and recognition from the Allies in return for helping the White Russians to attack Petrograd. He found the Estonians fighting off Bolshevik incursions. He found Latvia virtually occupied by the Bolsheviks. He found General Von der Goltz, who had led the German invasion of Finland, in charge of a German garrison in the Latvian port of Libau. This was in accordance with the Armistice which allowed the Germans to maintain order, but Von der Goltz had other ideas: when German reinforcements arrived – among them the re-nowned Iron Division – he set about clearing the Bolsheviks out of Latvia.

Cowan also found the White Russian Northern Corps. This had originally been formed by the Germans from prisoners of war and refugees from Bolshevism and was commanded by Tsarist officers. The German plan had been to use it to replace men withdrawn from the Eastern Front to bolster their crumbling Western Armies. But the war ended too soon and the Northern Corps, which at that time numbered less than four thousand men, was taken over by the Estonians who needed whatever men they could get to fight off the Bolsheviks.

In addition, there were various "Freikorps" and "Landeswehr" of Poles and Baltic Germans and Finns. One of the roughest of these fighting bands was composed of Red Finns from Maynard's army who had not been allowed to return to Finland because of the part they had played in the civil war in which they had been defeated by the White Finns. Put under a young British Lieutenant-Colonel attached to the Polish Relief Mission, who whipped them into shape, they became devoted to him and among the best disciplined soldiers in the area. His name was Alexander and he became Field-Marshal Earl Alexander of Tunis, that great leader in the Second World War. He later told how, in those extraordinary days in the Baltic, British and German officers, victors and vanquished, all with pistols at their belts, would frequent the same restaurants. But dislike was mutual and hands never strayed far from holsters.

The Germans, who were regarded in some British quarters as a useful bulwark against the Bolsheviks, rapidly became a murderous embarrassment. They took the view that although forced to admit defeat in the West they certainly had not been defeated in the East, and the infant states of Latvia and Lithuania looked easy meat to these hardened veterans. Their acquisition would go some way to compensate for Germany's defeat. They occupied Mitau in March, then Libau, Memel in Lithuania, Windau and, finally, Riga, the capital of Latvia, in May. They behaved atrociously – conquerors rather than a defeated army – and some three thousand people were killed during their occupation of Riga.

Cowan, threatening to use his cruisers' guns, wrung a promise from Von der Goltz to give back the captured towns to their inhabitants. But Von der Goltz was a master of procrastination and when the thaw came and Russian warships started to raid the Estonian coast, Cowan had to sail his ships away to face the Red Fleet, while Von der Goltz, defying everybody, even his own government, clung to his gains.

Meanwhile General Yudenich had proclaimed himself commander of the White Russians in the name of Admiral Kolchak. A burly, moustachioed, professional soldier, Yudenich had emerged as one of the few heroes of the Russo–Japanese war in 1905 and had risen to command the Russian forces in the Caucasus where he performed well against the Turks. He not only commanded a growing army, but also set up a Political Council composed of Tsarist refugees ready to form the civil government of Petrograd when, as he confidently expected, he marched in. Yudenich suffered however, like all the White Commanders, and, indeed, the Red Commanders, from indecision and quarrelling among his staff. He also had to cope with the tantrums and scheming of the émigrés; at times it seemed that they were more intent on doing each other down than in winning back Russia.

Operating with the Estonians, Yudenich launched an offensive in May which, while failing to reach Petrograd, won him a sizeable area for recruitment and established for the first time a solid defensive line which ran from Narva on the coast to Pskov at the southern tip of Lake Peipus. His offensive also brought about the desertion of large numbers of men who had been unwillingly conscripted into the Red Army. He promptly incorporated them in his own army and by the early summer he had the not inconsiderable force of 25,000 men.

That same month the British sent out a military mission of 44 officers and 45 other ranks to force Von der Goltz to obey his government's instruction to withdraw from the Baltic and to "galvanise" Yudenich into greater efforts. Lieutenant-General Sir Hubert Gough, a man not inexperienced in political and military controversy, was appointed to lead it. As a brigadier-general commanding the Third Cavalry Brigade in Ireland he had been the prime mover in the "Curragh Incident" when he and 57 of his officers stated that they would rather be dismissed from the Army than be used against Ulstermen who were threatening civil war over the government's plans to give Ireland Home Rule. Then in March 1918 when in command of the Fifth Army in France, he had the misfortune to receive the full weight of Ludendorff's attack. The Fifth Army disintegrated and he was sacked. But even in disgrace he had his supporters who argued that he had fought as well as he could and that his dismissal had been brought about by politicians still angry over his stand at the Curragh. Now he was being given another chance.

He based himself in Helsinki where Yudenich and Von der Goltz also had headquarters. The three generals each occupied one of Helsinki's best hotels and flew their national flags from their roofs. The Finns called them "The Three Fortresses".

Meanwhile Cowan was concentrating on the bottling-up of the Red Fleet in Kronstadt – the immensely powerful island fortress which guards the approaches to Petrograd. In 1919 Kronstadt was protected by forts and underwater breakwaters built across the bay, with further forts on the mainland. It seemed to be impregnable. No hostile ship could approach it without being blown out of the water. In addition, its well equipped harbour held a fleet which, on paper, was far superior to Cowan's. He had cruisers and destroyers, along with minesweepers and monitors, and was later joined by two of the Navy's new class of ship, the aircraft carrier. But the Russians had two battleships armed with 12-inch guns, the *Andrei Pervozvanny* and the *Petropavlovsk*, the cruiser *Oleg* with 6-inch guns, the submarine depot ship *Dvina*, now given back its old revolutionary name of *Pamiat Azova* – the ship whose crew had given Cromie so much trouble – as well as seven submarines, a squadron of destroyers, some auxiliaries and the minelayer *Narova*, which had sown fresh minefields round Kronstadt.

However, the effectiveness of this powerful fleet was undermined by shortages, especially of fuel and ammunition. And, as the sailors – the muscle of the Revolution – had murdered so many of their officers there was no discipline; orders were answered by debate rather than action. The command structure was so weak that the Bolsheviks had been forced to put officers of the Tsarist Navy back in command of some ships. But they were captains in name only, working under threat of death to themselves and their families and with political commissars watching their every move.

That the fleet existed at all was due to the brilliant staff work of an

Imperial Navy officer, Admiral A. M. Shchastny, who twice saved the ships from capture by the Germans, moving them from Reval to Helsinki in February 1918 and then to Kronstadt when the Germans invaded Finland two months later. By using ice-breakers and minesweepers, he was able to deliver almost the entire Russian Baltic Fleet to the Bolsheviks.

Shchastny became a hero among the Bolsheviks, despite remaining very much an Imperial officer. This, of course, was unbearable for the Bolshevik fanatics. They lured him to Moscow to be "decorated" for his work, arrested him on trumped-up charges of using his popularity to work against the Revolution and shot him.

The ships that he saved were those that Cromie had plotted to sabotage to prevent them falling into German hands. How strange that the man who saved them and the man who plotted to sink them should both be murdered by the Bolsheviks.

With the coming of spring and the breaking of the Baltic ice these big Russian ships started to show signs of life. The Bolsheviks would send out their destroyers, occasionally protected by the *Oleg*, to raid along the Estonian coast. When Cowan's ships chased them back to Kronstadt, the two battleships would poke their noses out from the minefields and bang away with their big guns. This proved to be a waste of ammunition and after the end of May the battleships stayed at home, hoping that the emboldened British would run their ships into the minefields.

This did not mean there was a lack of action as Bolshevik destroyers emerged to bombard the Estonian coast and White Russian positions. On one of these raids two destroyers, the *Lennuk* and the *Yombola*, set out to attack Reval, but were cut off by British ships and boarded from a trawler by John Pitka, the flamboyant commander of Estonia's infant navy who later became Sir John Pitka. He and his men captured them both in an old-fashioned hand-to-hand encounter and they became the nucleus of the Estonian Navy.

One of the men captured by Pitka was the Commissar of the Baltic Fleet, F. F. Raskolnikov, a former chief petty-officer who had played a leading role in the overthrow of the Provisional government and was one of Trotsky's most loyal supporters. He was among a small number of high-ranking Bolsheviks who were taken to England to be used as hostages to force the Soviet government into an exchange of prisoners. On February 1st, 1920, he sent a radio message from England – obviously at British instigation – to Trotsky telling him that he and a member of the Petrograd Soviet were being held as hostages for "all British civilian and military prisoners" held by the Bolsheviks. Eleven days later an agreement was signed by both countries for the exchange of all prisoners. Raskolnikov went home on May 26th. We shall meet him again later.

The submarines were also active. Two British destroyers, HMS *Valorous* and HMS *Vancouver*, severely damaged the *Ersh* which barely succeeded in limping back to Kronstadt. The trade was two-way, with the Bolshevik destroyer *Azard* sinking the British submarine *L55*. The Russians raised the *L55* in 1928, accorded the dead crewmen full naval honours and then used her as the prototype for their highly successful Leninetz class of submarine. It is sobering to think that the nuclear submarines which now have their missiles trained on London and New York had their origins in a British boat sunk so long ago.

Cowan had one weapon of which the Bolsheviks knew nothing. It was the Coastal Motor Boat, developed during the war for hit-and-run raids along the German and Belgian shores. These boats, forty and fifty-five footers, had hydroplane hulls and with engines of up to 500 hp were capable of over forty knots. They were armed with Lewis guns, depth charges and either one or two torpedoes. They could also carry specially designed mines instead of the torpedoes. During the raid on Zeebrugge on April 22nd, 1918 they performed well and, because of their ability to skim over minefields, were being prepared for attacks on German heavy ships inside their harbours when the war ended.

Lieutenant Augustus Agar, whom we met earlier through his description of the *Askold* at Murmansk, was then serving with the CMBs at Osea Island on the River Blackwater in Essex. He watched impatiently as boats were sent off to fight the Bolsheviks on the Caspian, the Dvina and Lake Onega and his chance came following a summons to London to meet "C", the head of the Secret Service.

"C" was busy rebuilding his Russian network. After the death of Cromie, Reilly's flight, the expulsion of Lockhart, Hicks and Boyce and the departure of Hill, "C" had only one asset left in Petrograd. John Merrett who, according to Soviet accounts, ran his own trading business, Merrett Jones and Company, as cover for his illegal activities, used the name of Ivan Ivanovich. Described as a "blond giant" in a Cheka report, he was an obvious target for Cheka agents who followed him and searched his office. Although he kept a flicker of secret service activity alive in Petrograd the Cheka was closing in on him and, according to the Soviet version, "he avoided arrest only by accident". It was essential, therefore, to get him out and replace him with an undercover agent.

"C" had chosen one of the most remarkable of his agents for this task, Paul Dukes, a slightly-built twenty-eight-year-old, who had first gone to Russia in 1909 to study music at the Conservatoire. While attached to the Marinsky Theatre he had joined the Anglo-Russian Commission and with a King's Messenger's passport had travelled throughout Russia for six months studying relief work. In June 1918 he was summoned to London and – believing his work to be unsatisfactory to the Foreign Office – presented himself at a building near Trafalgar Square where, to his surprise, he was offered a job with the SIS.

Dukes' task would be to return to Russia to report on Bolshevik policy, the attitude of the population towards the government, the possibilities for a change in the regimes, and the extent of German influence. He was also asked to provide military and naval intelligence. He agreed and, armed with the names of a "few English people" to contact, landed at Archangel in September 1918. Dukes then made his way in disguise to Petrograd where Merrett handed over his skimpy network to him and vanished from Russia in the guise of a coachman.

It was to be Lieutenant Agar's job to establish a secret base for two CMBs on the Finnish coast, close to Petrograd, and run in couriers and money to Dukes, a job which had become urgent since a number of his couriers travelling overland had been picked up by the Bolsheviks and shot. Agar was to be known as Agent ST 34 and he and his boats were to serve MI6 rather than Admiral Cowan.

On June 10th, 1919, he arrived at Terrioki, just three miles from the Russian border. There with six men, two boats and the help of British agents based in Finland and the co-operation of the local Finnish commandant, he set up his base in a disused yacht club.

He went to work immediately. On June 13th, guided by a smuggler, he threaded his way through Kronstadt's forts and the underwater breakwaters, waiting for the searchlights and the burst of gunfire which would signal the end of his mission. But he slipped through unseen, and landed his courier "Peter" on an island virtually in the suburbs of Petrograd. He turned for home and once more easing past patrol boats, minefields and forts, made his way safely back to Terrioki having arranged to fetch "Peter" out of Petrograd the following night.

Agar's situation had become complicated because the Fortress of Krasnaya Gorka on the coast to the west of Petrograd had rebelled against the Bolsheviks on June 10th and two battleships had been

sent out from Kronstadt to bombard it into submission. He could
see the battleships bombarding the fort throughout June 14th, but
nevertheless made his preparations. That night he went out again
and everything went like clockwork. The courier was picked up
with despatches from Dukes, including the message that Dukes did
not want to be lifted out for another month.

This brought an end to Agar's secret service work for the time
being and he turned his mind to other things. He had borrowed two
torpedoes from Cowan and now proposed to use them against the
battleships bombarding Krasnaya Gorka. But his request to London brought the instruction: "Boats to be used for intelligence
purposes only. Take no action unless specially directed by Senior
Naval Officer Baltic." To most young officers that would have
been an explicit order but Agar saw it as giving him permission to
go ahead as long as he could obtain Cowan's approval. Furthermore, although he had no way of contacting Cowan, he was sure
the Admiral would approve. So with that piece of Nelsonian logic
Agar made preparations to attack the battleships.

Both boats, Agar commanding No. 4 and Lieutenant J. Sindall
commanding No. 7, loaded their torpedoes and, changing their
civilian spy clothes for Royal Navy uniforms, set out, White
Ensigns flying, at midnight on June 16th. Almost immediately
Sindall's boat hit a floating mine. It failed to explode but broke his
propeller shaft. Agar towed him to safety but Sindall and his boat
were now out of the game. The following day, June 17th, the
Bolshevik battleships returned to harbour and their place was taken
by the *Oleg*. That night, in a heavy sea, Agar set out to attack the
Oleg with Sub-Lieutenant John Hampsheir and Chief Motor
Mechanic Hugh Beeley as his crew on CMB 7. They were sliding
slowly through the destroyers screening the *Oleg* when suddenly
the boat started to judder violently. The charge used to eject the
torpedo had fired. Luckily it was held firmly by two iron clamps.
Hampsheir then fought to fit a new charge while the boat lay rolling
between two Bolshevik destroyers. Eventually he succeeded and
Agar headed, engine roaring, at full speed towards the *Oleg*, fired
his torpedo and swung away. They now came under fire from the
cruiser, the destroyers and the forts but, miraculously, they were
untouched. Their torpedo ran true and burst against the *Oleg*'s side.
She rolled over and sank and forty crewmen died. Agar was
awarded the Victoria Cross for this exploit, but as the circumstances could not be revealed it became known as the "Mystery
VC".

There still remains something of a mystery about this action for in his book, *Baltic Episode*, Agar writes only about these two attempts to attack the Bolshevik ships, while his official report which is printed as an appendix to the book reveals that he had in fact made three attempts, the first one being made not on the *Oleg* but on the battleships as he returned from landing "Peter" on his first run to Petrograd. His report says: "On the morning of Friday, June 13th, after completing a special mission in the Bay of Petrograd, I recrossed the Eastern line of forts guarding Kronstadt in CMB No. 7 and proceeded to make a reconnaissance near Tolbouhin Lighthouse. There I saw anchored two Bolshevik Dreadnoughts, the *Petropavlovsk* and the *Andrei Pervozvanny*, with a destroyer guard both to the East and West of them. I decided to attack, the time being 2.00 a.m. (Finnish Time), but, when only 4 miles away, the engine failed and revolutions dropped below torpedo firing speed, so I had to turn 16 points and return to my base, arriving there at 3.15 a.m."

It would appear from this report that Agar had armed his boat with a torpedo and undertaken an attack while wearing civilian clothes before he had even sent his signal to London asking for permission to attack. If the mission had gone wrong it could have had a disastrous effect on his intelligence mission and he would probably have earned a court martial rather than a Victoria Cross.

In the next few weeks Agar, with both boats now operational, resumed his intelligence activities, running couriers to Dukes. It was a perilous occupation especially as the Bolsheviks now realised that the CMBs were operating virtually in their own front parlour. It also became necessary to try to get Dukes out earlier than planned as the Cheka was closing in. Operating in a variety of guises Dukes not only provided maps of the minefields guarding Kronstadt, but also financed an underground organisation formed by Tsarist officers, businessmen and former landowners. Called the National Centre, it was dedicated to the overthrow of Bolshevism. Dukes also acquired much valuable information about social and political conditions inside Russia.

Recent Soviet accounts refer to the existence of a "British File" drawn up at the time by Eduard Otto, of the Cheka's Special Department OO. Otto, nicknamed "The Professor", spent all his time trying to catch Dukes who was described in the Cheka files as: "Young, tall, slightly stooping, with a thin cleanshaven face and usually wearing a Red Army greatcoat and shabby boots."

Otto and Dukes came face to face when the Cheka was tipped off that Dukes had gone to a doctor for treatment of frostbite. The Cheka detachment burst into the room where Dukes lay on a couch. A man stared into Dukes' face. It was Otto. But Dukes had been taught by the doctor – an anti-Bolshevist – how to throw a fit. He did so most impressively and the Chekists left. But many of Dukes' contacts were arrested and shot. In July two of his National Centre couriers were caught crossing the border into Finland. One was killed and a capsule containing two slips of rice paper were found in the heel of his boot. They contained intelligence about Red Army defences and secret Bolshevik political decisions, and they were signed ST 25. The net began to close. When Dukes went to Moscow to seek information from the Reverend Frank North, the British chaplain and the only representative Englishman left in the city (his church, St Andrews, is now the recording studios of the Melodiya record company), North was picked up by the Cheka and spent several months in prison. When he was eventually released Dukes met him at Waterloo Station. North could be forgiven for showing his pique. His first words were: "By jove, Dukes, that interview with you all but put me up against the wall."

It was in these circumstances that Agar and Sindall made several attempts to get Duke out. They failed in a succession of hair-raising episodes which Dukes and Agar later recounted in their books, *The Story of ST 25* and *Baltic Episode*.

Agar made another run on August 8th, having sent word to Dukes that this would be the last attempt for some time because of "naval operations". This too failed because the small boat stolen by Dukes and his companion to row out to the CMB sank beneath them and they had to swim for the shore where they watched the CMB turn round and depart.

Agar's "naval operations" sprang from his success at sinking the *Oleg* and the plans made to attack German battleships at their moorings the previous year. Cowan had made up his mind to remove the threat of the two battleships, which had forced Krasnaya Gorka to surrender, and to do so he planned to use a flotilla of CMBs to make a high speed torpedo run into the harbour under cover of darkness. In the meantime he had been reinforced by another squadron of destroyers and by HMS *Vindictive*, a light cruiser which had been converted into an aircraft carrier and carried a fighting force of Camels, Griffins, 1½ Strutters and Short Seaplanes to the Baltic. Commanded by Captain Edgar "Dasher" Grace, son of the great cricketer "W.G." she disgraced herself on arrival by running aground. It took much effort over eight days to get her off.

The aircraft were unloaded and flown from a primitive aerodrome carved out of the scrub at Biorko in Finland. Two or three anti-submarine patrols were made every day and on July 30th, eleven aircraft carried out a dawn raid on Kronstadt and Squadron Leader D. G. Donald – later Air Marshal Sir Grahame Donald – reported that "a destroyer depot ship disappeared and was not seen again". Donald was not too happy with the situation: "Anti-aircraft fire improved daily. Inadequate aerodrome arrangements hampered operations; further, the aircraft were, without exception, old and unsuitable for the duties they were required to carry out." Nevertheless, they were to play a vital role in the Kronstadt Raid.

Seven CMBs arrived at Biorko – one had been lost in the North Sea – on August 2nd. Command of the enterprise was given to Commander C. C. "Dobbie" Dobson and Agar was asked to lead them through the chain of forts. It was planned that they would go in at full speed in two groups of three under cover of bombs and bullets from Donald's planes. The seventh boat would deal with the guard ship and Agar would lurk outside ready to cope with any ships which might come out to fight.

The CMBs went in at 0140 on August 18th. Helped by a strong westerly wind which raised the level of the water in Petrograd Bay, they were able to pass over the breakwaters without damage. The first boat to roar through the narrow entrance was No. 79 commanded by Lieutenant Bremner. He achieved complete surprise with the noise of his engines being lost among the racket made by Donald's aircraft. Bremner scored a direct hit on the *Pamiat Azova*. It was only then that the defences came to life. Dobson, in No. 31 was the next to strike, hitting the *Andrei Pervozvanny* with both his torpedoes. By now the air was full of shot and shell; searchlights combed the harbour, and tracers arrowed through the night. Lieutenant Dayrell-Reed was hit as he made his attack and slumped across the wheel. Sub-Lieutenant Steel left his Lewis gun and pulled his mortally wounded skipper from the controls. He was just able to fire his torpedoes and swing away; any later and he would have rammed the *Petropavlovsk*. One of his torpedoes was wasted on the anchor chain but the other hit the battleship full under its forward turret.

The second wave was not so fortunate, however. No. 86, commanded by Lieutenant Howard, broke down before reaching the forts. Then Lieutenant Brade in No. 62 was blinded by a searchlight as he swung into the harbour and collided with Bremner's No. 79 as it was coming out. Bremner's boat was almost cut in half, so, ordering his crew to climb aboard Brade's boat, he blew up his own craft with gun cotton.

All hell had now broken loose. Donald's planes were straffing the gun positions and searchlights, the CMBs were joining in with their Lewis guns and the Bolsheviks were firing everything at them. Lieutenant Napier in No. 24 had tried to follow his instructions to sink the guard ship, the destroyer *Gavriel*, but his torpedo missed and the *Gavriel* blew his boat out of the water. Brade, now unable to get into the harbour, decided to use his two torpedoes on the *Gavriel*. But both of them missed and the destroyer retaliated once again with accurate shooting, wrecking No. 62's engines and sinking her within minutes. Agar, in No. 7, fired his torpedo into a military harbour containing patrol boats and did considerable damage.

By the time the last boat, Lieutenant Bodley's No. 72, headed into the harbour to torpedo the dry dock, it seemed that nothing could live in the hail of bullets and shells sweeping across the water. Bodley got about halfway before the cockpit was hit by a shell splinter. No one was hurt but the torpedo firing mechanism was jammed, so Bodley got out of the harbour as quickly as possible. Fortunately for Lieutenant Howard and his crew, Bodley came across the disabled No. 86 and was able to tow her to safety. The survivors headed at speed to Cowan's waiting line of cruisers and destroyers while Donald's aircraft continued to harry the Bolshevik defences.

Later that morning they tallied the balance sheet. Three CMBs had been lost: four officers and four ratings had been killed, while three officers and six ratings had been taken prisoner – among them the severely wounded Bremner. On the other side of the ledger, aircraft reconnaissance showed both battleships settled on the bottom, out of action, while the *Pamiat Azova* had rolled on to her side. At one stroke the naval threat to Cowan's fleet and the new Baltic states had been removed.

Dobson and Steele were both awarded the Victoria Cross and a number of other sailors and airmen decorated for gallantry. Two reluctant heroes, Finnish smugglers who had been persuaded to go along as pilots in Dobson's and Agar's boats, were also rewarded. They got double pay – £25 – for the trip and two quarts of rum instead of one.

It was a brilliant coup in the full tradition of small ship actions with the added dimension of aerial support. Even those who were bitterly opposed to intervention could scarce forbear to cheer. The Navy was rightly proud of its success and the bravery and skill of its men. However it would be wrong to think that the Royal Navy did not suffer from the same malaises as the Army. In many ways the sailors had more cause for grievance than the soldiers. They still suffered from a hangover of Victorian conditions and pay. Life on board ship was still harsh and shore based living costs had soared while the sailors' pay lagged behind. The married sailors' families were ekeing out miserable existences. It was these grievances which were to erupt in the Invergordon Mutiny in ships of the Royal Navy in 1931.

Many of the sailors also objected to being sent to Russia. There were a number of cases of men refusing to sail their ships to the Baltic, and Admiral Sir Sydney Fremantle refers in his memoirs to a mutiny among a squadron of light cruisers which refused to sail from the Firth of Forth to the Baltic. The Bolsheviks attempted to capitalise on the sailors' grievances by aiming wireless broadcasts at them which urged them to refuse duty and hasten the cause of World Revolution. This was the first time radio had been used for propaganda purposes.

None of this became known to the British public. Strict censorship prevented any mention of disaffection and mutiny. But the extent of the problem may be judged from the second part of Sir Walter Long's statement in the Commons which had referred for the first time to the mutiny of the Royal Marines in North Russia. Turning from the marines to the Fleet, he listed a number of cases where men "had broken out of the ships which had received orders unexpected by them to proceed to the Baltic, with a result that the sailing of the flotilla was jeopardised . . ." In each case he announced the reduction of their sentences. And then he turned to what had obviously been a serious attempt to sabotage the aircraft carrier *Vindictive* while she was in the Baltic: "The men concerned were dealt with summarily except two of the ring leaders who attempted to stop the fan engines, thus endangering the lives of their shipmates below. They were sentenced to five years' penal servitude; and the Admiralty will review the cases of these men after two years and one year respectively."

On August 23rd Agar made one final attempt to bring Dukes out of Petrograd. It ended in disaster. The approaching CMB was seen by the defences who were now fully aware of the presence of the boats and it was lit up by searchlights until, as Agar wrote, it was like "a rabbit trapped between the headlights of a motor car". The forts opened fire, the boat's steering was damaged and it roared off at full speed, out of control, until it hit one of the breakwaters and came to a crashing halt. Luckily, the searchlights had lost it and, while the engine was useless, she still floated. Kronstadt was only a few hundred yards away; the Finnish coast, and safety, was fifteen miles, and they had just a few hours of darkness to reach it. They rigged a mast and a piece of canvas as a sail. The wind was in the right direction and gradually they began to draw clear of the forts. A mist at dawn gave them added protection and then they came across a boat in which two Red soldiers from one of the forts were enjoying a morning's fishing. Training the Lewis gun on them Agar forced them to tow the CMB to Terrioki. They reached safety with the boat sinking under them some twelve hours after they had set out. They then gave the bewildered soldiers some spare rations and set them free.

Agar was involved in one more operation in which the CMBs laid their special mines in the cleared channel leading into Kronstadt. It had an unexpected result. The *Gavriel* which had been missed by three torpedoes and had sunk two of the CMBs during the raid came out one night with an Azard class destroyer. Their mission was to patrol the area, but their Tsarist captains intended to hand their ships over to the British. However, before they could do so they ran on to the mines and sank with heavy loss of life.

As for Dukes, he made his way out overland through Estonia and was knighted for his work. He and Agar at last met in September 1919 at "C"'s office in London. That night they dined at the Savoy.

One memento of these stirring occasions survives – Agar's CMB 4 in which he sank the *Oleg*. Refurbished by Thornycrofts, it is now on exhibition at the Imperial War Museum in Duxford, Cambridgeshire.

While the Royal Navy was consolidating its hold on the Gulf of Finland, the political scene had become even more complex. Von der Goltz, frustrated in his attempt to establish German rule in the Baltic, had organised a Russo-German army of 42,000 men, 12,000 of whom were former Russian prisoners of war who had been sent from Germany. He set up a Georgian, Colonel Bermondt, as its commander and was proposing to march into Russia in an attempt to seize Moscow.

Mannerheim had been voted out of power in Finland and the new Finnish government had adopted a far less warlike attitude towards the Bolsheviks. The other Baltic states were demanding an undertaking of *de jure* recognition together with military and financial assistance from the British before agreeing to support Yudenich's march on Petrograd. Sir Hubert Gough had blotted his copybook once again by setting up a Russian government in exile in Estonia from which he hoped to get a guarantee of Estonian independence. Both Denikin and Kolchak, committed to the restoration of Russia's pre-war borders, angrily refused to recognise any such guarantee from any such government. The Baltic states, seeing no prospect of support from the Allies and fearing what would happen if they became involved in a losing war, began to talk peace with the Bolsheviks who were only too anxious to close off the threat to Petrograd while dealing with Kolchak and Denikin.

General Laidoner, Commander-in-Chief of the Estonian Army, explained his country's position to the *Berlingske Tidende* in these terms: "Admiral Kolchak did not recognise the independence of the Baltic border states. The Estonian peasant soldier could not, consequently, understand why he should fight the Bolshevists who proclaimed their readiness to recognise Estonian independence."

In London there was deep division between Churchill and the rest of the Cabinet. Lloyd George had already made his views painfully clear to him, but Churchill persisted in wanting to support every aspect of resistance to the Bolsheviks. It was essential for Britain to support Yudenich, he argued, because, at worst, Yudenich's activities outside Petrograd would draw off troops which would otherwise be used against Denikin and Kolchak and, at best, could deliver a stunning blow to the Bolsheviks by capturing Petrograd and Kronstadt. Lord Curzon, the Foreign Minister, was completely opposed to this view, insisting that Yudenich was a reactionary whose occupation of Petrograd would be disastrous for the whole of the Baltic.

Churchill even faced strong opposition within his own Ministry, with a General Staff Paper dated October 3rd proposing that in view of the peace talks between the Baltic states and the Bolsheviks, Yudenich's army should be withdrawn and sent to help Denikin. This argument became academic when Yudenich launched his offensive on Petrograd on October 11th. Whatever his failings it is difficult not to sympathise with the Russian for while almost everybody in the region wanted the Bolsheviks to be made harmless, few were prepared to help him. In September he told Hugh Muir of the *Daily Express*:

My army is ragged and practically barefoot while the Bolsheviks have a good army of 45,000 men comparatively well equipped with abundant artillery and machine guns and sufficient ammunition. We cannot take Petrograd in our present condition. My army has been constituted with material captured from the Bolsheviks. It is hungry and tobaccoless as well as ragged.

In fact the British Government had agreed in May to send an initial consignment of matériel sufficient to equip 7,500 men along with eight 6-inch howitzers, sixteen 18-pounder guns, twenty lorries and medical supplies for 10,000 troops. There were further shipments – mostly from surplus stores left over from the war – up till September when Yudenich wrote to Churchill thanking him for the supplies and expressing the hope that they would continue. Among the most important equipment sent to him were six Mark V composite tanks with a detachment of twenty-two officers and twenty-nine other ranks from the Tank Corps commanded by Lieutenant-Colonel E. Hope-Carson. He arrived with three of the tanks in a cargo of war matériel on board the SS *Davia*, a former German mine-layer escort, at Reval on the night of August 5th. Yudenich came to inspect the tanks and Hope-Carson suggested that one should be named after him. He insisted however it should be called "First Aid". The others were called "Brown Bear" and "Captain Cromie".

The intention was that the detachment would teach the White Russians how to use the tanks and then hand them over. Of course, it did not turn out like that. Hope-Carson was sent into action on Sunday August 21st, after attending a memorial service for the British sailors killed in the Kronstadt Raid. Two of the tanks were loaded on to a train and sent up to the front south of Pskov where the Bolsheviks had attacked the Estonians. But while Hope-Carson was scouting the ground under shell fire the Estonians pulled back and the train with the tanks still on board had to steam hurriedly back to Narva to avoid being cut off. The tanks first showed what they could do on September 13th outside Gdov some fifty miles south of Narva where, firing their six-pounders and machine-guns and supported by a newly formed "Tank Push Battalion" they routed a Bolshevik force established in a series of fortified villages.

From then until the end of the campaign the tanks were in almost continual action, being rushed to places where the Bolsheviks were threatening to break through and to lead attacks. They achieved a tremendous reputation for invincibility and the Bolsheviks usually ran when they appeared. But there were not enough of them. Of the detachment's three other machines one had broken its gear box and the remaining two had been sabotaged, either in Hull from where they had been shipped or after their arrival in Reval.

Hope-Carson, whose colourful and detailed account of the Detachment's campaign was printed in the *Royal Tank Corps Journal* in 1927, was therefore unable to meet all the demands made on him and the White Russians were later to blame the tanks for their eventual failure to take Petrograd.

One further drama had still to be played out before Yudenich launched his attack. On October 6th, Colonel Bermondt, now commanding a force of some 50,000 Russo-Germans and with ambitions to march not only on Petrograd but also on Moscow, decided first to occupy Riga. Once again Anglo-White Russian relations were confused. The Latvians who had been armed by Cowan, resisted stoutly and Cowan sent the British cruisers *Dragon* and *Cleopatra* along with a division of destroyers to help them. The ships, under the command of the French Commodore Brisson, bombarded Bermondt who replied with artillery fire from Von der Goltz's Iron Division causing 15 casualties on the British ships. But the Navy's guns proved too much for the Germans and they fled with the Latvian Army chasing them all the way back through Lithuania to East Prussia where they finally split up in defeat and ignominy. No one regretted their going. One report printed in London said: "Latest telegram received by Lithuanian Delegation in London states that the Russo-German forces in Lithuania fighting the Bolshevists are devastating the Lithuanian country, burning villages and plundering the property of the people. They are thus annihilating all sympathy among the Lithuanian population for the Russian cause."

Yudenich opened his offensive with a series of victories. Hope-Carson's tanks were in the forefront and, according to the *Daily Express*'s special correspondent:

The Tank Corps continues to win a golden reputation, indeed it appears to be considered impossible to take a step without their aid. Reliance is placed to such an extent on the Tanks that the crews find it difficult to obtain the necessary rest. A remarkable feat reflecting credit upon Colonel Carson and his men was performed in crossing the River Luga which was considered impracticable. Colonel Carson has received the Order of St. Anne.

The Navy was also in action, bombarding Krasnaya Gorka. The fortress, now manned by loyal Bolsheviks, was holding up an Estonian force which, despite the proposed peace negotiations, was supporting the coastal flank of Yudenich's drive. The Monitor HMS *Erebus*, mounting two 12-inch guns, was brought up to do the job, but, unable to take the fortress in its undefended rear as the

Bolshevik battleships had done, *Erebus* not only failed to put the fortress out of the fight but was forced to move because of some very accurate shooting from the defenders. The fort's guns were directed by observers in a kite balloon which, said one report, "was evidently filled with non-inflammable gas since it was frequently riddled by our airmen but continued working".

Squadron Leader Donald and his men were hard at work, dropping over 300 bombs on Krasnaya Gorka and another fortress holding up the Estonians in the first five days of the offensive. Donald had been most relieved to hear in September that HMS *Furious* – the first true aircraft carrier – was coming out with fresh pilots and planes, for both his men and his machines were getting very tired, having been in action almost continually since their arrival in July. But when the new machines arrived he found that nearly every one of the twenty aircraft "were in a bad condition and hardly one was fit for active service flying".

Continuous seaplane patrols were flown in spite of bad weather with "one particularly good action being fought by two seaplanes against a Bolshevik destroyer in a snowstorm". He was forced to use Camel fighters for daylight bombing raids and even at 15,000 feet they were being hit by anti-aircraft fire. By the time it was all over thirty-three of his fifty-five aircraft were "expended". Three were shot down, nine force-landed in the sea, seven more crashed owing to the uneven surface of the aerodrome and fourteen deteriorated owing to climatic conditions. Four pilots were killed and two were wounded. It was an unsung but gallant little campaign in the early history of the RAF.

Yudenich's troops made good ground at the start of their attack. They were led by the dashing cavalry general, Rodzianko, who, according to Hope-Carson "was well-known in sporting circles in England, having taken prizes in horse jumping competitions at Olympia". They took Yamburg and then Gatchina and pressed on to the suburbs of Petrograd. Among them was a unit of Swedish troops wearing their national uniform fighting in the front line and working with the tanks. In one small battle twelve out of a party of fourteen Swedes supporting the tanks became casualties. They were fortunate however in being looked after by their own nursing sister, Matart Kurkinen. According to Hope-Carson: "Where the Swedish troops went she went. If they were front line infantry, as on this occasion, she walked with the front line. She carried a heavy load of hospital stores and must have been the saviour of many a man . . . I am glad to say that later she was given a British decoration." How strange that Sweden, so careful to avoid involvement in two World Wars, should get itself involved in this imbroglio.

By the end of the second week of October the latest White Russian offensives seemed to be on the point of success. True, Kolchak had been pushed back across the Urals but Denikin was advancing on Moscow while Petrograd seemed to be at Yudenich's mercy. But it was all an illusion. Just as with Hitler's army years later, Petrograd was not for the taking.

Krasnaya Gorka had stopped the advance along the coast, and the indefatigable Trotsky had arrived on his mobile headquarters, the train which he described as "the vital shovelful of coal that keeps a dying fire alive". He brought up reinforcements along railway lines that Yudenich's cavalry had failed to cut and although, by October 20th, Yudenich's men were fighting among the factories on the outskirts of the city, the White Army was running out of men and time. And the Bolsheviks started to counter-attack.

By now the strain was beginning to tell on the tanks and their crews. Hope-Carson was alternating his British with Russian crews but his tanks were dropping out with mechanical defects having been fought hard for ten days. He had also come up against a powerful armoured train which was more than a match for his tanks. But still Yudenich's officers wanted him to press on:

> It was now obvious that the staff were relying on three lame tanks to get the column through. The infantry were thoroughly worn out and not willing to advance without them. Many of the senior officers were incapable of understanding that the tank was a machine and had its limitations. It was seriously suggested . . . that by placing a tank on either side of the line it would be an easy matter to catch the armoured train.

The retreat began. Yudenich lost Gatchina on November 3rd and Yamburg nine days later. Hope-Carson took his tanks and two French light tanks back to Narva. By November 25th it was all over. The White Russian Army streamed back over the Estonian frontier where it was disarmed while the Estonians closed their border against the advancing Bolsheviks.

A terrible outbreak of spotted typhus now swept the defeated army and its soldiers died in the most dreadful conditions, without shelter or medical attention. By the end of the year nothing remained of the White Russian Army. Yudenich sought asylum in Britain. And the British went home.

Admiral Cowan waited to leave until the last possible moment on

December 28th, the day the sea froze. In all, the Royal Navy lost seven ships in the Baltic and Gulf of Finland, among them one light cruiser – with another badly damaged – two destroyers and a submarine. One hundred and thirteen sailors died, forty-two were wounded and nine were missing. When Cowan steamed home, the new Baltic states were engaged in negotiating their freedom from Russia.

Joyful in their independence, they would perhaps have been wiser to have united to destroy the Communist threat, for Bolshevism gathered them back into the Russian Empire only twenty years later while Finland, having fought valiantly against the Red Army in 1939, was forced to accept Russia's terms and give up her strategic territory to the north of Petrograd. The Soviets never forgot nor forgave the fact that it was from Terrioki that Agar led the CMBs into Kronstadt. Terrioki is now Russian.

CHAPTER 19

The Bolsheviks Triumph
South Russia and the Caspian, December 1919–May 1920

We must return to "Z" Flight. Joe Archer and his by now some-what less than merry men had made good their escape from the battlefield and had spent Christmas 1919, at their old base of Valuyki. They did not stay there long. With Denikin's armies disintegrating and Budenny's Red Cavalry raiding deep into his territory, the RAF loaded up its trains again and set out for safety, aiming to cross the Don at Rostov. It was not the easiest of journeys. As they rolled through the southern steppes and looked out of the windows they could see Denikin's Cossacks retreating alongside the line, horses and riders with their heads slumped in utter weariness, like a cut-out frieze against the snow. Behind them were Budenny's raiding parties of horsemen and, on the line, a Bolshevik armoured train mounting a 9.2-inch gun. "A" and "Z" Flights' trains had taken on as many refugees and wounded as they could carry. Typhus broke out. Fuel was short. The line was crammed with trains puffing their way to safety. The driver of Vic Clow's train had to have a pistol put to his head to persuade him to carry on. Partisans sniped at the trains as they passed in the night. When a station master complained about supplying locomotives Collishaw passed on a message from that coldly efficient White general, Baron Wrangel, informing him that the Baron had hanged nineteen station masters on another front and that if it became necessary he would hang one hundred and nineteen here.

It is not surprising that by now Clow and his fellow pilots were beginning to have second thoughts about the wisdom of their presence in this vast, confusing and highly dangerous country. "To put it bluntly," recalled Clow, "we began to wonder what the hell we were doing there."

It had started with the Anglo-French agreement of December 23rd, 1917, in which the French were given responsibility for "activities against the enemy" in Russian territories west of the Don while the British would control operations east of the Don and in Trans-

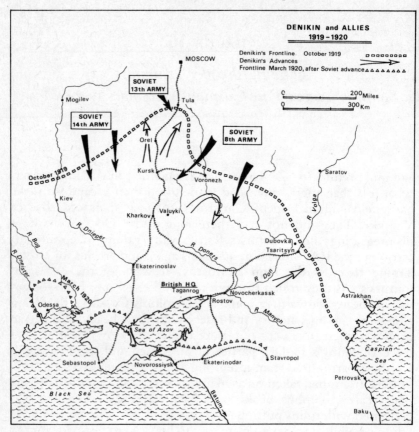

caucasia to the south. When this agreement was concluded it was
assumed that the "activities against the enemy" would be undertaken against the Germans and the Turks. But by the end of 1918,
the situation had, of course, changed drastically. Germany and
Turkey had been defeated and were no longer "the enemy".

In the British areas, the Transcaucasian states had declared their
independence and possessed governments of sorts while north of
the Caucasus, General Denikin was raising his White Russian forces
to fight the Bolsheviks and was recognised as the *de facto* ruler of the
area. But in the French area which had been occupied by the
Germans and Austrians there was nothing but chaos with Nationalist, Anarchist and Bolshevik bands all fighting one another in a
free-for-all, cut-throat war. On December 18th, on the heels of the
evacuating Germans, the French started to land troops at Odessa
with the expressed intention of saving the area from anarchy. In the

Soviet view, however, they were sent to create a protective shield behind which Denikin could form his army. Altogether the French landed a division of 10,000 men, many of whom were Algerian and Senegalese. The Greeks sent two divisions numbering 30,000 and the Poles a 3,000-strong brigade. In addition the Rumanians put 32,000 over their borders and Denikin sent in 15,000. Altogether some 90,000 men occupied a fifty-mile deep strip of territory along the Black Sea coast from the Rumanian border to Kherson on the Dnieper.

It should have been a formidable Army, well able to look after itself. But its morale was poor, and it was hit by fierce cavalry raids from all sides. The Cossack Ataman Grigoriev forced them to give up Kherson and then attacked them at Odessa. Their soldiers had no heart and their politicians no will to continue the fight. The French had had enough. They sued for peace and on April 5th the last French ship sailed from Odessa. They had evacuated 30,000 Russian civilians and 10,000 of Denikin's soldiers, but they had left behind six Renault tanks (which were later used against Denikin) and had destroyed huge quantities of stores which would have proved invaluable to the White leader. Not that they could have shipped these stores to him, for that same month the French Black Sea Fleet mutinied. The mutiny was led by André Marty, founder of the French Communist Party.

The British involvement in the Ukraine was of quite different complexion: unlike the French sphere of interest the British area had never been occupied and Denikin himself had sufficient force to be regarded as the representative of a Russian government. So the need for a British occupying force never materialised.

Consequently, Collishaw's squadron, "Z" Flight and the Royal Tank Corps training detachment were the only British units to become involved in the fighting in South Russia. Their comparatively marginal activities were heavily criticised by the Opposition in the House of Commons and provided the source of misgiving within the Cabinet.

What Denikin needed from the British was recognition, money, a training mission and supplies. And he got all of these. Drawing on the arms dumps in the Middle East left over from the war, the British sent him shiploads of matériel. All told, he received enough to arm and equip a quarter of a million men. The shipments, which started to arrive on April 15th, 1919, included some 1,200 guns, among them 6-inch howitzers, 60-pounders and a large number of 18-pounders. The ammunition for these guns included a liberal proportion of gas shells. The supplies formed a complete quartermaster's list: Two tons of assorted nails, 1,500 curry combs, one million pounds of preserved meat, one million pounds of biscuits, 25,000 tins of tea, sufficient mule shoes for six months. There was even "stationery on a 50 per cent basis for 1 Army HQ, 3 Corps HQ, one Cavalry Division and five Infantry Divisions".

Six heavy and six light tanks were sent as a first shipment and, eventually, more modern aircraft followed to supplement the 100 RE8s. Uniforms, rifles, machine-guns, ammunition, transport, hospitals, engineering equipment; the cost price of this great military cornucopia spilled out on the dockside at Novorossiysk eventually amounted to £35.9 million. Much of it was, as Churchill argued in the House of Commons, largely unsaleable. Nevertheless, it was a great deal of money and it provided Denikin with sufficient "sinews of war" to beat the Bolsheviks.

But, while he had the sinews he had neither the manpower, the organisation nor the qualities of leadership to do the job. He did not have enough men to secure his rear and his lines of communications when he began his march north – partisan bands were raiding into the outskirts of Novorossiysk itself – his supply lines were virtually non-existent and he had no reinforcements. The White Russian General Wrangel and the British General Holman advised him against his headlong dash but he was blinded by the thought of taking Moscow. In typical Russian fashion he gambled everything on one throw of the dice.

The disorganisation and corruption behind the lines horrified Holman and his officers at the Military Mission. While the fighting soldiers were barefoot and ragged in the field, British uniforms were being sold on the civilian black market. Novorossiysk prostitutes plied their trade dressed in British nurses' uniforms. Corruption is always prevalent in wartime but in South Russia in 1919 it was especially blatant.

As for the leadership, the portly, bald, bearded Denikin relied on the Tsarist methods of driving men rather than leading them. He could not see that the world had changed since 1917. He believed passionately in a Greater Russia restored to its pre-war frontiers and would not countenance the independence of the Baltic or the Transcaucasian states. He was also violently anti-Semitic. Like most of the White Russian leaders and their British army friends he equated Bolshevism with Jewishness and his rule of South Russia was marked by a series of pogroms in which some 100,000 Jews were killed. They were not, however, all victims of his Army. The Anarchists and Ukrainian nationalists killed their quota too. But the murders created a feeling of disgust in Britain and the belief grew in the face of this cruelty that there was little to choose between the Bolsheviks and the White Russians.

Given these basic weaknesses, it was not surprising that Denikin's cause collapsed once the Bolsheviks stopped his drive on Moscow. He had brave men – good soldiers – serving under him. But there was little they could do except die as they were harried back to Rostov.

The transition from imminent victory to disaster took just two weeks. On October 15th Denikin was preparing to march into Moscow from Orel. A week later he was forced to abandon Orel. Two days after that, on the 24th, Budenny's Red Cavalry defeated the White Cavalry under General K. K. Mamontov and occupied Voronezh. Makhno's anarchists wrought havoc in the White rear and on October 26th the Don Cossacks turned against Denikin. In those two short weeks the White cause was lost.

As Denikin's tired and dispirited men pulled back, with typhus and hunger beginning to thin their ranks more effectively than the Bolsheviks' bullets, the British Tank Corps detachment abandoned their base at Taganrog. They had enjoyed their time in this pleasant town on the Sea of Azov. When the great tank exponent, General Fuller, went out to visit them he described the conditions:

The personnel of our Tank Detachment in Taganrog is very comfortably quartered and cared for. To all intents and purposes there is no work to be done in the afternoons, and there is both time and facilities for sport and amusements. Football is very popular, even under the almost tropical heat which prevailed whilst I was in the country, and I was lucky enough to be able to witness a couple of games between the British "Tanks" and the local Taganrog team. These people play a perfectly good game of football, but their interpretation of some of the more elementary rules is so very grotesque that it becomes a practical impossibility for them to leave the field other than as victors.

There is also plenty of swimming, boxing and boating to keep our fellows fit and happy. The officers are honorary members of the local Yacht Club, at which there is plenty of sailing to be had, and, into a hull presented to them by an admirer, the ingenious Workshops have fitted an engine – I did not care to enquire too closely into the antecedents of said engine, but, having been "Workshops" myself once, I have my own theories on the subject. Anyway, the result is a roomy, comfortable, and very fast motor-boat, the sole property of "Tanks", and the envy of all Taganrog.

For the delectation of the troops in the evenings there is a very excellent garden, where plays a band and where may be found most of the youth and beauty of the neighbourhood. There are several cinemas also in Taganrog, and, greatest joy of all, a theatre in which Denikin's own string orchestra plays two or three times a week. Here the music is perfectly wonderful, and it is an inspiration to observe the reverent attention which the entire audience bestows upon the whole performance.

Although the tank detachment had been sent to Taganrog only to train the White Russians, inevitably they could not resist taking their beloved tanks into the fighting on the excuse that they were giving their students "battle training". Like the RAF they went to battle with their machines loaded on to trains, unloading them when they got to the fighting and then trundling off along the railway line to look for another scrap. Their field of operations was perfect tank country, the rolling steppes where Hitler's Panzers were to fight another war. Wherever they appeared they seemed to bring success and Fuller reported, "in more than one instance, it has been unnecessary to detrain the tanks, since the Bolsheviks bolted at the mere report that a tank train was approaching their positions."

But that was before the great retreat started. The Tank Detachment abandoned their idyllic existence at Taganrog and joined the scramble for safety across the bridges at Rostov. Captain Marion Aten, an American flying with No. 47 Squadron, gave a graphic account of the desperate train ride to safety by part of the Squadron in his book *Last Train over Rostov Bridge*. Vic Clow, on "Z" Flight's train with General Holman on board, also got safely across, passing the hat round for the driver whose co-operation had been ensured by a cocked revolver placed to his ear.

Unfortunately "C" Flight's train with Collishaw on board did not make it across the bridge and had to run for safety to the Crimea. It was chased all the way by a Bolshevik armoured train which could sometimes be seen in the distance. One night some local Bolsheviks sent an unmanned engine careering down the line to smash into the rear of "C" Flight's train. The last eight coaches were smashed to matchwood. Luckily, they held only stores. The rest of the train, loaded with sick and wounded, was full of horrors and littered with dead. It eventually reached safety in the Crimea on January 4th, 1920. The respite was short. The pilots resumed operations but they had lost a number of aircraft in the retreat and the pilots themselves were getting worn out. Clow who had gone down with malaria, opted to go home and was shipped out to Constantinople.

The Daily Routine Orders of the Kuban Group (as it was now called) records that on January 19th, 1920, Clow was awarded the Order of St Stanislaus with Swords and Bow. But it was never confirmed and he never received the medal.

The remaining pilots continued to fly. They dropped leaflets in an attempt to induce the Kuban Cossacks to fight for Denikin but their propaganda had no effect. On January 30th General "Cissy" Maund left them with the following monumentally daft farewell message: "Although the fortunes of Russia are temporarily clouded I hope you will continue to show the same excellent qualities and high endeavour under my successor and thus continue to set the example necessary to restore the spirit of victory in our Russian allies."

Far more to the point was the order issued on February 21st, that "All officers and ORs must be in possession of a Rifle, Bayonet and 150 rounds of ammunition. These must in all cases be carried when travelling."

At the beginning of March Budenny struck again, crossing the Don and outflanking Denikin's strongpoint at Bataisk. On the 9th he occupied the railway junction at Tikhoretsk and then all that was left was a mad scramble to safety on the boats at Novorossiysk. During this period the British military mission, the Tank Detachment, and 47 Squadron did sterling work in keeping order as the beaten army and the terrified refugees funnelled down to the coast behind a thin screen of those Don Cossacks who, to their great credit, had remained loyal to Denikin when so many had changed sides.

Novorossiysk itself was like a foretaste of hell. The all pervasive typhus killed thousands of the refugees who crowded the streets fighting to get to the docks to board a ship, any ship going anywhere to escape the Bolsheviks. The bitter wind known as the "Bura" scoured the streets. On the dockside the British, reinforced by a battalion sent from Constantinople, struggled to organise the evacuation and to destroy the vast quantities of supplies – the last ship had unloaded only three months previously – which Denikin's men would never be able to use. No. 47 Squadron's Camels were taken off their flat cars and crushed by brand new tanks. The tanks then rolled over DH9s still in their factory packing cases and then the tanks themselves, their engines roaring, were sent on their last mission, off the dockside into the sea to join the cannon which had already been pitched over the side.

Inevitably, huge stocks of guns and ammunition and clothes and boots fell into Bolshevik hands, as on every other front. Indeed, by the end of the intervention a large part of the Red Army had been outfitted by the British taxpayer and it was armed with the latest of British weapons.

The last ships sailed away on the night of March 26th. Shells dropped into the harbour from Bolshevik guns in the hills around the port while the British battleship *Emperor of India* and the cruiser *Calypso* along with the French cruiser *Waldeck Rousseau* kept the Red Cavalry at bay with their big guns. They left behind a mass of refugees with nowhere to go and the Don Cossacks who fought it out, sabre to sabre, with the Red horsemen. Denikin had been ousted as commander. He went to live in exile first in France, then in America, and the far more able Wrangel took over to make a last stand in the Crimea.

Collishaw had already been making his own last stand in the Crimea, flying as often as he could. On one of his missions, flying a DH9 bomber, he was hit by anti-aircraft fire and forced to land. But as his engine was still running he taxied twenty miles back to his base across the hard packed snow. He made his last flight "in anger" on March 26th, crossing to the mainland where he bombed and straffed a cavalry troop and a field battery and scored direct hits with bombs on an armoured train. The following day he flew a long reconnaissance, really a sort of farewell to Russia for on his return orders were waiting for him to leave. He turned his aircraft over to the White Russians. The British went home.

The gaunt, shaven-headed Baron Wrangel did a tremendous job of turning the defeated mob he had inherited into a disciplined army. But he had assumed command too late; the British government had decided to end the Russian adventure and had started trade talks with the Bolsheviks so that even the role played by the British forces in the evacuation was an embarrassment to the British government. At the War Office Churchill had at last abandoned all hope that the Bolsheviks could be overthrown. Thus, when, in early June, Wrangel launched a successful offensive which left him in possession of a large arc of territory on the mainland, the British government was horrified, fearing that their new and fragile contacts with the Bolsheviks would be endangered. The small British military mission to Wrangel was pulled out and the Royal Navy withdrew its protection. Wrangel, however, maintained his position on the mainland, refusing offers by the British to mediate with the Bolsheviks on his behalf. The Bolsheviks themselves were preoccupied with their campaign against the Ukrainians and the

Poles and it was not until that was settled that they were able to turn their attention to Wrangel. In October they drove him back into the Crimea and then, in the second week of November, they crossed into the Crimea itself. Recognising the inevitability of defeat, Wrangel ordered his men to make their way to the ports. There, under French protection, they embarked on the remnants of the Black Sea Fleet and civilian ships which eventually carried a total of 146,200 disarmed soldiers and refugees away to Bizerte in Tunisia where they and the ships were interned.

The Civil War was over. The White Russians had been defeated. Bolshevism had triumphed in Russia.

Meanwhile the last act of the Intervention was played out at a scene outside Russia. It took place in May 1920 at Enzeli, the Persian town on the Caspian which had served as Dunsterville's base for the defence of Baku.

After the Armistice in 1918 British troops had returned to Transcaucasia to oversee the Turkish withdrawal but they stayed only until August 1919 and with the collapse of Denikin the Red Army started to move across the Caucasus. On April 27th, 1920 the Bolsheviks of Baku, the capital of Azerbaijan, gave an ultimatum to the Azerbaijani parliament demanding that power be handed over to the Communists. That night the Red Army poured over the frontier and by the next day Baku was Communist. It was an event of a singular misfortune for a party of five Royal Navy officers and twenty-seven ratings on their way to take charge of the remains of Denikin's fleet which had sought refuge at Enzeli – for they stepped off the train at Baku straight into the arms of the Bolsheviks. The men were arrested and, along with other British prisoners, including women and children, were carted off to Baku's Central Prison which became notorious as the "Black Hole of Baku". Among them was a young naval officer who afterwards became Admiral of the Fleet, Lord Fraser of Inchcape. He lived for months with the ratings of his party, sharing their misery among the lice and rats and hunger and the indignities imposed on them by their captors. It was during this period that, like Horrocks in similar circumstances, he developed the regard for those who served under him that became such a hallmark of his career.

The Bolshevik occupation of Azerbaijan meant that the Caspian was now completely under their control and the British garrison at Enzeli, although on Persian territory, was in a very uncomfortable position. While the British had maintained their Coastal Motor Boats on the Caspian the Bolshevik Fleet had been worsted more often than not and for a time after the British withdrew the White

Fleet maintained this superiority. But by early 1920 the Bolsheviks had increased their fleet to eleven destroyers and torpedo boats and four small submarines and a number of smaller vessels.

The commander of this formidable fleet was none other than Commissar F. F. Raskolnikov, the Baltic sailors' leader who had been captured with his destroyer and taken to England as a hostage. Once he had been exchanged he had plunged back into the fight.

With Petrovsk and Baku in his hands Raskolnikov saw the opportunity to strike. On May 18th Major General H. B. Champain, commander of British forces in North Persia, was at Enzeli to watch the test-firing of some guns which had been taken off the White Russian ships and mounted to protect the port. It was these same guns that Fraser and his men had been on their way to serve when they were arrested in Baku. The garrison of some 500 men of the joint British and Indian Army North Persia Force at Enzeli had its positions on a neck of land encircling the harbour. It had never been expected that this small detachment could withstand a determined Bolshevik attack but it was thought that with the guns it could run a bluff to frighten off the Red Navy. However that sort of bluff did not work with Raskolnikov. He put his fleet into the harbour and landed troops to cut off the garrison. There was little fighting. Champain was in an impossible position and had no option but to negotiate under a flag of truce. Raskolnikov, no doubt relishing the irony of the situation, agreed to allow the British to leave for the mainland as long as they surrendered all Denikin's ships and left behind their heavy equipment.

That night the garrison marched out in compliance with Raskolnikov's terms and thus, the intervention – which had started with a similar small movement of British troops two years before – ended in humiliation. But, while it marked an end, the Enzeli incident also signified a beginning. As the first incursion by the Red Army into territory which had not belonged to Tsarist Russia, it heralded the beginning of the Soviet Empire.

Selected Bibliography

Agar, Captain August. *Baltic Episode*. London, Hodder and Stoughton, 1963.

Aten, Captain Marion and Arthur Ormont. *Last Train over Rostov Bridge*. New York, Messner, 1961.

Coates, W. P. and Zelda K. *Armed Intervention in Russia, 1918–22*. London, Gollancz, 1935.

Deacon, Richard. *A History of the British Secret Service*. London, Frederick Muller, 1969.

Dukes, Sir Paul. *The Story of ST 25*. London, Cassell, 1938.

Dunsterville, Major-General L. D. *The Adventures of Dunsterforce*. London, Edward Arnold, 1920.

Ellis, C. H. *The Transcaspian Episode, 1918–19*. London, Hutchinson, 1963.

Erickson, John. *The Soviet High Command*. London, Macmillan, 1962.

Gilbert, Martin. *Winston S. Churchill*. Vol. IV. London, Heinemann, 1975.

Hill, George. *Go Spy the Land*. London, Cassell, 1932.

Horrocks, Lieutenant-General Sir Brian. *A Full Life*. London, Collins, 1960.

Ironside, Field-Marshal Lord. *Archangel 1918–19*. London, Constable, 1953.

Jackson, Robert. *The Red Falcons*. Brighton, Clifton Books, 1970.

Kazemzadeh, Firuz. *The Struggle for Transcaucasia, 1917–21*. Oxford, George Ronald, 1951.

Kendall, Walter. *The Revolutionary Movement in Great Britain, 1900–21*. London, Weidenfeld and Nicolson, 1969.

Kennan, George F. *Soviet-American Relations, 1917–20*. Princeton University Press, Vol. I, 1956. Vol. II, 1958.

Kettle, Michael. *Sidney Reilly*. London, Corgi Books, 1983.

Knightley, Phillip. *The First Casualty*. London, André Deutsch, 1975.

Kochan, Lionel. *Russia in Revolution*. London, Weidenfeld and Nicolson, 1967.

Laue, Theodore H. von. *Sergei Witte and the Industrialisation of Russia*. New York and London, Columbia University Press, 1963.

Leggett, George. *The Cheka*. Oxford, Clarendon Press, 1981.

Lockhart, Robin Bruce. *Reilly, Ace of Spies*. London, Hodder and Stoughton, 1967.

Lockhart, R. H. Bruce. *Memoirs of a British Agent*. London, Putnam, 1932.

Luckett, Richard. *The White Generals*. London, Longman, 1971.

Maisky, Ivan. *Journey into the Past*. London, Hutchinson, 1962.

Select Bibliography

Maynard, Major-General Sir C. *The Murmansk Venture*. London, Hodder and Stoughton, 1928.

Mitchell, Donald W. *A History of Russian and Soviet Sea Power*. London, André Deutsch, 1974.

Moorehead, Alan. *The Russian Revolution*. New York, Harper and Brothers, 1958.

Nabakov, Konstantin. *The Ordeal of a Diplomat*. London, Duckworth, 1921.

Norman, Aaron. *The Great Air War*. New York, The Macmillan Company, 1968.

Paléologue, Maurice. *An Ambassador's Memoirs*. London, Hutchinson, 1923.

Rothstein, Andrew. *When Britain Invaded Soviet Russia*. London, The Journeyman Press, 1979.

Rumbelow, Donald. *The Houndsditch Murders*. New York, St Martins Press, 1973.

Schapiro, Leonard. *The Communist Party of the Soviet Union*. New York, Random House, 1960.

Singleton-Gates, G. R. *Bolos and Barishnyas*. Privately printed in England 1920.

Sokolov, Nicholas. *The Murder of the Imperial Family*. Berlin, Slovo, 1925.

Toland, John. *No Man's Land*. London, Eyre Methuen, 1980.

Tuchman, Barbara W. *The Guns of August*. New York, The Macmillan Company, 1962.

Ullman, Richard H. *Anglo-Soviet Relations 1917–21*. Princeton University Press, Vol. I, 1961. Vol. II, 1968. Vol. III, 1973.

Walker, Christopher J. *Armenia*. London, Croom Helm, 1980.

Ward, Colonel J. *With the Die-Hards in Siberia*. London, Cassell, 1920.

Soviet Publications

Chekisty. Leningrad, 1982.

Chekisty Raskazyvayut. Moscow, 1983.

Grazhdanskaya Voina i Voiennaya Interventsia v SSSR. Moscow, 1983.

K Istorii Rossiskoi Revolutzii. Vadim Chaikin. Moscow, 1922.

Kniga o Murmanske. Murmansk, 1977.

Krusheniye Antisovyetskovo Podpolya v SSSR. Moscow, 1978.

Poluchitelny Urok. General A. Samoilo, Moscow, 1962.

Severny Front. Moscow, 1961.

V Boi Rokovoi. M. Sboucharkov, Moscow, 1981.

Vystrel v Serdtse Revolytzii. Moscow, 1983.

Ya Yemu ne Mogu ne Verit. Gladkov, Moscow, 1983.

Zapiski Komendanta Moskovskovo Kremlya. P. Malkov, Moscow, 1969.

Index

Page-references for maps, in *italics*, precede other page-references. References to illustrations are given as plate-numbers: *Pl 1A* etc. Place-names and spellings are those principally used in the book; common variants are indicated. Main references are given in **bold** type.

Index

Index

Index

Index

Index

287

Index

H50 925 079 X

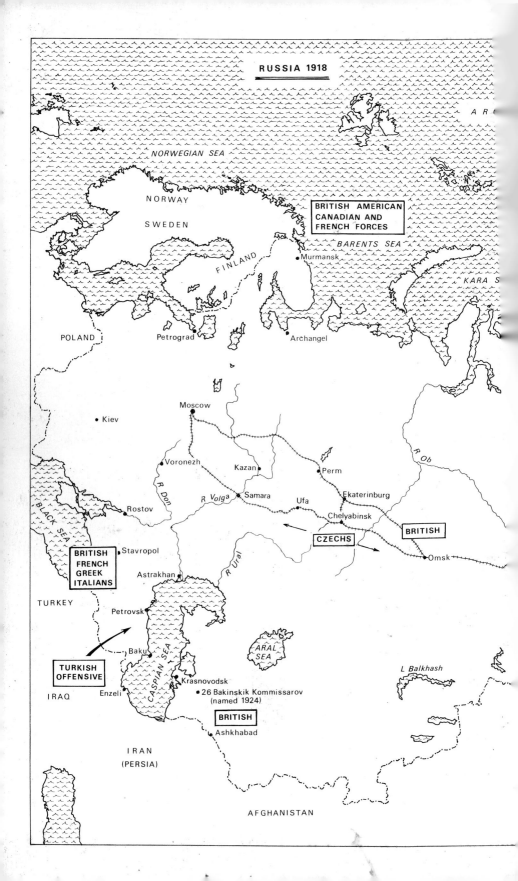

RUSSIA 1918

NORWEGIAN SEA

NORWAY

SWEDEN

FINLAND

BARENTS SEA

BRITISH AMERICAN
CANADIAN AND
FRENCH FORCES

KARA S

A R C

• Murmansk

POLAND

Petrograd

• Archangel

Moscow

• Kiev

R Ob

• Voronezh

Kazan

• Perm

R Don

R Volga

Samara

Ufa

Ekaterinburg

Chelyabinsk

Rostov

BRITISH

CZECHS

Omsk

BLACK SEA

BRITISH
FRENCH
GREEK
ITALIANS

• Stavropol

R Ural

TURKEY

Astrakhan

Petrovsk

ARAL
SEA

L Balkhash

TURKISH
OFFENSIVE

Baku

CASPIAN SEA

Krasnovodsk

• 26 Bakinskik Kommissarov
(named 1924)

IRAQ

Enzeli

BRITISH

• Ashkhabad

IRAN

(PERSIA)

AFGHANISTAN